Praise for *The Empathic God*

"*The Empathic God* is a masterpiece. In this groundbreaking contribution, Frank Woggon skillfully engages pastoral, theological, and clinical perspectives from his experiences as a spiritual care provider, educator, administrator, and researcher to explore new understandings of *at-onement*. This book will stimulate new conversations among theological educators and students, clergy and chaplains, and other readers who seek to interpret human experience with fresh insights into a classical theological doctrine."

—**Kenneth J. McFayden**, vice president for academic affairs and academic dean, and professor of practical theology, Union Presbyterian Seminary

"Frank Woggon redefines the narrative of the concept of atonement in a way that liberates it from traditional themes that often suppress and oppress. In the context of spiritual care, this reframing invites all to see this move as a means of healing of body, mind, and spirit. Practitioners in both the clinical and congregational setting can utilize this text to enhance their care of persons who are seeking to integrate faith practices into their lives."

—**Bishop Teresa E. Snorton**, Clinical Pastoral Educator (ACPE and BCC) (retired), Ecumenical Bishop, the Christian Methodist Episcopal Church

"Atonement theology has fallen on hard times, it seems, but Frank Woggon's book *The Empathic God: A Clinical Theology of At-Onement* breaks open this central Christian understanding with freshness, clarity, and comprehensiveness. This book will remain a valuable resource that touches this core Christian understanding with theological and spiritual integrity as well as grounded life-praxis. Pastoral practitioners as well as theological and spiritual seekers—even those soured on the question—will find a guide and a friend in this book."

—**William S. Schmidt**, professor, Loyola University Chicago

"Human flourishing is a buzzword of the day, yet how is it possible? Frank Woggon brings years of clinical engagement in hospital chaplaincy and palliative care to explore existential questions of shame, guilt, personal trauma, and social fragmentation that haunt our lives and make flourishing feel impossible. In *The Empathic God*, he first deconstructs and reconstructs a theology of *at-onement*, illuminating God's union with Jesus and solidarity with humanity. Then he urges us toward empathic spiritual care for ourselves and others and invites us to embrace a salvation that embodies wholeness, healing, and flourishing."

—**Rev. Dr. Eileen Campbell-Reed**, visiting associate professor of pastoral theology and care, Union Theological Seminary, and author of *Pastoral Imagination: Bringing the Practice of Ministry to Life*

"A brilliant reinterpretation of the Christian understanding of atonement. Dipping deftly and in great depth into the best of Christian theological reflection as well as actual life experiences, Frank Woggon demonstrates the value of seeing God as a God of empathy to address our human struggle with shame. *The Empathic God* should be a must-read for all persons engaged in spiritual and pastoral care."

—**E. Glenn Hinson**, professor emeritus of spirituality and church history, Baptist Theological Seminary at Richmond

"Frank Woggon's book *The Empathic God: A Clinical Theology of At-Onement* is faithfully researched and thoughtfully presented, describing the painful and universal human experience of shame and varied therapeutic responses that are grounded in a nuanced practice of empathy and a theology of wholeness. Woggon powerfully envisions a movement away from shame- and guilt-inducing theologies of redemptive violence to a form of spiritual care that is informed and supported by the restorative, revolutionary, and radically inclusive life of Jesus. *The Empathic God* is a call to a deeper understanding of Jesus's essential message of healing and wholeness, and to the practice of that empowering love in our daily encounters with others and ourselves. As an artist who sings and writes about human condition, spiritual practice, and the ongoing process of healing and becoming, I found this work professionally intriguing, personally encouraging, and artistically inspiring."

—**Carrie Newcomer**, Emmy- and Grammy-recognized songwriter, author, activist

"Dr. Woggon demonstrates the power of pastoral theology to weave together theological and psychological scholarship, stories from Scripture and contemporary life, and empathic healing practices. His singular focus on the destructive power of shame and the healing power of divine and human empathy drives broad and deep examinations of Scripture, theology, human suffering, and salvation-healing. Those who practice spiritual care, theological construction, and contemporary meaning formation will be informed and challenged."

—**Steven Ivy**, professor of the practice of pastoral care, Baptist Seminary of Kentucky

The Empathic God

FRANK WOGGON

The Empathic God

A CLINICAL THEOLOGY OF AT-ONEMENT

Fortress Press
Minneapolis

THE EMPATHIC GOD
A Clinical Theology of At-Onement

Copyright © 2024 Frank Woggon. Published by Fortress Press, an imprint of 1517 Media. All rights reserved. Except for brief quotations in critical articles and reviews, no part of this book may be reproduced in any manner without prior written permission from the publisher. Email copyright@1517.media or write to Permissions, Fortress Press, PO Box 1209, Minneapolis, MN 55440-1209.

All Scripture quotations, unless otherwise indicated, are from the New Revised Standard Version Bible, copyright © 1989 National Council of the Churches of Christ in the United States of America. Used by permission. All rights reserved worldwide.

Excerpts from *Telling Secrets* by Frederick Buechner, copyright (c) 1991 by Frederick Buechner, used by permission from HarperCollins Publishers and Frederick Buechner Literary Assets, LLC.

Library of Congress Cataloging-in-Publication Data

Names: Woggon, Frank, author.
Title: The Empathic God : a clinical theology of at-onement / Frank Woggon.
Description: Minneapolis, MN : Fortress Press, [2024] | Includes bibliographical references and index.
Identifiers: LCCN 2023034816 (print) | LCCN 2023034817 (ebook) | ISBN 9781506496689 (print) | ISBN 9781506496696 (ebook)
Subjects: LCSH: Christian life. | Spiritual life--Chrsitianity. | Empathy. | Atonement.
Classification: LCC BV4501.3 .W63 2024 (print) | LCC BV4501.3 (ebook) | DDC 234/.5--dc23/eng/20231122
LC record available at https://lccn.loc.gov/2023034816
LC ebook record available at https://lccn.loc.gov/2023034817

Cover design: Ashley Muehlbauer
Cover art: Standing Still - stock illustration by AEvenson/Getty Images

Print ISBN: 978-1-5064-9668-9
eBook ISBN: 978-1-5064-9669-6

In memory of
Edward Thornton and Andrew Lester,
teachers, mentors, and friends,
who encouraged me to write about what (I think) I know.

CONTENTS

Preface	ix
Introduction	1

Part One
A Problematic Atonement

1. Tradition	25
2. Re-Visions	47

Part Two
Life Narratives of Shame, Salvation, and Redemption

3. Frederick Buechner: *Telling Secrets*	73
4. Toni Morrison: *Beloved*	89

Part Three
Shame

5. Psychological Perspectives	109
6. Theological Approaches	139

Part Four
Empathy

7. Clinical Theories and Applications	181
8. A Theological Interpretation	213

Part Five
Practicing At-Onement

9. Toward an Empathic Praxis of Spiritual Care	245
Bibliography	275
Index of Names, Scripture References, and Subjects	293

PREFACE

Sitting in the black, wooden pew during Sunday morning worship at Immanuel Baptist Church, my eight-year-old self *knew* that I was sinful and that I was at the same time loved by a God who sacrificed his son to save me. The crosses carved in three layers into the wood at both ends of the pew were symbolic reminders of that vicious act of love. At that time in my life, my religious knowledge was not yet a heartfelt conviction but more of an awareness of sorts of how the message proclaimed from the pulpit pertained to me, and it certainly was not anything that preoccupied me Mondays through Saturdays. It took five more years and many more indicting reminders about my corrupt nature until I publicly declared in front of the congregation that I wanted to be saved and desired to be baptized. To be sure, the congregation that worshiped at Immanuel Baptist Church was a loving group of believers, truly a family of faith, and I am grateful for many expressions of nurture and pastoral care that I experienced among this community during my early faith journey into young adulthood. However, the message that I received from the pulpit about the human condition—my condition—and the possibility of redemption was in line with traditional teachings about the verdict of eternal damnation and the possibility of salvation.

This book is about salvation. Given my early experience with the topic, it may not come as a surprise that I would eventually write about it. But my argument in this book is about a different kind of salvation and a different kind of God than I knew as an eight-year-old. In fact, I argue that what we need to be saved from is the shame that certain Christian teachings instill or perpetuate. More precisely, I propose to reinterpret the Christian teaching of atonement and the God event in the Jesus story from a clinical perspective, suggesting a corresponding empathic praxis of care. I primarily address spiritual care practitioners in the Christian tradition and learners in the field of spiritual care who strive to pursue a reflective practice. Chaplains, ministers of pastoral care, pastoral counselors, and spiritually integrated psychotherapists may fall into this category as do students in pastoral care and pastoral theology, clinical pastoral education, or similar praxis-oriented training programs. My hope is that pastoral theologians in the academy and others who are interested in studying alternative models of salvation will also consider this model as a theoretical basis for a faithful Christian praxis.

While I am academically trained in pastoral theology and the psychology of religion, I am not an academic theologian. I work as a clinical theologian in a regional health care system. I am a board-certified health care chaplain and a clinical educator of aspiring chaplains and seminary students enrolled in Clinical Pastoral Education. I am also an administrator for spiritual care services in an academic health care system and teach at a medical school where I am primarily involved with interprofessional palliative care education and research. The task of reinterpreting a central Christian doctrine such as the teaching about the atonement might seem ostensibly to be out of my lane. However, if the doctrine of atonement is about a God event that initiated salvation, it should be of concern to spiritual care practitioners in the Christian tradition how the teaching about salvation interprets the human condition and the possibility of transformation. After all, we attend daily to persons and to communities in need of healing and restoration.

I began working on the manuscript for this book when the COVID-19 pandemic reached the United States and when a renewed racial reckoning began in many U.S. cities. In our hospitals, patients faced serious illness and death in isolation, separated from the care of loved ones, lonely and often afraid, if they were alert. Our chaplaincy team had to provide care in new ways and needed to accept limitations that were inherent in this new form of crisis care. Much of our care for months was provided through teleconferencing and phone calls, which seemed often less than what we wanted to offer and, at the same time, was strangely rewarding when family members who could not visit the hospital felt connected to their loved ones through our initiative. The COVID-19 crisis marked the human condition as frightfully vulnerable, confronted us with unforeseen limitations, and left us often feeling helpless.

Along with a global pandemic, the killings of Breonna Taylor, Ahmaud Arbery, and George Floyd by police officers and by self-appointed community guardians forced us to face a national epidemic of structural and institutional racism. My own community, home of Breonna Taylor, was one of the cities that saw prolonged protests for justice and also experienced escalations of violence. I remember being paged to the hospital one evening in May 2020, after seven people had been shot during protests, to support family members of victims and anxious hospital staff who were frightened, angry, and divided about the events in our community. The human condition showed up unmistakably fragile, fragmented, and in need of healing, restoration, and reconciliation. In light of racially motivated violence that we witnessed in the news and on our streets, the notion that violence could be ultimately redemptive and heal the human condition seemed incredulous, and the task of constructing a therapeutic theology of the atonement that could guide a praxis of spiritual care, not just for individuals but also for communities, appeared to be not only a worthwhile undertaking but a theological imperative.

I am grateful for the support of many colleagues, friends, and my family who listened to my emerging ideas and engaged my argument with curiosity and with critical questions. Their feedback has been invaluable, and the dialogue has been energizing all along the way. Eileen Campbell-Reed, Glenn Hinson, Bob Cunningham, Bill Thomason, and Chris Conver read drafts of chapters or the whole manuscript, provided insightful feedback, offered critique, and asked the right questions that helped me clarify my argument. I am grateful for their commitment and willingness to dialogue despite their own busy teaching schedules, writing projects, and professional commitments. Riley Sumner of the *Rowntree Medical Library* assisted me with literature searches and supplied the literature that I requested, often at lightning speed, proving her to be a librarian extraordinaire. The teams of chaplains on the UofL Health downtown campus have provided collegiality over the years, and much of my perspective on spiritual care has evolved in dialogue with them. My colleagues in the Interdisciplinary Program for Palliative Care and Chronic Illness at the University of Louisville School of Medicine—Barbara Head, Carol Jones, Bonika Peters, Mark Pfeifer, Tara Schapmire, along with Karen Black and Monica Shaw—have taught me much about interdisciplinary dialogue, which is a central aspect of constructing a clinical theology.

I am deeply grateful to Clarence Barton, my first clinical pastoral education (CPE) supervisor at Central State Hospital, who provided early guidance in my professional training. He died just a few months before this book was scheduled to be published. He lived long and well. Clarence met this German student, who often masked his insecurities through pretentious theological reflections, with curious and compassionate empathy and challenged me during my first unit of CPE to develop my own clinical theology in dialogue with others. His challenge was a turning point and has guided much of my theological work over the last three decades. Clarence continued to offer his friendship through the years, and it has been a precious gift. Many of the students I worked with in CPE programs, still heeding Clarence's challenge, have helped me to learn about constructing a clinical theology even as I tried to instruct them in that very task. They are too many to name, but some of their stories appear in clinical vignettes throughout the book.

Yvonne D. Hawkins at Fortress Press received and accompanied this project with much enthusiasm and encouragement. She has been a skilled and helpful guide through the publication process. Her suggestions for tightening my Germanic style polished my writing and sharpened my argument. This book would not have seen the light of publishing day without her dedication and commitment to making it happen, and I am grateful for our collaboration.

Finally, I am deeply thankful for my family, who encouraged and supported my investment in this project even as it took time away from spending time together. Our daughters, Hannah and Erin, cheered me on, not quite getting into the depth of my argument but appreciating my enthusiasm. They shine bright and beautiful as they make their way and a difference in the world. Kelley has been a fun, loving, gracious, and challenging partner in marriage, parenting, and in professional ministry for more than thirty years. She patiently read and commented on the various versions of each chapter. My argument is more clearly developed, and the book has much less Latin with shorter sentences because of her input, which, I am sure, readers will appreciate. More importantly, her dedication to her calling and commitment to service and to the ministry of caring for others exemplifies the praxis of at-onement that I propose.

All those who have come alongside to help me explore the possibility of salvation through a different lens may not have kept me on the straight and narrow—I consider that a good thing—but they helped to make this a better and more readable book. Any erroneous statements I made or blind spots in my argument are, of course, entirely my own responsibility. A final comment about my use of language when it comes to writing about individuals, particularly as it applies to clinical-therapeutic situations. Throughout the book, I switch between male and female pronouns in no specific order and employ in places plural pronouns in reference to individuals. This use of plural pronouns is my attempt to acknowledge that not everyone identifies with binary gender categories.

INTRODUCTION

"Gloria enim Dei vivens homo."

— Saint Irenaeus

SAINT IRENAEUS'S OFTEN-QUOTED statement from his fourth book *Against Heresies* is about the interrelatedness of God's being and human life.[1] It literally translates "for the glory of God is a living human being," and it is frequently rendered as "the glory of God is a human being fully alive." In context, the statement intimately links the work of creation with the incarnation and with revelatory knowledge of God. Regardless of what the exact translation is, Irenaeus's declaration suggests that human life and its flourishing are not only theologically relevant but also theologically significant. The flourishing of human life signifies God's ongoing work toward salvation and to restore wholeness. Consequently, questions about conditions and dynamics that inhibit the flourishing of life and how those conditions and dynamics can be transformed become equally important and should be a focus of theological inquiry. This book examines shame as a major life-inhibiting force and considers therapeutic, restorative responses to the human condition in the grip of alienating shame.

Traditionally, the proclamation that God saves through the Jesus event is at the center of Christian faith (Matt 1:21). However, the proclamation is not self-explanatory and requires interpretation, particularly in light of changing paradigms that explain human experience for the sake of a relevant Christian praxis. This book develops an understanding of salvation through a clinical theological paradigm that holds that shame more so than guilt is a central dilemma and source of suffering inherent in human experience. I argue that such a clinical theology requires a new interpretation of God's

---

1 Saint Irenaeus, *Five Books against Heresies: The Standard Greek and Latin Text for Over a Century with Detailed English Commentary*, vol. 2, ed. W. Wigan Harvey (1857; repr., Rochester: St. Irenaeus Press, 2013), 219.

saving response to the human condition in the Jesus event. I will introduce the clinical theological method in detail later in this introduction. For now, it may suffice to say that a clinical theology takes its point of departure in lived human experience, particularly experiences of travail, suffering, and struggle, to explore how a creative and saving God event can address such experiences and may call upon us to participate in the ongoing work of salvation.

The Self in Need of Salvation

In Christian theology, the restoration of the human condition has traditionally been explained through the concept of *atonement*, which refers to the reparation or expiation of sin and is closely related to the notion of *salvation*, God's initiative to deliver humanity from sin and its consequences. Traditional interpretations have emphasized that human atonement is an impossible possibility; therefore, God's saving initiative became necessary to redeem humanity. Although the concept of atonement in Christian thought has taken on a specific and narrow meaning that is primarily defined through a particularND crucicentric interpretation of the Jesus story, I continue to use that terminology of atonement and interpret the Christian story about salvation from a clinical perspective and the practice of spiritual care. I use the word *at-onement* as a clinical-theological construct that refers to the empathic process that supports the flourishing of life by functioning to restore personal and relational wholeness in individuals and communities. Such wholeness, I contend, is the essence of salvation.

The next two chapters discuss traditional models of the atonement as well as contemporary interpretations. Traditional models are based on the premise that humanity is in need of salvation because of its inherent sinfulness understood as willful rebellion against God. According to those theological paradigms, humanity has been infected with sin and is guilty due to violating God's commands and dishonoring God through disobedience. The notion of *original sin* is closely tied to a traditional understanding of the atonement. It defines the human condition as an intrinsic state of estrangement and rebellion against God, set into motion by Adam's disobedience and his yielding to temptation. The original version of this teaching by Augustine of Hippo declared that the transmission of the sinful nature happened physically through sexual intercourse and, more specifically, that the male semen was the culprit. Thus, the virgin birth and the belief in the immaculate conception of Jesus became important underlying concepts for an understanding of the atonement, as the early Christian creeds document.

How we understand sin will determine how we understand salvation and whether such understanding can be relevant to contemporary human experience in travail. Traditional understandings about sin and forgiveness may not alleviate inner turmoil and spiritual pain but may indeed intensify them.

> Ken[2] had voluntarily entered an outpatient treatment program at a hospital for chemically dependent patients. He was addicted to alcohol. His decision to seek treatment followed a serious bout with pancreatitis and his wife's threat to end their marriage if he continued to drink. Ken had been raised in a Baptist family, and participation in church life had been both time-consuming and meaningful for him until he started to drink in high school and increasingly withdrew from his religious community. At the time of his treatment, he was not actively involved in any church activities, except that he nominally belonged to the community church where his wife and her family were members. When he met for his spiritual assessment with the chaplain assigned to the treatment program, he was tearful with many regrets about decisions made and actions taken under the influence of alcohol. Ken was clearly experiencing spiritual pain, and eventually gave words to it, saying, "I know that God can forgive me. I just cannot forgive myself."

Ken remembered the teachings of his church about salvation and God's forgiveness, but this knowledge did not help to overcome his agonizing regrets. While he was familiar with the concept of a forgiving God and had believed it to be true since childhood, his belief ultimately did not affect how he felt

---

2 Names and identifying characteristics of persons mentioned in clinical vignettes as well as details in the description have been changed to protect individuals' rights to privacy while preserving the essence of the clinical situation.

about himself. In clinical practice, I have heard similar statements about patients' struggles with their past many times. I have learned that the inability to forgive oneself is typically not evidence of an exceptionally heavy burden of guilt, but rather it typically is evidence of crippling shame and self-judgment.

In *Christ and Selfhood*, pastoral theologian Wayne Oates argues that a Christian understanding of the self needs to be focused on a person's encounter with Christ and its transformative effects. "Jesus Christ is the historical Event and transforming Person from whom all distinctly Christian notions of selfhood are derived."[3] While Oates employs established Christological concepts to explore the transformation of selfhood and identifies human sin essentially in traditional terms as human hubris, he was ahead of his times in suggesting that contemporary psychological perspectives "have something to offer to our day in the recital and proclamation of redemption in Jesus Christ."[4]

Expanding Oates's argument through a contemporary, clinical interpretation of the atonement, I argue that the human condition in need of salvation and healing is first and foremost defined by the psycho-social-spiritual experience of shame and its alienating effects. This assessment requires us to rethink how we understand God's saving initiative through the Jesus event. In other words, the self in need of salvation is not in a state of inevitable and inherent corruption but in a state of fragmentation that marks the human condition afflicted by alienating shame. Shame essentially signals a loss of wholeness. The self in need of salvation is first a fragmented, alienated, and defeated self and not a morally corrupt self. The psycho-spiritual experience of self-fragmentation may include or lead to acts that can be judged as morally wrong, and from a clinical perspective, the experience of guilt certainly must not be dismissed. However, while guilt may co-exist with shame, it is a secondary emotional response.

If shame is indeed a primary affective experience that defines the human condition, the notion of *self* appropriately refers to the human subject, and I will use the term *self* throughout the book to refer to the essence of a person. Both shame and guilt are *self*-conscious experiences. However, while guilt

---

3 Wayne R. Oates, *Christ and Selfhood* (New York: Association Press, 1961), 22.
4 Oates, *Christ and Selfhood*, 23.

references behavior, shame is focused on the self. Shame determines how we perceive and construct ourselves to be and our relationships with others. Shame identifies the self as lacking in value, as blemished, and even as unacceptable. It alienates the self from others, from its true self, and from God. Psychologist Gershen Kaufman highlights the close connection between shame and the self and identifies shame as an entrance to the self. "It is the affect of indignity, of defeat, or transgression, of inferiority, and of alienation. No other affect is closer to the experienced self. None is more central to the sense of identity. Shame is felt as an inner torment, a sickness of the soul. It is the most poignant experience of the self by the self. . . . Shame is a wound felt from the inside, dividing us both from ourselves and from each other."[5] The self that is tormented by shame is not in need of salvation from God's eternal judgment as much as it is in need to be saved from defeating self-judgment and restored to wholeness in relation with self, God, and others.

Shifting the Atonement Paradigm

Admittedly, I am not the first to suggest a paradigm shift from guilt to shame in understanding the human condition and the meaning of atonement. Pointing to the fact that, on the one hand, theological reflections about the atonement have not paid attention to the implications of shame, and that, on the other hand, theories of shame do not consider the implication of the atonement, pastoral theologian Brad Binau asks, "When shame is the question, how does the atonement answer?"[6] He presents elements of a relational, theological anthropology, arguing that human beings are essentially created for relationship, that the experience of estrangement defines the human condition existentially, and that shame is the primary force that disrupts relationships and shapes existential, human experience. Binau does not see that the paradigm shift requires a radically new interpretation of the atonement but explores the relevancy of traditional atonement models as a response to

---

5 Gershen Kaufman, *Shame: The Power of Caring*, 3rd rev. ed. (Cambridge, MA: Schenkman Books, 1992), xix–xx.
6 See Brad A. Binau, "When Shame Is the Question, How Does the Atonement Answer?" *Journal of Pastoral Theology* 12, no. 1 (January 2002): 89–113.

shame. In particular, he suggests that the notion of recapitulation, which was prominent in the theologies of Irenaeus of Lyon and Athanasius, provides a corrective response to the problem of shame and corresponds to interventions for shame in contemporary psychotherapeutic approaches.[7]

Similarly, theologian Mark McConnell has drawn on social science research and suggests that the reality and experience of shame is the problem of the human condition. Like Binau, McConnell offers an account of the atonement that builds upon a theological understanding of Jesus's saving work as an act of recapitulation and of the vicarious humanity of Christ. According to McConnell, in "Christ's identification with humanity, God fully moves toward humanity even though humanity is lost in sin. Our humanity does not repel God. Our humanity leads God to embrace us in our shame. If the location of the first Adam was paradisiacal Eden, the location of the second Adam is shame-filled humanity."[8] While Binau and McConnell shift the understanding of the human condition from guilt to shame, their theological frameworks still characterize humanity as corrupted and affirm a traditional model of the atonement that ultimately culminates in sanctioned violence as a remedy. Both offer a modified interpretation of traditional doctrine that views Christ's work of recapitulation as taking on human shame to transform it into a restored relationship with God. The solution they suggest, however, seems unsatisfying as a merely updated answer from the past to a question that is raised by a contemporary understanding of the human condition.

Philosopher Eleonore Stump presents an interpretation of the atonement based on Thomas of Aquinas's ethics of love and his satisfaction model, maintaining that the atonement is a remedy that offers humanity a way to be united with God by providing a solution for shame *and* guilt, both of which result primarily from moral wrongdoing and separate humans from God. She acknowledges that among the two experiences that define the human

---

7 See Binau, "When Shame Is the Question," 103. For a more detailed discussion of the *Christus Victor* model and Irenaeus's understanding of recapitulation, see the next chapter.
8 T. Mark McConnell, "From 'I Have Done Wrong' to 'I Am Wrong': (Re)Constructing Atonement as a Response to Shame," in *Locating Atonement: Explorations in Constructive Dogmatics*, ed. Oliver D. Crisp and Fred Sanders (Grand Rapids: Zondervan, 2015), 183.

condition, shame is more complex than guilt and that it is more difficult to overcome and creates a divided self.[9] Shame, as Stump points out, does not exclusively result from moral transgression, even though one's own or someone else's evil acts against a person may cause shame. Shame may also be the consequence of limitations or defects of nature that lead to considering oneself or being considered by others for various reasons as deficient. Additionally, it may result from the awareness or perception of one's social location that leads to self-judgment of inferiority or deserved rejection. "Consequently, shame can be a potent source of distance between the shamed person and others, and it can also introduce distance between a shamed person and God. A shamed person's repudiation of himself as ugly, or otherwise meriting rejection, is as effective as the inner dividedness generated by moral wrongdoing at preventing or undermining union between himself and God."[10] Stump notably distinguishes between various sources and manifestations of shame as defining aspects of the human condition and adopts the concept of a divided self as a result. At the same time, however, she also affirms the traditional account of the atonement and sees the solution to all variations of shame in the bestowing of honor. Stump interprets both the incarnation and the shame of the cross through the shame-honor principle. In light of Jesus's sharing of human shame, she holds that "it is reasonable to conclude that this sharing defeats the shame attaching to the species itself. That is, it is reasonable to think that the honor of having God out of love share human shame as well as human nature is greater than the good lost, namely, the honor that the species lost in virtue of its deplorable history."[11] Focusing on the atonement in the event of the cross, Stump explains God's work of salvation that defeats shame as a restored union, God's indwelling within persons through the divine spirit, allying the "truest or deepest self with the God who joins himself on the cross to every post-Fall person and shares all that is in that person's psyche, including the shame."[12] Like Binau and McConnell, Stump shifts the assessment of the human condition from guilt to shame but does not shift an understanding about a salvific, restorative response.

---

9 See Eleonore Stump, *Atonement* (Oxford: Oxford University Press, 2018), 50.
10 Stump, *Atonement*, 52.
11 Stump, *Atonement*, 354.
12 Stump, *Atonement*, 361.

If shame is regarded as a cultural and interpersonal phenomenon, the social construct of honor may be deemed an antidote to shame. However, if we consider shame in terms of Kaufman's explanation above as an existential, psycho-spiritual experience that may have social causes and implications but is primarily a disturbance within the self, a sickness of the soul, honor does not promise a restorative solution. For honor is a public claim to worth or value that may not transform the existential experience of the self as defeated and deficient. In fact, public honor may increase a sense of shame by contrasting an admiring outside perception with self-judgment of inferiority and deficiency, enhancing the fear of "being found out" and rejected. A mere reinterpretation of a traditional, crucicentric version of the atonement through the lens of shame is not sufficient to explain God's saving response to the fragmented self. If our understanding of the human condition changes, so must our understanding of God's response, since the therapeutic solutions to shame and guilt are distinctly different. Guilt is overcome through repentance, forgiveness, and, if it is possible, by making amends. Shame is not primarily a response to behavior or an internal, emotional reaction of the self to moral decisions but involves the whole self in what Kaufman calls "a torment of *self*-consciousness."[13] It is the excruciating experience of judging oneself as inadequate, wrong, unworthy, or unacceptable, and I shall argue that the restorative, therapeutic response to shame is through empathic attunement to the self and to its narratives and through acceptance.

Theology as Therapeutic

In his now classic essay about anxiety, guilt, and shame in the atonement, clinical psychologist Paul Pruyser explored the psychological substrate of traditional atonement models and argues "that the idea of God must be therapeutic and that the imagery and language in which he is to be pondered must be therapeutic imagery and language."[14] Since Pruyser made his argument, research about neuroplasticity has shown how neural networks within the brain can grow and change as a result of new learning, environmental influences, and psychotherapy. Recent scholarship in *neurotheology* has used

---

13 Kaufman, *Shame*, 9.
14 Paul W. Pruyser, "Anxiety, Guilt, and Shame," *Theology Today* 21, no. 1 (April 1964): 29.

research on neuroplasticity to support the idea of a therapeutic theology by examining the relationship between the brain and the mind on the one hand and theology and religion on the other hand. One of the principal goals of neurotheology is to improve the human condition by examining the impact of theology and religious and spiritual practice on human experience as reflected in brain functioning.[15] Models of God, therefore, not only affect individual faith experience and shape personal values and behavior, but they also impact physical and emotional well-being. They influence cultural systems and the values those systems espouse. Furthermore, they create and install symbols that can powerfully shape how we understand and interact with ourselves and others.

Traditional models of atonement have created symbols—most prominently the symbol of the cross—that promote redemptive violence and implicate God in a violent atonement, at best, as a bystander who allows violence to take its course and, at worst, as a perpetrator or abuser. The narrative of salvation too often has been reduced to its violent end and miraculous resurrection. However, the *whole* Jesus story is both about a response to the human condition in need of salvation and about a response to the God event that called upon Jesus. A theology of the atonement that is therapeutic creates a new symbol system by interpreting God's saving initiative in the Jesus event through therapeutic wisdom, theory, and practice. A therapeutic theology provides a theoretical framework that promotes the restoration of wholeness in persons and communities. Personal wholeness integrates various aspects of one's life story and experience into a cohesive self and reflects the ability to flourish in one's relationships with self, others, and God. Communal wholeness restores inclusive and wholesome relationships in communities and accesses resources that support flourishing life.

The Jesus story has therapeutic intent. The story is an exemplary theological narrative about one whose mission was determined by his sensitivity to God's love and empathy for humanity. In speaking of the Jesus *event* or the God event in the Jesus story, I draw upon John Caputo's theology that understands God as the name of an *event* that calls upon us rather than as a supreme being that controls the world and acts in our favor or against us,

---

15 See Andrew B. Newberg, *Principles of Neurotheology* (London & New York: Routledge, 2016), 18.

doing or undoing things.[16] God does not exist, according to Caputo, but rather *insists* and calls into existence. "God is a spirit that calls," explains Caputo, "a spirit that can happen anywhere and haunts everything, insistently."[17] God as the name of an event does not just name that which is happening but rather is the name for the *essence* of what is happening and, perhaps most importantly, is the call ushered by the event. The Jesus event is at once about one who was called upon and responded in a radical fashion, and it is about a call that is ushered upon us through that event. It remains to be seen what exactly the nature of that call is, how it will be disturbing for us, and how it insists. I interpret the meaning of the Jesus event from a clinical-therapeutic perspective and explore how that event calls upon us to imagine a faithful practice of care in response.

A theology that is therapeutic is a practical theology. While it interprets the tradition through the lens of therapeutic knowledge and practice, it also provides a theological narrative, a symbol system, and an ethics that guide those who follow in the way of Jesus how to engage the world and the human condition in healing ways. Practical theologian Stephen Pattison holds that the question "So what?" is crucial to claim relevancy when reflecting theologically.[18] In order to answer this question, he outlines the movement of practical theology from *description* ("What is the case?") and *understanding* ("Why is it this way?") to *prescription* ("What might be done and considered differently?") and *action*. He identifies practical theology as "a searching, critical, interdisciplinary conversation between contemporary human experience, the insight of modern non-theological disciplines and practices and aspects of the theological tradition."[19] Therefore, the so-what of re-interpreting the atonement through the lens of shame and empathy is a praxis of spiritual care that participates in God's saving response to the human condition.

---

16 For the most part, I refer to the content of the gospel narratives as "the Jesus story." In a few places, I use "the Jesus event" interchangeably with "the Jesus story" and to abbreviate the phrase "the God event in the Jesus story."
17 John D. Caputo, *The Insistence of God: A Theology of Perhaps* (Bloomington & Indianapolis: Indiana University Press, 2013), 13.
18 See Stephen Pattison, *Saving Face: Enfacement, Shame, Theology* (Farnham & Burlington: Ashgate Publishing, 2013), 4.
19 Pattison, *Saving Face*, 5.

I use the terms *practice* and *praxis* both throughout the book. While the two are related concepts, they have distinct meanings. *Practice* is the skilled and customary or repetitive, practical application of theory or doctrines. *Praxis*, on the other hand, is the synthesis of theory and practice and a continuously reflective practice.[20] I argue that a contemporary praxis of spiritual care that is informed by a therapeutic, clinical theology participates in God's ongoing work of salvation. In traditional Christian perspective, the salvific change in the life of individuals is a *result* of salvation from divine judgment and the consequences of sin. In the classic distinction between justification and sanctification, doctrinal theology identified the change of juridical standing before God through *justification*, which became a condition for *sanctification*, the transformation from sinfulness and a self-centered life to a God-centered life. In the context of a therapeutic, practical theology and a related and relational praxis of spiritual care, the transformation of the self *is* the salvific event, even as God's saving response has been previously expressed in an exemplary way in the Jesus event. How we interpret the God event in the Jesus story does not only explain God's saving initiative toward humanity, but it also creates a theological narrative that impacts spiritual and existential meaning-making in contemporary human experience and can guide the empathic praxis of spiritual care.

Constructing a Clinical Theology

A theology that aims to be therapeutic is ideally constructed as a clinical theology. A clinical theology adopts processes and principles that are used in clinical contexts to provide therapeutic interventions and applies them to the task of theology. I use the term *clinical* in a broad sense to refer to different therapeutic contexts where practitioners from various healing professions work together to provide treatments and care. A clinical theology is not constructed in the academy but is grounded in clinical experiences and constructed by clinicians, expert practitioners of spiritual care who may be chaplains, pastoral counselors, spiritually integrated psychotherapists, and the like. More specifically, a clinical theology is a reflective and constructive

---

20 See Paulo Freire, *Pedagogy of the Oppressed*, trans. Myra Bergman Ramos (New York & London: Continuum, 2000), 125–126.

theological process by which practitioners of spiritual care explore how a creative and saving God event becomes present to lived human experiences of suffering and spiritual struggle and how an understanding of such presence can inform a praxis of spiritual care.

Influences of a Clinical Theology

A clinical theology starts with human experience to arrive at a theological perspective that informs a relevant and faithful praxis. It aligns with the assertations of constructive theologians Stephen Ray and Laurel Schneider, both members of the Workgroup on Constructive Theology, who argue that theology must be relevant to the human experience and reflect the incarnational Jesus story.

> *Theology that gets its own hands dirty with the real pain and the real joy of life in* this *very world in* this *very time comes closer to expressing something meaningful about the God who became fully and fleshly present in* that *real time and real place two thousand years ago, a place so much like our own, a place and a time as much in need of new pathways to healing as ours is now.*[21]

Ray and Schneider conclude that if "we do not begin with the reality of human experience in the world as it is, theologians cannot hope to speak with any wisdom to that world."[22] Using the metaphor that Ray and Schneider offer, a clinical theology is a theology constructed with dirty hands and firmly rooted in the at times messy practice of spiritual care and in experiences of human solidarity. It is a constructive theology in that it constructs a theory of the ongoing work of salvation through the practice of spiritual care.

A clinical theology also resembles a pastoral theology.[23] Both approaches to theological reflection focus on lived experience and are grounded in the

---

21 Laurel C. Schneider and Stephen G. Ray, eds., *Awake to the Moment: An Introduction to Theology* (Louisville: Westminster John Knox Press, 2016), 3.
22 Schneider and Ray, *Awake to the Moment*, 3.
23 The mission statement of the *Journal of Pastoral Theology* describes this branch of theology in a way that closely resonates with the above description of a clinical theology. It defines pastoral theology as a "constructive theology growing out of the exercise of caring relationships, with attention both to present lived experience and to knowledge

actual practice of care, in theological theories past and present, and in interdisciplinary dialogue. However, while pastoral theology ideally explores a wide range of human experiences, a clinical theology has by definition a more narrow, reflective focus on aspects of the human condition that are in some ways characterized by travail or distress and are in need of care or healing. While life-affirming themes are not absent from the clinic, it is, after all, a place to attend to injuries, illness, and pain.

The clinical theology that I propose also draws from John Caputo's distinction between a *confessional theology* and a *radical theology*. As Caputo puts it, confessional theology is "what we ordinarily call just theology, period, plain and simple, without adjective, the sort of thing the various religious communities do in their seminaries."[24] Confessional theology, even though it clarifies and interprets the tradition, is a practice of genuflection that bows to the tradition as normative. Radical theology, on the other hand, is the radicalization of confessional theology that explores the tradition as a formative but not as normative source. According to Caputo, it is a disciplined practice of theological inflection, "constituted by the distance it creates between itself and confessional theology, the disturbance it creates within confessional theology."[25] By shifting the atonement paradigm using a clinical perspective, I address a certain community like a confessional theologian to propose a theology in which that community can hopefully recognize itself. At the same time, I do not consider a cruricentric interpretation of the Jesus event as normative. Rather, like radical theologians, I propose a theological perspective that may disturb a traditional reading of the Jesus story. Furthermore, I follow the approach of a radical theology by not observing a strict separation between theology and other disciplines. In fact, interdisciplinary dialogue and the input from other disciplines are crucial elements of a clinical theology and provide important data to re-interpret aspects of the Christian tradition.

---

derived from the past." Accessed August 23, 2020, http://societyforpastoraltheology.org/journal-of-pastoral-theology/.
24 John D. Caputo, *In Search of Radical Theology: Expositions, Explorations, Exhortations* (New York: Fordham University Press, 2020), 3.
25 Caputo, *In Search of Radical Theology*, 3.

Clinical Theology as Dialogical

A clinical theology emerges through dialogue. In the clinic, interdisciplinary dialogue and collaboration that attend to the whole person produce the most effective care. Interdisciplinary care provided by interdisciplinary teams is a best practice that produces better outcomes than specialized or multidisciplinary care and is more cost-effective. Applying principles and processes from clinical practice to the task of theology, I suggest that interdisciplinary dialogue is an essential part of a clinical theology. Clinical theologians particularly seek out dialogue partners from other healing professions who have knowledge about theories and therapeutic processes that have the capacity to explain and alleviate distress, painful limitations, and suffering within the human condition. A clinical theology constructs an understanding of the God event in the Jesus story and corresponding concepts and models of caring and healing through appreciative dialogue with other disciplines. Such dialogue is not just an attempt to listen for supportive evidence but is open to discovering new perspectives that may emerge in the process and thus becomes a means for theological exploration and theological learning.

However, a clinical theology does not only engage in appreciative interdisciplinary dialogue between experts; it also enters into dialogue with life narratives of individuals and the narratives that shape the life and identity of communities. Educator and philosopher Paolo Freire's philosophy of education adds an important perspective to an understanding of such dialogue. In *Pedagogy of the Oppressed*, he characterizes education as a dialogical collaboration to name and transform reality that requires critical thinking and a love for the world and those who inhabit it. Freire insists that "dialogue cannot exist . . . in the absence of profound love for the world and for people. The naming of the world which is an act of creation and recreation is not possible if it is not infused with love."[26] If we apply Freire's reflection about the importance of love in dialogical education to the construction of a clinical theology, it suggests that clinical theologians do not only need to have faith in God but also faith in humanity and in the ability of individuals and communities to construct knowledge; to change, create, and recreate; and to engage the possibility of transformation toward wholeness.

---

26 Freire, *Pedagogy of the Oppressed*, 89.

Love sees others as intrinsically valuable and with dignity and possibilities. A pessimistic assessment, on the other hand, which insists with certitude that the human condition is inherently corrupted, cannot support an open, appreciative, and dialogical approach to understanding human experience and possibilities for transformation. Appreciative dialogue that is rooted in love for the world and its inhabitants transcends dogmatic certitude about the human condition and is open to discover new possibilities of seeing and naming the world, including one's theological world.

Clinical Theology as Contextual
All theology is ultimately contextual, constructed at a certain time and in a certain place and utilizing in one way or another metaphors, concepts, and stories from that time and place. The question is whether the contextualization of theology is intentionally claimed or whether context is in the theological blind spot. Angie Pears, a leader in organizational equity, diversity, and inclusion initiatives in Great Britain, raises the question whether a distinction between content and context is even possible when reflecting theologically. She argues that "contextual theology interacts with the traditions of Christianity through the engaged reflection of the theologian and the theological community. . . . It recognizes that both context and human experience along with other more traditional theological sources are significant components of contemporary Christian theologies."[27] A clinical theology claims a particular perspective that is rooted in clinical processes, practice, and experience, and it uses clinical-therapeutic concepts and stories along with concepts and metaphors from the Christian tradition. It explores the meaning of Christian teachings with a focus on real-life human experience, particularly experiences of suffering and spiritual pain. As all contextual theologies are by definition limited and not universally "true," a clinical theology, too, may not be applicable to all contexts.

Catholic theologian Stephen Bevans has classified and examined in detail various models of contextual theology. A clinical theology, as I propose it, fits most closely Bevans's category of a *praxis model*. However, while traditional praxis models of contextual theology, such as liberation theologies,

---

27 Angie Pears, *Doing Contextual Theology* (New York: Routledge, 2010), 2.

emphasize the integrated praxis of theological reflection and action to create social change, a clinical theology focuses primarily on therapeutic change but has also implications for a praxis of spiritual care in response to structural sources of shame. "When we speak of the praxis model of contextual theology," Bevans explains, "we are speaking about a model the central insight of which is that theology is done not simply by providing relevant expressions of Christian faith but also by commitment to Christian action."[28] The praxis model aims at social transformation by using social science insight in a reflective and transformative Christian praxis. Clinical theology, as a praxis model of contextual theology, aims at therapeutic transformation by employing dialogue with other healing disciplines to understand how the alienating effects of shame can be transformed and how to develop a praxis of spiritual care accordingly. The praxis model of contextual theology presupposes that God is present in history and that "God's presence is one of beckoning and invitation, calling men and women of faith to locate God and cooperate with God in God's work of healing, reconciling, liberating. We best know God," Bevans states, "by acting in partnership with God."[29] God's beckoning presence to cooperate with God, not unlike John Caputo's notion of God as the name of an event that calls upon us, means that salvation is an ongoing process in history. I shall argue that an empathic praxis of spiritual care is an important way that spiritual care practitioners participate in that process.

Clinical Theology as Experience-Near

A clinical theology starts with human experience and observations about that experience. In other words, a clinical theology applies an experience-near approach to explore the meaning of the God event or of aspects of that event. The term *experience-near*, to my knowledge, originated with psychiatrist Heinz Kohut's psychoanalytic psychology of the self.[30] Kohut introduced it to distinguish his understanding of the self that was rooted

---

28 Stephen B. Bevans, *Models of Contextual Theology*, rev. ed. (Maryknoll: Orbis Books, 2020), 72.
29 Pears, *Contextual Theology*, 75.
30 See Heinz Kohut, *The Analysis of the Self: A Systematic Approach to the Psychoanalytical Treatment of Narcissistic Personality Disorders* (1971; repr., Chicago: University of Chicago Press, 2009), xv.

in a practice of empathic understanding of how emotions form in human experience from a traditional abstract psychoanalytic model of the psychic apparatus made up of ego, superego, and id. A clinical theology takes an experience-near approach in identifying its point of departure and to find focus but not necessarily to define the entire process of theological inquiry. For example, in relating contemporary human narratives to sacred stories, exploring how they intersect and how one is implicated in the other, a clinical theology applies both an experience-near and an experience-distant perspective.

The clinical pastoral education (CPE) movement has used an experience-near theology since the 1930s, albeit without using this particular terminology. Anton Boisen, a pioneer in the twentieth-century chaplaincy movement and one of the founders of clinical pastoral education, taught his students the case-study method, which he had adopted from physician Richard Cabot, who was another pioneer in the CPE movement and in medical education. Boisen proposed that clinical theological education needed to use the study of the living human document as a primary educational resource. Clinical pastoral educator Charles Gerkin examined Boisen's notion for another generation of theologians and clarified its meaning and intent.

> *Anton Boisen's image of the human person as a "document" to be read and interpreted in a manner analogous to the interpretation of a historical text has, up to the present, simply been taken as an admonition to begin with the experience of persons in the development of ministry theory. That certainly was central to Boisen's intention. Boisen, however, meant more than that. He meant that depth experience of persons in the struggles of their mental and spiritual lives demanded the same respect as do the historic texts from which the foundations of our Judeo-Christian faith tradition are drawn.*[31]

---

[31] Charles V. Gerkin, *The Living Human Document: Re-Visioning Pastoral Counseling in a Hermeneutic Mode* (Nashville: Abingdon Press, 1984), 38. Bonnie Miller-McLemore has offered a critique of an individualistic approach in pastoral theology and spiritual care and has suggested that the concept of the "living human web" provides a more relevant contemporary paradigm to address spiritual needs and social injustices from a

Boisen collaborated with theologian-physician Helen Flanders Dunbar to create clinical theological training and with physician Richard Cabot, who called for the development of an experience-near theology in the early 1930s. As Cabot understood it, an experience-near theology was one that tested its convictions in the clinic for relevance, "a theology brought to the bedside, to the bereaved, to the dying, to the invalid, to the aged, and to the delinquent."[32] Cabot envisioned a theology at the bedside that would create a theological understanding that was relevant to medical crises and, at the same time, would create a profound understanding of the human condition in the face of suffering. While I agree with Cabot's view about the dyadic nature of a clinical, experience-near theology, a clinical theology is not just purposefully tested at the bedside and applied to clinical practice. Rather, it is a constructive theology, generating theological insight, principles, and models that inform ministry practice.

Clinical Theology as Purposeful
Therapeutic processes in the clinic are typically guided by interdisciplinary plans of care that are established based on clinical assessments. These care plans are outcome-oriented. I suggest adopting this aspect of clinical protocols to the construction of a clinical theology. In doing so, I am making a distinction, albeit subtly, between practical theology and purposeful theology. If practical theology examines, in general, the practices of Christian communities to aid the flourishing of persons and communities, then the notion of a clinical theology as purposeful theology adds the dimensions of hope, meaning, and vocation.

First, living and working with purpose means living and working with hope. Pastoral theologian Andrew Lester makes the point that future consciousness and future orientation are the essence of hope, but that hope is deeply rooted in the present. "Used theologically," Lester explains, "the word hope describes a person's trusting anticipation of the future based on an understanding of a God that is trustworthy and who calls us into and

---

systemic perspective. See Miller-McLemore, "The Living Human Web: A Twenty-Five Year Retrospective," *Pastoral Psychology* 67, no. 3 (June 2018): 305–321.

32 Edward E. Thornton, *Professional Education for Ministry: A History of Clinical Pastoral Education* (Nashville & New York: Abingdon Press, 1970), 48.

open-ended future. This God keeps promises of deliverance, liberation, and salvation."[33] Hope is critical to the therapeutic process and, if we translate the theological, transfinite concept of hope into finite processes of change and growth, it means envisioning a future realistically and identifying possibilities to move with purpose into that future. In other words, hope is an outcome-oriented practice. It does not merely await the future with passive anticipation but actively engages possibilities. A clinical theology aims to create a hopeful practice of participating in God's initiatives of deliverance, liberation, and salvation.

Second, clinical theology as a purposeful activity explores the meaning of the God event and of a corresponding, faithful praxis in response to human experiences of struggle, pain, and suffering. Meaning and purpose are closely related. We might say that purpose is the call to action that the discovery of meaning ushers. As a clinical educator, I draw on transformative educational theory, which understands meaning making as the essential task of the educational process. It is an act of interpretation and a constructive process to give coherence to human experience that may be expressed through symbols, rituals, or conceptual language.[34] According to transformative educational theory, meaning-perspectives that are either affirmed or developed by engaging disorienting dilemmas serve to guide future decision-making and action. The traditional Christian doctrine of the atonement presents a disorienting dilemma because it implicates the God who Jesus proclaimed as loving and compassionate, who "sends rain on the righteous and the unrighteous" (Matt 5:45), in an act of so-called redemptive violence. I endeavor to engage the dilemma and construct an alternative meaning-perspective through clinical-theological reflections that explore human stories in dialogue with the Jesus story and clinical knowledge and experience.

Finally, the notion of purpose suggests that the praxis of spiritual care, which results from clinical theological reflection, is a vocation. A clinical theology is in its essence a listening process. It listens as God calls upon us through human stories of suffering and through the Jesus story and other

---

33 Andrew D. Lester, *Hope in Pastoral Care and Counseling* (Louisville: Westminster John Knox Press, 1995), 62.
34 See Jack Mezirow, *Transformative Dimensions of Adult Learning* (San Francisco: Jossey-Bass, 1991), 4.

incarnational stories throughout the bible. It seeks to understand how we are to respond. The call that echoes in those different stories and that is upon us is what identifies a praxis of spiritual care as a vocation. It does not elevate spiritual care to a special status among the helping professions as if it were inherently more valuable or required more dedication than other professional activities. Rather, it directs practitioners of spiritual care into the messy depth of human experience and to attend to that experience with empathy and compassion.

Overview of the Chapters

The argument in this book develops in five parts. Each part reflects an aspect of a clinical theology. Part One identifies the problem and introduces theological perspectives that have emerged as attempts to present solutions. In this part, Chapter 1 offers a discussion and critique of crucicentric interpretations of the Jesus story, and I argue that these interpretations overshadow narratives about Jesus's life and liberating public work. In turn, these interpretations end up justifying death-dealing politics and campaigns in the history of the church. In Chapter 2, I examine more recent theological themes and perspectives that interpret the possibility of salvation in the Jesus event without a focus on redemptive violence. Contrasting traditional interpretations and re-visions, I conclude that the construction of a clinical theology of the atonement requires a shift from interpreting the Jesus event with a focus on Jesus's atoning death to a focus on the atoning life of Jesus.

Part Two begins the reflective-constructive process by attending to lived human experience as a point of departure for re-interpreting the need, the means, and the meaning of salvation in Christian experience and practice. In this part, Chapters 3 and 4 present and examine two literary case studies from a clinical perspective, claiming my context as a clinical theologian. Theologian and writer Frederick Buechner's memoir *Telling Secrets* gives an autobiographical account about family dynamics in the wake of traumatic loss, the power of a shameful secret, and the masks that cover the shame. It also documents a personal journey of healing through the discovery of accepting communities. The novel *Beloved* by Nobel Prize-winning author Toni Morrison, on the other hand, is an exemplary story about oppression, trauma, and shame; about the intergenerational reach of shame; and about courage in the face of dehumanizing adversity. While it is an imaginative story and a piece of creative writing, it is based on the true story of an enslaved woman, Margaret Garner, from Kentucky. One might with good reason raise the question as to how creative writing can provide experience-near data. I argue that literary narratives, even though creatively imagined, can provide relevant, experience-near data for theological reflection.

Part Three presents an assessment of the human condition based on interdisciplinary dialogue and argues that shame presents a universal and painful dilemma in human experience, detailing various aspects of the life-limiting and alienating effects of shame. In this part, Chapter 5 explores psychological perspectives on shame as a master emotion, drawing on a variety of theories and psychotherapeutic approaches. I discuss the difference between shame and guilt and how shame presents phenomenologically. The discussion pays particular attention to the relationships between shame and narcissism, trauma, addiction, and oppression. In Chapter 6, I attempt to understand the meaning of shame in human experience from a theological perspective. I revisit in some detail the so-called parable of the prodigal son as a master story about the human condition affected by shame and guilt and discuss seven modern theological approaches to shame that are rare examples of reflections on shame in the history of theological inquiry.

Part Four continues the interdisciplinary dialogue by examining the concept and practice of empathy as an imaginative, therapeutic response to the human condition and particularly to the experience of shame, both psychologically and theologically. In this part, Chapter 7 offers an overview of several theories of empathy. The discussion focuses on the therapeutic role of empathy in response to shame, considers the meaning of vulnerability as it relates to the practice of empathy, and considers the difference between empathy and compassion. In addition to presenting theoretical perspectives on empathy, I discuss what empathy looks like in clinical practice. In Chapter 8, I explore the meaning of the Jesus event as God's empathic initiative toward humanity and in the context of an understanding of God's vulnerability. The discussion focuses on the symbol of the incarnation, the centrality of Jesus's healing activity, his empathic imagination as a storyteller, as well as his prophetic empathy. I interpret Jesus's death in the context of his life, specifically as a consequence of his atoning life, and his resurrection as symbol of transformation and restoration from trauma and shame. My argument is that salvation, as it was proclaimed and enacted through the Jesus event, restores wholeness of self and wholeness in relationships rather than providing salvage from divine judgment.

Part Five addresses the "so-what?" of a clinical theology, presenting an understanding of spiritual care as a faithful response to the saving God event that calls upon us in the Jesus story. In this part, the final chapter marks this clinical theology as purposeful and lays out a praxis of spiritual care that corresponds to an understanding of the atonement as God's empathic initiative toward humanity. Both psychological and theological perspectives come together as I propose an empathic praxis of at-onement that is rooted in a hermeneutic of curiosity. Spiritual care as a praxis of at-onement, I argue, participates in the ongoing work of salvation, which seeks to restore wholeness in individuals and communities. The discussion highlights five facets or functions of spiritual care that each employ and exemplify a praxis of compassionate empathy.

Throughout the book, I have included short stories about the praxis of spiritual care, brief clinical tales, as neurologist and writer Oliver Sacks calls them. They illustrate my argument or a particular aspect of the discussion from a clinical praxis perspective. Yet, they also serve a larger purpose and invite an empathic connection with the experiences of human pain and distress that they convey. In that sense, they offer an opportunity to readers to practice what this book is all about.

Part One

A PROBLEMATIC ATONEMENT

NEXT TO THE doctrine of the trinity, the doctrine of atonement is arguably the most distinctive Christian teaching. Traditional theological atonement models pose a problem in that they raise the question of whether God's love can ultimately be expressed through an act of violence. The dominant teaching has focused on the meaning of the cross of Christ for the redemption of humanity, and the problematic theological argument has been that God's saving love for humanity was necessarily conveyed through an act of abandonment and deadly violence. An often-quoted passage from the Gospel of John has been interpreted accordingly and has served as a prominent biblical example of this teaching. "And just as Moses lifted up the serpent in the wilderness, so must the Son of Man be lifted up, that whoever believes in him may have eternal life. For God so loved the world that he gave his only son, so that everyone who believes in him may not perish but may have eternal life" (John 3:15–16). God's love for the world and for humanity thus was conveyed through the sacrificial gift of Jesus in the crucifixion, which, as an act of salvation, was reminiscent of the Hebrew people having been saved from God's wrath during the Exodus (Num 21:9). The problem with the atonement is that the notion of redemptive violence has pervaded interpretations of the Jesus event throughout most of the history of Christianity and has become acceptable by way of a myopic reading of the gospel narratives.

In the following two chapters, I discuss the consequences of a cruciform interpretation of the Jesus story through traditional atonement models. I also consider more recent theological perspectives that re-vision the meaning of Jesus's life, death, and resurrection and a Christian understanding of salvation. Both traditional and contemporary interpretations suggest that an interpretation of the atonement is ultimately shaped by the context of inquiry and the perspective it provides to those who seek to explore the meaning of the Jesus event. While traditional models were clearly products of their times and their places, they have not claimed their context intentionally but rather have staked a universal claim to truth. They have shaped proclamation and practices within the church over centuries and have inspired the piety of individual believers and a variety of spiritual disciplines. The contemporary perspectives that I discuss are in one way or another a response to the problem posed by traditional interpretations of the atonement and by and large account for context and for the perspectives that guide their inquiry and their argument. Understanding both tradition and re-visions will help us construct a clinical theology that can respond to historical perspectives and engage perspectives that include contemporary narratives and symbols.

1

TRADITION

IN A FOOTNOTE to his classic essay about the historical Jesus and the historic biblical Christ, theologian Martin Kähler famously stated that one could characterize the gospels as "passion narratives with extended introductions."[1] Kähler's focus on the cross and his characterization of the gospel narratives may very well describe the interpretation of the Jesus story through most of the history of Christian theology, since that story became identified primarily as a crucicentric event that overshadowed traditions about Jesus's life, healing work, prophetic stance, and teachings. Jesus's death on the cross has been traditionally understood as the center and purpose of his mission. As such, it has been interpreted as a theological requirement for the justification of sinners willed by a God who was offended by human transgression, rather than as a consequence of Jesus's life of prophetic and compassionate agency. The cross became the hermeneutical key to unlock the mystery of incarnation and turned into *the* trajectory target of the God event in the Jesus story. Moreover, it did not only define the interpretation of the Jesus story but also the appropriation of Hebrew scriptures in Christian interpretations to support the notion of prophecy and fulfillment.

The Jesus Event in the Shadow of the Cross

The cross became central in interpreting the Jesus story. It defined the story's meaning as one of sacrifice and atonement, even though the Jesus story itself was much larger, and the passages about Jesus's suffering and death in the gospel narratives are comparatively short. A generous review of the Gospel of Mark, for example, will find that the whole narrative devotes three out of sixteen chapters to the story about the conspiracy against Jesus, his death,

---

1 Martin Kähler, *The So-Called Historical Jesus and the Historic Biblical Christ*, trans. Carl E. Braaten (Philadelphia: Fortress Press, 1964), 80 n. 11.

and resurrection. On the other hand, stories about Jesus's public activity, his healing work, and his teaching constitute a much larger part of the gospel narratives. Moreover, Jesus's teachings did not seem to focus on his atoning sacrifice. As philosopher of religion John Hick points out, it is clear that

> *in the teaching of Jesus himself, insofar as it is reflected in the synoptic gospels, the juridical conception was entirely or almost entirely absent. Virtually the whole weight of Jesus' message came in the summons to his hearers to open their hearts now to God's kingdom, or rule, and to live consciously in God's presence as instruments of the divine purpose on earth. . . . there is no suggestion in Jesus' recorded teaching that the heavenly Father's loving acceptance of those to whom he was speaking was conditional upon his own future death.*[2]

In Luke's account about Jesus's mission announcement with reference to the prophet Isaiah, the theme of a sacrificial atonement is completely absent. Instead, the passage defines Jesus's mission as a work of liberation and healing, "to bring good news to the poor . . . to proclaim release to the captives, and recovery of sight to the blind, to let the oppressed go free, to proclaim the year of the Lord's favor" (Luke 4:18–19). According to Luke, Jesus did not identify his mission with the cross or the bloody sacrifice of his life, but with hope for the poor, with liberation for the oppressed and imprisoned, with healing, and with restorative justice that was associated with the Year of Jubilee (cf. Lev 25:8–12). However, in the history of the church, a crucicentric definition of Jesus's saving mission became prevalent over one that centered on good news for the poor, on healing, liberation, and just relations. Passages like Luke's version of Jesus's programmatic announcement became spiritualized and interpreted through a hermeneutic of the cross, and dissenting voices such as those of philosopher Peter Abelard or religious teacher Pierre de Bruys were deemed heretical and often violently silenced.

Pauline theology represents the earliest systematic teachings of the Christian movement and introduced the original version of a crucicentric

---

2 John Hick, *An Interpretation of Religion: Human Responses to the Transcendent* (New Haven & London: Yale University Press, 1989), 44–45.

explanation of the Jesus event that powerfully shaped a Christian theology of salvation. Paul did not pass on Jesus's story or message but interpreted the *kerygma* (proclamation) about the crucified and risen Christ, anchored in an essentially apocalyptic world view.[3] Questions remain about Paul's background in Palestinian or Hellenistic culture that influenced his theology and about how much he knew about Jesus's life and teachings. In his initial letter to the believers in Corinth, Paul emphasized that he "did not come proclaiming the mystery of God to you in lofty words or wisdom. For I decided to know nothing among you except Jesus Christ, and him crucified" (1 Cor 2:1–2). At the center of his message about God's reconciling initiative toward humanity was the scandalous event of Christ crucified. Paul explicitly rejected for the early Christian communities the notion of knowing "Jesus according to the flesh" (2 Cor 5:16), that is, in his humanity and his earthly existence.[4] Even when he directly or indirectly referred to Jesus's teachings (cf. Rom 12:17–18; 1 Cor 7:10; 1 Thess 5:15), he transposed them to become part of the *kerygma* about Christ. The Christ that Paul proclaimed and believed in was "essentially a rejected, crucified, and then divinely vindicated one, in whose death and new life those who believe in him may share."[5]

The early Christian creeds similarly professed the crucified and resurrected Christ without much or any attention to other aspects of the Jesus story. The Apostles' Creed in its earliest version dates to the Old Roman Creed of the second and third centuries; it developed through several stages into the final version of the confession we know today.[6] None of the versions

---

3 See Denny J. Weaver, *The Nonviolent Atonement* (Grand Rapids & Cambridge, UK: William B. Eerdmans Publishing Co., 2001), 49.
4 The interpretation of 2 Corinthians 5:16 depends on whether one determines that *kata sarka* is used in an adverbial sense to negate a certain way of knowing, or whether it refers to "Christ" as the object of knowledge. In Romans 9:5, the phrase clearly refers to Christ as "the Messiah," explaining his lineage and earthly existence. In other Pauline writings, the phrase refers to physical existence, to the human body, or to the whole person (cf. 1 Cor 6:16; 2 Cor 12:7; Eph 5:31), and there is no reason to suggest a different reading for 2 Corinthians 5:16.
5 J. A. Ziesler, *Pauline Christianity*, rev. ed. (Oxford & New York: Oxford University Press, 1990), 30.
6 See Donald Fairbairn and Ryan M. Reeves, *The Story of Creeds and Confessions: Tracing the Development of the Christian Faith* (Grand Rapids: Baker Academic, 2019), 110–115.

nor the final creed acknowledge that Jesus lived a life, taught, and healed in a community of disciples. The creed moves right from affirming Jesus's miraculous birth to the crucifixion, referencing his death explicitly as a historical event, declaring that Jesus "was conceived by the Holy Spirit, born of the Virgin Mary, suffered under Pontius Pilate, was crucified, dead and buried."[7] Jesus's life and ministry remained unrecognized and hidden in a wide gap between his birth and death. The Creed of Nicaea was first adopted by the Council of Nicaea in 325 in response to Arian theology that interpreted God's work of salvation through Platonic philosophy. It was modified in 381 and became known in its modified version as the Nicene Creed. The creed focused on the identity between Christ, the Son, and God, the Father, and the full equality of the Son, the Spirit, and the Father.[8] While the Nicene Creed affirmed that Christ "for our salvation came down from heaven and was incarnate by the Holy Spirit and the Virgin Mary and became human,"[9] it did not give any specific testimony to Jesus's human life and agency. Like the Apostles' Creed, it proceeded right to Jesus's suffering and resurrection. In 451, the Council of Chalcedon finalized the dogma of the two natures of Christ, "without confusion, without change, without division, without separation."[10] Even though the Chalcedonian definition acknowledged that Jesus was truly God and truly human, its declaration did not give any attention to Jesus's human story, as if it was irrelevant to an understanding of the Jesus event at large.

Early in the history of the Protestant Reformation, in the Heidelberg Disputations of 1518, Martin Luther juxtaposed a *theologia crucis*, a theology of the cross, to the *theologia gloriae*, the theology of glory of the official church, which emphasized human rationalism and moralism. Neither one paid particular attention to Jesus's life, teachings, or his prophetic and healing work. For Luther, the "cross alone is our theology."[11] In defense of his

---

7 John H. Leith, ed., *Creeds of the Churches: A Reader in Christian Doctrine, from the Bible to the Present*, 3rd ed. (Atlanta: Westminster John Knox, 1982), 24.
8 See Fairbairn and Reeves, *Story of Creeds*, 58–63.
9 Leith, *Creeds of the Churches*, 30.
10 Henry Bettenson, ed., *Documents of the Christian Church*, 2nd ed. (London, Oxford, & New York: Oxford University Press, 1963), 51.
11 Mary M. Solberg, "All That Matters: What an Epistemology of the Cross Is Good For," in *Cross Examinations: Readings on the Meaning of the Cross*, ed. Marit Trelstad (Minneapolis: Augsburg Fortress Press, 2006), 139.

theses during the disputation, Luther argued that God could only be found through the cross and through suffering and not through "good works" or human effort.[12] He depicted humanity as completely depraved, passive, and lacking free will, only able to sin, even as they attempted to do good. Caputo summarizes Luther's theology of the cross and states that "the way of the cross is to let God be all in all, *sola fide, sola gratia*, where we are strictly passive recipients of divine action. . . . For Luther, the cross is first of all Christ's cross, but it is also ours; it is not only an objective event in history but the personal cross each of us bears."[13] Thus, following in the way of Jesus did not mean to contemplate and obey his teachings or imitate his life but to be convicted by Jesus's suffering and to desperately seek God's grace.

In a controversial theological treatise, theologian Theodore Clark argued in 1959 that "the meaning of the Incarnation does not depend on any *direct* or *exclusive* reference to the cross as such. One must go *beyond* the cross, if the fullest meaning of the Incarnation is to be found."[14] Clark identified the preoccupation with the cross as the source of significant distortions in Christian theology and contested the cross being the central event of God's saving initiative in Christ. An understanding of the atonement based on New Testament theology, Clark argued, needed to consider all aspects of God's revelation in Christ and keep the incarnation, cross, and resurrection in a constant and mutually inclusive tension.

At the time, however, Clark's argument was a lonely voice in the discussion about the meaning of the Jesus event, and crucicentric interpretations remained dominant. Moreover, Jesus's crucifixion had long become an object of adoration, and the veneration of the cross has had a long history in Christianity. Both served to instill a piety of fear of God's judgment in believers and supported, at other times, the call to arms for Christian militias and soldiers to follow Jesus's example and give their life fighting non-Christians in what was considered righteous warfare. "Killing and being killed," as theologians Rita Nakashima Brock and Rebecca Parker explain,

---

12 See Martin Luther, *Die Reformatorischen Grundschriften*, vol. 1, ed. Horst Beintker (Munich: Deutscher Taschenbuchverlag, 1983), 44.
13 John D. Caputo, *Cross and Cosmos: A Theology of Difficult Glory* (Bloomington: Indiana University Press, 2019), 80.
14 Theodore R. Clark, *Saved by His Life: A Study of the New Testament Doctrine of Reconciliation and Salvation* (New York: Macmillan Co., 1959), 16.

"imitated the gift of Christ's death, the anguish of his self-sacrifice, and the terror of his judgment."[15]

If the Jesus story is read as a necessarily violent drama of redemption, Jesus's life and message of non-violence (cf. Matt 5:38–45) and his transforming initiatives for peace do not fit the script and are purged. When the Jesus event is reduced to a passion narrative with a lengthy introduction, distortions in the religious practice of those who claim to follow Jesus are inevitable and the history of the Church does not lack examples. Systematic theologian Mark Heim aptly identifies the cross as "a religious symbol soiled with persecution and psychological conflict. It entangles destructive ideas of original sin and overpowering guilt with unhealthy fixation on blood and death."[16]

Given the history of interpretation, I distinguish between the *Jesus event* and the work of Christ. I identify the work of Christ primarily as the post-resurrection, crucicentric interpretation and proclamation of God's saving initiative. The Jesus event encompasses more than the traditional narratives about Jesus's crucifixion and resurrection and their interpretations among early Christian communities. It comprises primarily the storied traditions about Jesus's life and public work. It is about the mystery of incarnation, the call to prophetic agency, and the parabolic wisdom of stories that reveal subversively the surprising truth about God's call upon us. It is about communion with those who were excluded and marginalized, about healing those who were hopelessly afflicted, and about a passion for just relations among humans and with God that provoked an oppressive and violent response from those who held dominant power. Finally, it is about the resonance that this event found in form of a hope that created and still creates a future and a community beyond oppression and fearful withdrawal.

Recognizing that the Jesus event is larger than the story about Jesus's suffering and death allows for consideration of the entire tradition of that event, and particularly what biblical and political theologian Ched Myers calls the ideological narratives of the Gospels[17] as relevant to

---

15 Rita Nakashima Brock and Rebecca A. Parker, *Saving Paradise: How Christianity Traded Love of This World for Crucifixion and Empire* (Boston: Beacon Press, 2008), 270.
16 Mark S. Heim, *Saved from Sacrifice: A Theology of the Cross* (Grand Rapids & Cambridge, UK: William B. Eerdmans Publishing Co., 2006), 3.
17 Myers argues that the gospel narratives are both symbolic and realistic in that they are "reworking traditions about *real* (not make-believe) events, sayings, and personalities"

understanding the atonement. Religious scholar Pamela Dickey Young has argued that we need to understand the atonement broadly in the context of the incarnation rather than narrowly through the crucifixion of Jesus. She contends that the "atoning is in the graciousness of God as seen in the whole event of Jesus Christ rather than in a graciousness seen only in death and resurrection as the overcoming of the powers of sin, death, and evil."[18] To understand the dynamics of salvation, we would thus need to consider the atoning life of Jesus and not merely focus on his atoning death.

To be clear, I am not advocating for a revival of nineteenth-century research aimed at reconstructing a biography of Jesus and projecting the ideals of liberal Protestantism onto the story and the person of Jesus, turning Jesus's proclamation of the reign of God into a set of inner values and truths. The Gospels simply do not provide the information to reconstruct a biography of Jesus's life. Too many details about his life and his person are missing. The evangelists were not biographers. Rather, they proclaimed good news. However, while their narratives are *kerygma*—proclamation—and do not portray the "real Jesus," as biblical scholar William Herzog argues, they provide glances and in places perhaps even a clear view at the historical Jesus.[19] "What we call the historical Jesus," Herzog explains, "is the composite of the recoverable bits and pieces of historical information and speculation about him that we can assemble, construct, and reconstruct."[20] According to Herzog, the historical Jesus was not one who sacrificed himself for sinful humanity but rather "a prophetic figure, a subversive pedagogue, a healer and exorcist, and a broker of God's reign and reputational leader."[21] I argue and will discuss in detail that these four aspects of the historical Jesus are essential to the salvific God event in the Jesus story.

---

and put each detail in narrative form for a reason. See Chad Myers, *Binding the Strong Man: A Political Reading of Mark's Story of Jesus* (Maryknoll: Orbis Books, 1988), 21–31.
18 Pamela Dickey Young, "Beyond Moral Influence to an Atoning Life," *Theology Today* 52, no. 3 (October 1995): 350.
19 See William R. Herzog, II, *Prophet and Teacher: An Introduction to the Historical Jesus* (Louisville: Westminster John Knox Press, 2005), 5.
20 Herzog, *Prophet and Teacher*, 6.
21 Herzog, *Prophet and Teacher*, 24.

Traditional Images of Salvation: A Trinity of Atonement Models

Theologian Gustaf Aulén presented a summary of traditional models of the atonement that is still relevant today for understanding the history of crucicentric interpretations of the Jesus event. Aulén distinguished between three types of interpretations: the classic or *Christus Victor* model, the Latin or objective view with the satisfaction model being its most prominent example, and the subjective or ethical effect model, which interpreters of Aulén also called the moral influence model.[22] All three types of interpretations essentially present contextual theologies, albeit without acknowledging their contextual nature. The three models do not present distinct, singular theological positions. Rather, they offer clusters of interpretations over time that present the Jesus event in similar terms, utilizing particular symbol systems.

Christus Victor
The *Christus Victor* interpretation of the atonement was a predominant view in patristic theology, proposed by leaders within the early Christian church in the East like Origen of Alexandria and Athanasius, the Confessor. The different versions, in one way or another, point to the cross as the paradoxical sign of Christ's victory over the devil or the forces of evil. This view was based on an understanding that humanity was enslaved by the devil. The human condition was seen as deeply corrupted and "infected by sin, and as such was prey to death and the powers of darkness."[23] Christ entered the realm of corruption and a cosmic battle between God and the forces of evil, seemingly defeated on the cross but claiming victory through the resurrection and liberating humanity from the devil's bondage. In a variation on this theme, Christ's death became the ransom paid to Satan to free those who were captives to sin, but through the resurrection, Christ escaped Satan's power and established freedom for sinners.[24] The ransom theory

---

22 See Gustaf Aulén, *Christus Victor: An Historical Study of the Three Main Types of the Idea of Atonement*, trans. A. G. Herbert (1931; repr., Eugene, OR: Wipf & Stock, 2003), 1–4.
23 James A. McClendon, *Doctrine: Systematic Theology*, vol. 2 (Nashville: Abingdon Press, 1994), 199.
24 See Weaver, *Nonviolent Atonement*, 15.

received a modern and popular treatment in C. S. Lewis's children's books about the *Chronicles of Narnia*. In *The Lion, the Witch, and the Wardrobe*, Aslan, the Christ-figure lion, savior of Narnia and the son of the Emperor beyond the sea, presents himself as a ransom for Edmund, the fourth son of Adam. Edmund has fallen under the spell of the Witch Queen of Narnia and become a traitor, and Aslan offers himself in a bargain with the Witch to have her agree to renounce her claim on Edmund's blood.[25] As the story goes, Aslan's humiliating self-sacrifice and subsequent resurrection through deep magic not only save Edmund but defeat the Witch and restore the whole realm of Narnia to life.

The theme of restoration and renewal was prominent in the theology of Irenaeus, bishop of Lyon, in the second century. In his *Books against Heresies*, he established a theology of salvation against Gnostic teachings and adopted the ransom model alongside his doctrine of recapitulation. His doctrine is a rare example of an understanding of the atonement that considered all of Jesus's life as relevant to God's work of salvation. According to Irenaeus, Jesus's "obedience on the tree renewed [and reversed] what was done by disobedience in [connection with] a tree; and [the power of] that seduction by which the virgin Eve, already betrothed to a man, had been wickedly seduced was broken when the angel in truth brought good tidings to the virgin Mary, who already [by her betrothal] belonged to a man."[26] It should not come as a surprise that his argument to locate the origins of human corruption with Eve's seduction was not an exception but became a common and oppressive stance against women in the history of the church. Irenaeus's doctrine tried to explain how Jesus recapitulated through his life and death the story of humanity in a restorative way. By entering human life and passing through every stage of life perfectly and according to God's original intent, Jesus sanctified those in every stage and overcame the corruption of humanity.[27] Through his life and death, he renewed all of creation and united humanity with God's spirit. Not just Jesus's death but his whole life was a ransom, according to Irenaeus, because a just victory over Satan

---

25 See C. S. Lewis, *The Lion, the Witch, and the Wardrobe* (1950; repr., London: Fontana Lions/Williams Collins Sons & Co., 1980), 130.

26 Ray C. Petry, ed., *A History of Christianity: Readings in the History of the Church*, vol. 1 (1962; repr., Grand Rapids: Baker Book House, 1981), 96.

27 See Bettenson, *Documents of the Christian Church*, 30.

required a human agent, born of a woman, since Satan had gained power over humanity through a woman. Thus, Jesus's ransom progressively restored humanity's status with God in himself, "and as death won the palm of victory over us by a man, so we might by a man receive the palm of victory over death."[28]

The *Christus Victor* interpretation of the atonement was rooted in a dualistic world view, where the Kingdom of Light was opposed by the Kingdom of Darkness and God-in-Christ fought the battle against the forces of evil to liberate humanity from Satan's grip. The socio-political context, in which this model of the atonement emerged in the pre-Constantinian area, makes a mythical, dualistic interpretation plausible. James McClendon explains how the early Christian communities existed as a minority in a world where oppressive powers of darkness, identified with the state and society, disadvantaged and persecuted them.[29] According to the *Christus Victor* narrative, the shame and seeming defeat of the cross was turned into a symbol of God's power to overturn evil. The narrative thereby not only explained the biblical story of Jesus's sacrifice in a dramatic fashion but also gave significance and relevance to a community that was despised and marginalized.

Satisfaction Model and Penal Interpretations

Within the context of missionary Christianity and the feudal system of the eleventh century, Anselm, archbishop of Canterbury, developed an interpretation of the atonement as systematic apologetics that influenced the history of the Christian church like no other. He introduced what became known as the satisfaction theory of the atonement in his treatise *Cur Deus Homo*, which can be translated "Why did God become human," or simply "Why a God-human." Anselm's treatise employed the Chalcedonian definition, and it attempted to make a logical and rational argument that proved why Christ's incarnation and death were necessary for the salvation of humanity. Anselm wrote the treatise in the form of a dialogue between himself and Boso, who was one of his students, his successor as abbot of Bec in Normandy, and a conversation partner in real life. As a literary figure in his treatise, Anselm had Boso present the perspectives, questions, and objections of unbelievers

---

28 Petry, *History of Christianity*, 97.
29 McClendon, *Doctrine*, 202.

trying to oppose the Christian faith. Anselm rejected a dualistic worldview and disputed an understanding that the devil had gained a right to all of humanity through the sin and the fall of the first humans and that Christ served as a ransom to Satan to liberate sinful humanity. Rather than attributing power to the devil to hold humanity captive, Anselm argued that both the devil and humanity were under God's power and had equal standing before God, one as seducer and torturer and the other as corrupted and rightly being punished.[30]

Anselm's argument is at once brilliant and peculiar. It is brilliant in its hairsplitting and logical sequence; it is peculiar in its underlying speculation about shifting roles in God's celestial city. Behind Anselm's satisfaction theory stands the belief that a selection of humanity was supposed to substitute for the fallen angels and join God's good angels in the celestial city. For humans to take their place alongside the pure and perfectly created angels, however, human sin could not simply be forgiven through God's compassion alone without cleansing and giving satisfaction to God, because forgiveness would create inequality between the angels and humans and leave the stain of sin.[31] Rather, it required a great and voluntary act of satisfaction to repay the debt that human sin had created. Anselm emphasized that the cross was not a punishment but rather a necessary act of satisfaction for humanity's offense against God through willful disobedience that dishonored God. So great was the debt that only God could settle it, even though humanity had incurred it and thus needed to repay it. In order to resolve this dilemma, Anslem argued, God had to become human through Christ and, as a *Deus-Homo* combining two natures, fulfill the human duty of rendering satisfaction for the debt of sin on the cross, while accomplishing what only God could do.[32]

Anselm's view that God's compassion was not sufficient for salvation stands in tension with Jesus's own message (Luke 6:36; 15:11–32) and illustrates how a crucicentric and violent interpretation of the atonement is liable to ignore the contributions of Jesus's life and teachings. Anselm understood Jesus's life as an expression of his obedience to God's will and emphasized

---

30 See Anselm of Canterbury, *The Major Works*, ed. Brian Davies and G. R. Evans. Oxford World's Classics (Oxford & New York: Oxford University Press, 1998), 272–273.
31 Anselm of Canterbury, *Major Works*, 301.
32 Anselm of Canterbury, *Major Works*, 48.

that Jesus's death to render satisfaction was not forced but was a voluntary act.[33] At the same time, he maintained that God willed and ordered Jesus's death and, through the Father's will, "drew or impelled" the Son toward the act of self-sacrifice.[34] Despite this seeming contradiction, Anselm interprets God's involvement in the drama of atonement not as forceful or violent but in terms of the relationship between the Father and the Son. "In view of the fact, therefore, that the Son's will was pleasing to the Father, and the Father did not prevent him from willing or fulfilling what he desired," Anselm explains, "it is a correct assertion to say that he 'wished' his Son to endure death in this way, so dutifully and so beneficially—even though he did not like his punishment."[35]

Anselm's treatise and the model of the atonement it espoused reflected a changed socio-political context from the one that had given rise to the *Christus Victor* interpretation. The Christian church had evolved from a marginalized and disadvantaged community into the ruling power and had become a missionary church that was making converts. Anselm's argument directly supports in form and content the purpose of convincing non-believers to accept the reasonable truth about the Christian message of salvation. Furthermore, a feudalistic system that ordered relationships and obligations within medieval society shaped his understanding of salvation and redemption with the notion that satisfaction was required by an offender according to the status of the one who had been offended. Thus, humanity's offense against God required a great recompense that could restore the right order within the relationship between God and humankind. I agree with theologian and ethicist James McClendon that Anselm's understanding of the atonement is too complex to be reduced to an analogy between God and a feudal lord who defended his honor and demanded satisfaction at a considerable price for his family.[36] Given the metaphors and argument in *Cur Deus Homo*, however, it seems apparent that his social and cultural context informed Anselm's understanding of ultimate and eternal relationships within a justly ordered universe.

---

33 Anselm of Canterbury, *Major Works*, 277.
34 Anselm of Canterbury, *Major Works*, 280.
35 Anselm of Canterbury, *Major Works*, 281.
36 See McClendon, *Doctrine*, 205.

Some interpreters of Anselm's theory place it in the context of substitutionary atonement.³⁷ This may make sense in a general way if one understands Jesus's act of salvation as offering satisfaction as a substitute for humanity, who was incapable of satisfying God's honor. However, given that the notion of substitutionary atonement means that Jesus accepted and endured God's penalty for sin in place of humanity, substitutionary atonement does not seem to characterize Anselm's theory accurately. Anselm insisted that Jesus's death had been not an act of punishment but the rendering of satisfaction. The belief that Jesus offered himself as a substitutionary sacrifice and accepted God's punishment in the place of humanity was prominently adopted during the Protestant Reformation by John Calvin and in Martin Luther's theology as a mixture of the classic and the Latin interpretation.³⁸ Of course, the notion that Jesus "gave himself up" for humanity's salvation (Gal 2:20) was already present in the early Christian writings. As the teaching goes, in an act of substitutionary atonement, Jesus accepted God's wrath against sinful humanity upon himself and, though innocent, died a shameful death to appease God. Thus, the God who "gave his only Son" (John 3:16) would prove to be both just in demanding retribution and merciful by sparing humanity the violent fate that Jesus suffered instead.

The notion of substitutionary atonement seems more closely related to the scapegoat phenomenon or mechanism that linguist and literary scholar René Girard explored and documented in detail than to Anselm's satisfaction theory. Girard traced the phenomenon of victim substitution as it appears in the Christian passion narrative to the ancient Israelite ritual of atonement (Lev 16:21), when a goat was driven into the wilderness to carry the sins of the people.³⁹ He identified the source of such substitution as an "appetite for violence that awakens in people when anger seizes them and when the true object of their anger is untouchable."⁴⁰ While the designation of scapegoat is not explicitly used to identify God's supposed act of salvation though the crucifixion, Girard identified language of rejection and victimization throughout the Gospel narratives.

---

37 See, for example, Heim, *Saved from Sacrifice*, 4–5.
38 See McClendon, *Doctrine*, 206.
39 See René Girard, *I Saw Satan Fall Like Lightning*, trans. James G. Williams (Maryknoll: Orbis Books, 2001), 154–155.
40 See Girard, *I Saw Satan Fall Like Lightning*, 156.

The scapegoat motif, as Girard pointed out, is most prominently replaced in Christian scripture by the lamb of God metaphor. "Like 'scapegoat,' it implies the substitution of one victim for all the others but replaces all the distasteful and loathsome connotations of the goat with the positive associations of the lamb. It indicates more clearly the innocence of this victim, the injustice of the condemnation, and causelessness of the hatred of which it is the object."[41] Substitutionary atonement, then, is the victimization of the innocent, a sacrificial offering in place of others, and an act of violence out of anger. The Gospel stories cite the anger of the religious and civil leaders about the scandal that Jesus represented as a reason for his death sentence. Prominent theological theories argue that the anger was on God's part against humanity, but that God could not punish humanity lest God was found to be unmerciful, and thus a substitute had to stand in to suffer the punishment that humanity deserved.

Moral Influence Model

Aulén identified the third, so-called subjective, type of atonement models initially in Abelard's protest against Anselm's satisfaction theory. Abelard agreed with Anselm that the devil had no active part in the atonement but disputed the idea of satisfaction. Abelard rather saw the redeeming work of Christ as one that set an example through his enduring love and thus had an ethical effect on humanity and aroused "responsive love."[42] Abelard formulated his critique of a violent atonement in his commentary on Romans. "How very cruel and unjust it seems," he writes, "that someone should require the blood of an innocent person as a ransom, or that in any it might please him that an innocent person be slain, still less that God should have so accepted the death of his Son that through it he was reconciled to the whole world!"[43] Reconciliation with God, according to Abelard, rather came through the grace of incarnation and through Jesus's teaching by word and example in human nature, thus revealing God's unmatched love that persevered to his death. Jesus's death, according to Abelard, was not necessary as

---

41 René Girard, *The Scapegoat*, trans. Yvonne Freccero (Baltimore: Johns Hopkins University Press, 1986), 117.
42 See Aulén, *Christus Victor*, 96.
43 Peter Abelard, *Commentary on the Epistle to the Romans*, trans. Steven R. Cartwright (Washington, DC: The Catholic University of America Press, 2011), 167.

satisfaction to restore God's honor or as an unfair act of divine vengeance but was necessary to create a greater love for God and a change of heart in humanity.[44]

Abelard's view would not become widely influential and was essentially an outlier among atonement interpretations until liberal Protestant theology of the post-Enlightenment period, most notably Friedrich Schleiermacher and Albrecht Ritschl, revived it. Aulén assessed the third type of atonement interpretations as a humanistic or humanizing theology that weakened the idea of sin and of God's opposition to evil by locating redemption within the realm of human ability to change in response to the example that Christ gave and the love that he expressed. The atonement therefore became "a matter of an approach of man to God, from below upwards, and not from God to man."[45] Christ's redeeming work thus produced primarily a change in humanity and secondarily a change in God and how God regarded humankind.

Systematic theologian and ethicist James McClendon also saw Abelard's influence and Aulén's third subjective type reflected in the theology of Horace Bushnell, an American Congregationalist pastor and theologian who has been sometimes considered the father of American religious liberalism.[46] Bushnell saw Jesus primarily as a healer, who "took our infirmities and bore our diseases" (Matt 8:17). Jesus's redemptive work was not substitutionary in nature but vicarious. He was not punished for the sins of humanity, nor did he contract diseases in a physical sense, as McClendon summarizes the argument in Bushnells's *The Vicarious Sacrifice*. Rather, Jesus "bore them vicariously in the sense that he 'took them on his feeling, had his heart burdened by the sense of them.' He suffered the impact of others' sickness and others' sin in his work of taking them away. By his sympathy and friendship, and in his chosen role as the people's Healer, Jesus expressed the identifying love that ultimately entailed the loss of his life."[47] God's sympathy and love for humanity was expressed in the Jesus event that culminated in his death,

---

44 See Abelard, *Romans*, 162–163.
45 Aulén, *Christus Victor*, 146–147. While I am committed to the use of inclusive language, direct quotes that do not reflect such use due to linguistic standards at the time of publication are cited in their original form.
46 See McClendon's discussion of Bushnell's expanding theology in *Doctrine*, 210–213.
47 McClendon, *Doctrine*, 211.

and God's forgiveness through Christ's work creates in turn an attitude of forgiveness and love in those who have been redeemed.

While interpretations of the atonement have changed throughout the history of Christianity and various arguments have been brought against previously asserted premises, in general they have been in agreement about the dilemma inherent in the human condition. Sin and salvation became a matter of guilt and forgiveness. Humanity was guilty of disobedience against God, caught in a cycle of sin and unable to restore itself to a state of reconciliation. In the classic view, guilt was the perpetual manifestation of humanity's enslavement to the devil, and forgiveness was achieved through Christ's death and resurrection victory over the devil or the ransom of his suffering, which freed humanity from the bondage of sin. The Latin view saw human guilt as the debt owed to God. The solution was an act of rendering satisfaction to a God offended by human willful disobedience by a two-natured God-human or through Jesus's substitutionary capital punishment. Even the subjective version identified the predicament of guilt as a response to moral failure and the answer to it as the ethical example that Jesus gave and the influence his example and love had in eliciting humanity's love in response.

An Abusing God and Religious Violence

The problem with traditional interpretations of the atonement is not just that they attribute an act of violence to God, but that the violence is considered redemptive and a manifestation of God's saving love. To be sure, the Hebrew tradition and Christian theology both acknowledge the dark side of God. The God event in the Exodus narrative is in several places portrayed as terrifying (Exod 19:16; 20:21), and the God that liberated the Hebrew people is at times described as jealous (Exod 20:5) and as one who brings destruction to those outside the chosen community (Jer 45:4–5). Martin Luther's notion of the *Deus absconditus*, the hidden and remote God, pointed to the incomprehensibility of a mysterious God who extended grace and could be destructive.[48] In his classic essay about *The Idea of the Holy*, scholar of religion Rudolf

---

48 See Caputo, *Cross and Cosmos*, 73–75.

Otto described this kind of religious experience of a God event as both a fascinating and a frightening mystery that could induce dread.⁴⁹

The traditional atonement narrative, however, does not simply fit the template of a mysterious, dark, or even frightening God event but suggests a more disturbing understanding of an abusing God. The belief that love's purpose is achieved through an act of violence reflects a reasoning reminiscent of the justification of violence in abusive relationships. Jewish theologian David Blumenthal, in presenting a theology of protest in response to the Holocaust, maintains that abusiveness is indeed an attribute of God. *"God is abusive but not always* [sic]. God, as portrayed in our holy sources and experienced by humans throughout the ages, acts, from time to time, in a manner that is so unjust that it can only be characterized by the term 'abusive.' In this mode, God allows the innocent to suffer greatly."⁵⁰ While the narratives about Jesus's life and teaching do not seem to support Blumenthal's conclusion, one may understand his argument through the lens of traditional readings of the atonement narrative and in light—or rather, in the darkness—of the Holocaust and of anti-semitic pogroms throughout history.

Traditional, crucicentric models of the atonement have provided the template for a theology that explained how God used or allowed violence to achieve God's purpose. Liberation theologian Dorothee Sölle, in her critique of Jürgen Moltmann's theology of the cross, pointed out how God's brutality became a fascination for some theologians and was regarded as a normal aspect of the salvation story. Sölle pointed to dynamics within abusive relationships when she identified the notion of redeeming violence as theological sadism. Sölle explained that theological sadism "does school people in thought patterns that regard sadistic behavior as normal, in which one worships, honors, and loves a being whose 'radicality,' 'intentionality,' and 'greatest sharpness' is that he slays. The ultimate conclusion of theological sadism is worshipping the executioner."⁵¹

---

49 Rudolf Otto, *The Idea of the Holy: An Inquiry into the Non-Rational Factor in the Idea of the Divine and Its Relation to the Rational*, trans. John W. Harvey, 2nd ed. (Oxford & New York: Oxford University Press, 1950), 13–20.
50 David R. Blumenthal, *Facing the Abusing God: A Theology of Protest* (Louisville: Westminster John Knox Press, 1993), 247.
51 Dorothee Sölle, *Suffering*, trans. Everett R. Kalin (Philadelphia: Fortress Press, 1974), 28.

Somewhat polemically, Sölle's point sheds light on a clinical tale about a woman experiencing spiritual pain in addition to the physical pain she suffered after a violent attack.

> Margaret was brought to the emergency room after experiencing violent trauma. Her former husband came unexpected to her apartment, surprised her, and forced his way in to attack her brutally with a baseball bat. A neighbor likely saved her life when he responded to her cries for help, which caused her attacker to stop the assault and flee from the apartment. When she came to the hospital, Margaret's face was covered with blood, and one side was almost grotesquely swollen. She was incessantly whimpering until medication somewhat numbed the pain. After a medical resident had stitched her head wound and her nurse had cleaned her with much care, Margaret asked to see a chaplain. The nurse informed the chaplain briefly about the circumstances of her injuries. Margaret spoke with the chaplain with great difficulty and tears about the pain of her soul. "I wanted you to come because I keep asking God 'Why?'," said Margaret. "Why did this happen to me? I didn't deserve this." "No," responded the chaplain after listening to her, "you did not deserve this. You did not deserve this." As she continued, Margaret became more agitated. "I swear, my ex, he would have killed me. He's twice my size. Why would he do that to me? It's not fair. I just don't know why God did this to me? I mean I know God uses bad things to teach us something, but I don't know what God wants me to learn. Can you tell me what God wants me to learn?" The chaplain was silent. Then she said, "I don't have an answer, Margaret. I hear that you ask about God's purpose in what happened to you. I don't know about that, but what I imagine is that God is crying and hurting with you tonight. I am so sorry that this has happened to you. You are right, you did not deserve this." Margaret looked at her and replied: "I know you can't answer my question. I'm just so scared right now, and I don't feel safe to go home."

Margaret's adopted theology deepened her pain rather than providing her comfort or hope. In her account, God and the perpetrator became one, merged into one almost indistinguishable image of an attacker. To make meaning of a traumatic and brutal attack on her life, she identified God as one who pursued a mysterious purpose through an assault that left her violated, confused about God's intention, and unsafe in her world.

The notion of an abusing God who achieves sacred purposes through violence has not only shaped personal theologies and faith narratives but has greatly impacted the history of the church after the Constantinian shift when the persecuted church became the persecuting church. In examining the roots and expressions of religious violence across cultures, anthropologist Jack David Eller draws upon psychological research that identified sets of conditions that contribute to incidents of violence. Among contributing factors to violence, such as dehumanizing of victims, diffusion of responsibility, gradual escalation, and blind obedience to authority, Eller lists "an ideology or set of justifying beliefs" for violent action and "verbal distortions that obscure the real nature, for example, calling harm 'discipline' or 'purification.'"[52] Traditional atonement narratives certainly have provided justifying beliefs or ideologies and verbal distortions about redemptive violence. The previously mentioned adoration of the crucifixion and veneration of the cross in the history of the church are only two examples that illustrate such distortions. An act of abandonment and public, lethal violence became the object of glorification and even love and has been proclaimed as an act of salvation and redemption.

Theologians Rita Nakashima Brock and Rebecca Parker discuss Bernard of Clairvaux's erotic theology of the cross as an ideology that fused love and the crucifixion and that provides an example of verbal distortions that justified religious violence. Based on the Song of Songs, Bernard taught in the monastery at Clairvaux a path of mystical, erotic union with God. The Black lover in the poem became in his sermons the bride of Christ, a model of devotion for monks to imitate, and a bride that Bernard identified as wounded, disfigured, and humiliated on basis of her skin color. As Brock and Parker explain, suffering, "which he called sweet, and torture, which he eroticized, were integral to his idea of love. . . . The bride shared with Paul in the scorn and the persecution of the crucified Christ. For Bernard, the

---

52 Jack David Eller, *Cruel Creeds, Virtuous Violence: Religious Violence across Cultures and History* (Amherst, NY: Prometheus Books, 2010), 17–18.

bride's black skin was a sign of her deep pain and therefore her deep love, like the blows Christ endured on the cross.... Torture and abuse marked the bride of Christ, who gloried in the cross of affliction because it united her to Jesus in mystical, erotic union."[53] They argue that Bernard's glorification of suffering led logically to his appointment as the preacher for the Second Crusade in 1146. In providing a theological rationale for religious violence against non-believers, he both motivated and justified religious violence. In participating in the armed pilgrimages to Jerusalem, lay people could achieve the same mystical union with Christ through suffering and death that monks accomplished in the monasteries. *Malecide*, as Bernard coined it, the killing of an evil person, was a spiritual act in the battle against a malevolent, spiritual army. By eroticizing violence and pain in spiritual terms, Bernard identified that "killing, dying, and suffering were spiritual modes of communion with Jesus—aspects of salvation. He insisted that the 'knight of Christ' could kill and die with confidence, 'for he serves Christ when he strikes, and saves himself when he falls.' His killing profited Christ, and his death profited himself."[54] In the joining of love with violence, Bernard's erotic theology reflected the confused argument and perverted dynamics of abusive relationships, based on a model of atonement that proclaimed salvation through the loving act of an abandoning and abusing God.

Conclusion

Tradition can be at once a gift and a liability. It is what has been handed over to us as an inheritance, connects us to those who came before, and provides continuity with the past. As such, traditional theological perspectives may provide rich meaning and guidance for the life of faith and the practice of ministry. They may convey to us the very lifeblood of the Christian faith, challenging us and instructing us to live in the way of Jesus. At the same time, tradition is not self-explanatory, and traditional interpretations of the Christian narrative may become a liability in the sense that we have responsibility for them as stewards, including the responsibility to re-interpret them. Tradition can prove to be like an outdated map, which may picture the

---

53 Brock and Parker, *Saving Paradise*, 283–284.
54 Brock and Parker, *Saving Paradise*, 287.

general terrain but fail to give accurate direction in contemporary contexts where the theological and cultural territory we navigate has changed. If so, the map needs to be updated or drawn anew.

Some traditional interpretations of Christian doctrine do not only fail to give directions in a contemporary context but have inflicted grave harm and injustice on individuals and whole populations through the centuries. Repenting for those theological sins cannot simply mean to stop teaching those aspects of the tradition or to purge them from the repertoire of Christian doctrine. Repentance is active and not just a resolve to cease believing or behaving in certain ways. It is an act of change, a turn-around, a re-engagement with God, others, and self under different terms. Theological repentance, from a Christian perspective, is a constructive effort to understand the meaning of the God event in the Jesus story as a non-violent, empathic, and accepting initiative toward individuals and communities.

2

RE-VISIONS

SINCE THE MIDDLE of the twentieth century, interpretations of the cross and the meaning of salvation have emerged that critique traditional perspectives and re-vision the atonement from the vantage point of unique historical and cultural experiences. Most of these interpretations explicitly claim their contextual approach and use the symbols of particular cultural communities or theologies and socio-political movements to gain a new perspective. Rather than affirming the necessity of violent sacrifice, satisfaction, or retribution, these theological models, for the most part, interpret God's initiative toward salvation in non-violent ways. They explore the image of God's compassionate suffering through contemporary narratives and symbols related to the experiences of marginalization, solidarity and liberation, life-affirming incarnation, and trauma to come to terms with a difficult doctrine in the history of Christian theology. The following discussion of theological perspectives about the God event in the Jesus story is not exhaustive but introduces important themes that influence a way to re-vision the possibility of salvation and restoration with regard to the human condition.

The Jesus Story as a Relational Event

In the gospel narratives, the Jesus story unfolds within a relational matrix that consists of family and family of choice, a growing community of disciples and followers, helping and caring relationships, as well contentious and hostile relationships. At the heart of story, however, is the relationship between Jesus and the God who called upon him. In the synoptic Gospels, the story of Jesus's baptism marks this relationship as special by declaring Jesus as the beloved Son (Matt 3:17; Mark 1:11; Luke 3:22). The Gospel of John describes the intimate relationship between Jesus and his God as oneness or at-onement (John 10:30; cf. 17:11). Based upon the notion that the Jesus event was intrinsically relational, Moltmann insists that Christian theology that seeks to be relevant to contemporary life and societies necessarily needs to be relational, and he argues that this principle also applies to an interpretation of Jesus's death.[1]

In his influential treatise *The Crucified God*, Moltmann states that "this book was part of my personal 'wrestling with God,' my suffering under the dark side of God, the hidden face of God, the *hester panim*, as the Jews say, the godforsakenness of the victims and the godlessness of the guilty in the human history of violence and suffering."[2] The horrors of the Second World War and the atrocities witnessed in Germany provide the background for Moltmann's interpretation of the meaning of Jesus's suffering. Moltmann contends that if "the Christ of God was executed in the name of the politico-religious authorities of the time, then for the believer the higher justification of these and similar authorities is removed. In that case, political rule can only be justified 'from below.'"[3] Consequently, any notion of Christianity as a national religion needs to be rejected. "The crucified God," Moltmann concludes, "is in fact a stateless and classless God. But that does not mean he is an unpolitical God. He is the God of the poor, the oppressed, and the humiliated."[4]

Moltmann arrives at his interpretation by exploring Jesus's suffering and death as a trinitarian and therefore relational event. He argues against a theological stance that views God as impassible and immovable. The notion of God's apathy was challenged by Jesus's passion, which was an expression of the *pathos* of God, God's openness to the world, and God's willingness to be affected by human affairs and suffering in history. "The Son suffers dying, the Father suffers the death of the Son. The grief of the Father here is just as important as the death of the Son. The Fatherlessness of the Son is matched by the Sonlessness of the Father, and if God has constituted himself as the Father of Jesus Christ, then he also suffers the death of his Fatherhood."[5] While Moltmann affirms Jesus's death as an act of suffering love on part of

---

1 Jürgen Moltmann, *The Crucified God: The Cross of Christ as the Foundation and Criticism of Christian Theology*, trans. R. A. Wilson and John Bowden (New York: Harper & Row, 1974), 11.
2 Jürgen Moltmann, "The Crucified God—Yesterday and Today: 1972–2002," trans. Margaret Kohl, in *Cross Examinations: Readings on the Meaning of the Cross*, ed. Marit Trelstad (Minneapolis: Augsburg Fortress Press, 206), 127.
3 Moltmann, *Crucified God*, 328.
4 Moltmann, *Crucified God*, 329.
5 Moltmann, *Crucified God*, 243.

the Father and of the Son, his interpretation of Paul's cruciform theology in Romans 8 and Galatians 3 is rather traditional, in that he affirms that God effectively willed Jesus's death. God abandoned Jesus and delivered him up in an act of all-encompassing suffering within God to spare and justify humanity, who had abandoned God.

This insistence on God's ability and willingness to suffer the deep pain and grief of abandonment, dying, and separation distinguishes Moltmann's paradoxical interpretation from traditional views. God's pathos was painfully embodied in Jesus's passion. "Through his own abandonment by God, the crucified Christ brings God to those who are abandoned by God. Through his suffering he brings salvation to those who suffer. Through his death he brings eternal life to those who are dying. And therefore, the tempted, suffering, rejected and dying Christ came to be the centre [sic.] of the religion of the oppressed and the piety of the lost."[6] At the heart of Moltmann's political theology is the notion that God is deeply affected by suffering, be it Jesus's suffering on the cross or the suffering of those who have abandoned God or have been oppressed by evil powers.

The argument in *The Crucified God* was foreshadowed in Dietrich Bonhoeffer's prison theology, which used a similarly paradoxical reasoning. Not long before his own execution, Bonhoeffer reflected on the execution of Jesus and suggested that the cross was at once a symbol of Godforsakenness and of God's solidarity and help in suffering.

> *The same God who is with us is the God who forsakes us (Mark 15:34!). The same God who makes us to live in the world without the working hypothesis of God is the God before whom we stand continually. Before God, and with God, we live without God. God consents to be pushed out in the world and onto the cross; God is weak and powerless in the world and in precisely this way, and only so, is at our side and helps us. Matt. 8:17 makes it quite clear that Christ helps us not by virtue of his omnipotence but rather by virtue of his weakness and suffering!*[7]

---

6 Moltmann, *Crucified God*, 46.
7 Dietrich Bonhoeffer, *Letters and Papers from Prison*, trans. Isabel Best, Lisa E. Dahill, Reinhard Krauss, and Nancy Lukens. *Dietrich Bonhoeffer Works*, vol. 8, ed. Christian

For both Bonhoeffer and Moltmann, it is not *Christus Victor* who brought hope of salvation, but rather the suffering God and the marginalized Christ who identified and joined with human suffering.

Like Moltmann, theologian Frank Tupper discusses Jesus's suffering in the context of the pathos of God and the mystery of God's death. In *A Scandalous Providence*, he presents a postmodern, narrative interpretation of the doctrine of God's providence based on a critical reading of the Gospel traditions as well as contemporary narratives of lived experience, including his own experience of suffering the loss of his spouse. However, focusing on Jesus's life of compassionate relationships and not just his death, Tupper explicitly rejects the idea that Jesus's execution was in any way part of a divine plan for the salvation of sinful humanity because the God that Jesus related to as *Abba* could not cooperate with, participate in, or contribute to his violent death. Rather, the plan that led to Jesus's death was entirely a human plot and the "path of Jesus after entering Jerusalem to his death on the cross happened in the contingency of history, the human calculation and strategy to eliminate Jesus already after his protest in the Temple and prophecy of the destruction of the Temple."[8] According to Tupper, salvation did not come through Jesus's death but through Jesus's life of compassion and more specifically through his message of the coming kingdom of God and God's grace. Jesus's death was not in agreement with or in submission to God's will but rather ended his *Abba* relationship in an experience of absolute rejection and Godforsakenness.

Tupper identifies Jesus's seeming blasphemy as the main indictment that led to his death. In claiming the authority to proclaim the coming kingdom as the non-discriminatory reign of God's grace, the prophet from Nazareth provoked a confrontation with the religious authorities. "Jesus stood with the prophets calling people to repentance, but Jesus *relativized* repentance through the priority and primacy of grace: Salvation is a gift, and Jesus extended God's gift of salvation to everyone in the openness of grace without any semblance of inequity: When Jesus offered the gift of

---

Gremmels, Eberhard Bethge, and Renate Bethge, with Ilse Tödt (Minneapolis: Fortress Press, 2010), 478–479.

8 E. Frank Tupper, *A Scandalous Providence: The Jesus Story of the Compassion of God*, new ed. (Macon, GA: Mercer University Press, 2013), 457–458.

salvation—unprecedented in the history of Israel—Jesus stunned, even shocked his opponents and others through the ambivalence intrinsic in his message."[9] In offering salvation in the name of God, Jesus sealed his fate. He did not bear the wrath of God on all of humanity but suffered the wrath of religious authorities that guarded the understanding of God among the people.

The entire Jesus event, as Tupper understands it, unfolded in the context of Jesus's relationship with God as *Abba*. He explains that, even though the term suggested a parental model of providence, it was a subversive naming of God that replaced patriarchal and monarchical models by introducing God's essence as unconditional love, the Motherly Father and the Fatherly Mother of all.[10] Jesus's *Abba* experience was a complete openness to God's loving presence, a deep intimacy that realized God's claim on his life, identified Jesus as "the Son," and "proved indispensable for comprehending his confident proclamation of the imminent coming of the kingdom of God."[11] Jesus's experience of God's unconditional love, exemplified in his baptism (Mark 1:9–11), his experience of being beloved, Tupper explains, is the paradigm for God's providence. It brought about his ministry, which actualized God's compassion and provision, particularly for those who were marginalized and experienced various forms of suffering and oppression.[12] Jesus was at once *the* human being who fully and constantly lived in community with God until his last days and thus actualized God's intention for humanity and *the* one who fulfilled God's compassionate mission among humanity.

Tupper places his understanding of providence, God's loving care in relation to creation, history, and each person's life, within a framework of God's self-limiting power. The withdrawal of God's omnipotence was God's choice for the relative independence of the world and genuine human freedom as demonstrated eventually in the event of the cross. In Tupper's concluding analysis, God's providence means that in "the given of a specific historical situation of desperate human need—with the particular limits and transforming possibilities intrinsic within it as well as the transcendent

---

9 Tupper, *A Scandalous Providence*, 464.
10 See Tupper, *A Scandalous Providence*, 95–97.
11 Tupper, *A Scandalous Providence*, 75.
12 See Tupper, *A Scandalous Providence*, 74–75.

possibilities available only to God beyond it—God always does the most God can do."[13] In Jesus's suffering and death, God experienced the ultimate self-limitation and what Tupper calls "the Godforsakenness of God from God" or "God's Self-abandonment."[14] For Tupper, this does not contradict that God was not an agent in Jesus's suffering and death. Paradoxically, God's experience of Godforsakenness from God was ultimately not the result of separation but rather the demonstration of continuity and unity since Jesus experienced the agony of the silence of his *Abba* God and God experienced the negation of unbroken community with the Beloved.

In other words, the experience of Godforsakenness was a reciprocal event of intimate pathos that bound God and Jesus together in shared but distinct agony that was the result of a human plot leading to the death of Jesus and his *Abba* relationship. The concept of Godforsakenness as a theological datum and not merely as an experience within God points, for Tupper, to the truth that God's love for us cannot be separated from God's suffering with us. "The God who loves us," concludes Tupper, "shares our agony and pain, helping us to bear its travail. Indeed, the suffering solidarity of the suffering love of God with human sufferers helps to sustain us and empower us to overcome suffering that hinders joy in life."[15]

Trauma and the Cross

The cross is a symbol of violent historical trauma to the body, the psyche, and the spirit. Not unlike lynchings of African American people during the period of reconstruction and the Jim Crow era, under Roman occupation of Palestine, public crucifixions were a way to inflict violence, terror, and control upon an oppressed people group. In the history of the church, the trauma memory quickly faded and the cross soon became a theological symbol of salvation, the possibility that sinful human existence can be restored for eternal glory. Pastoral theologian Shelly Rambo has reclaimed the trauma history of this central Christian symbol and interprets the Jesus narrative from a trauma-informed perspective, which in turn suggests a

---

13 Tupper, *A Scandalous Providence*, 402.
14 See Tupper, *A Scandalous Providence*, 465–466.
15 Tupper, *A Scandalous Providence*, 434.

pastoral theology for trauma-informed spiritual care and has implications for a contemporary understanding of the atonement.

While Rambo finds the notion of redemptive suffering problematic and shares the critique about traditional atonement models for their death-focused narratives, Rambo wonders if re-interpretations that simply assert life over death "exchange one set of images for another, albeit more nourishing and sustaining ones. In the search for pristine beginnings and the recovery of images that counter death, might these critiques fail to speak to the experiences in which death and life are peculiarly entangled?"[16] A linear interpretation that views death and life in opposition or understands the atonement as a gradual and purposeful salvific movement from the agony of abandonment and death to victorious life cannot account for the experience of trauma, where death lingers.

Rambo follows contemporary trauma theory and understands trauma as a typically violent encounter with death, where death is not necessarily defined in a literal way. Rather, it may be "a way of describing a radical event or events that shatter all that one knows about the world and all the familiar ways of operation within it."[17] Important and central to the experience of trauma is that an excess of death remains in life in the aftermath. Trauma is not the wound that is healed by time. Fragments of the violent experience that caused trauma, remnants of death, remain and return from the past to disturb the present. An understanding of salvation that is relevant to those experiencing traumatic suffering must therefore account for the remainder of death.

Rambo draws on Hans Urs von Balthasar's theological reflections about Holy Saturday, Adrienne von Speyr's mystic passion experiences, and the post-crucifixion narratives about witnessing in the Gospel of John to develop a theology of the middle, which she understands as a possibly redemptive space in the aftermath of death. Experiences in the middle, as Rambo explores them, seem at first glance like experiences of liminal space in that they instill a sense of disorientation. However, liminality identifies a threshold experience that purposefully awaits a transition and may or may

---

16 Shelly Rambo, *Spirit and Trauma: A Theology of Remaining* (Louisville: Westminster John Knox Press, 2010), 155.
17 Rambo, *Spirit and Trauma*, 4.

not involve suffering, while the middle is a space that may hold a tentative hope for redemption and always involves suffering. Rambo explores the Christian tradition of Holy Saturday and the teaching about Jesus's descent into hell to understand suffering in the aftermath of death to identify the middle as a place of theological significance.

For Rambo, the idea that Jesus descended to hell does not speak of Jesus's mission into the underworld to bring salvation to the dead. It rather intensifies the theme of Godforsakenness, for Jesus joins the dead as one of them in separation from God. Like Moltmann and Tupper, Rambo argues that the promise of redemption lies paradoxically in the very experience of forsakenness, which she also interprets from a trinitarian perspective.

> *The picture of forsakenness that the Son experiences in hell is interpreted redemptively as the complete solidarity of God with humanity. Divine love is revealed at the point at which it is most threatened. God experiences, within God's inner life, the forsakenness of those in hell. Instead of heroically rescuing the forsaken in hell, the Son identifies with them. Becoming one of the forsaken, he is without the father. This translates into a picture of love traveling to a place where there is no love, and this is the central force of Holy Saturday. There is no place that God does not go.*[18]

The symbol of Holy Saturday, the mysterious day in the middle between the day of crucifixion and the day of resurrection, thus points to an event where death remains, but where God's presence and love are expressed through an act of suffering solidarity.

Rambo formulates a pneumatology of witness based on her reading of the Johannine passion narrative, focusing on the characters of Mary Magdalene and the beloved disciple. She interprets the mention about Jesus handing over his spirit on the cross (John 19:30) through the lens of trauma theory as an indication that the passion narrative in the Gospel of John does not have a clear ending but that there "is, instead, an unclear beginning. Death and life are, in this space, unmarked. The significance lies, however,

---

18 Rambo, *Spirit and Trauma*, 68.

in the fact that death is witnessed not as something conclusive but, instead, as something that continues."[19]

While the Spirit is usually not center stage in interpretations of the atonement and salvation, the *paraclete* is crucial to Rambo's argument. What Rambo calls "middle spirit," exhaled on the cross and inhaled by the witness becomes "the breath of witness to what remains . . . the breath that moves between death and life, hovering over the deep not as a mastering or commanding presence but as a testimony to the inextinguishable remainder of divine love."[20] At the same time, the Spirit witnesses, in the territory marked by trauma, also the remainder of death and the abyss of suffering, which is necessary for the reconstruction of life in the aftermath and for healing. The Spirit in the middle thus becomes the symbol of therapeutic agency. As Rambo puts it, as "the breath of witness, the Spirit oscillates between formlessness and form, making visible what has been repressed, but never with certainty that form will come."[21]

Salvation and redemption from the middle can perhaps best be described as a sacred possibility that does not depend on forgiveness but rather on what remains. It does not lead to victorious new life but to survival and to the reconstruction of life infused with death after trauma. Such possibility is neither accurately grasped through interpretations of Jesus's death nor through interpretations of the resurrection. Rather, redemption is possible through the simultaneous witness to suffering and to God's love that remains in the middle between death and life. The middle Spirit, according to Rambo, "testifies to death's persistence and also points to distinctive movements of life in the aftermath. Fragments of death remain, yet the breath of witness remains there as well. The cross haunts the territory of remaining, yet this haunting is met with pneumatological possibility."[22] Through the lens of trauma, salvation is a messy possibility, not a neat transition from death to life, from forsakenness to communion, from judgment to redemption. Rather, it is a Spirit-witnessed transformation of life that arises out of the depths.

---

19 See Rambo, *Spirit and Trauma*, 107.
20 Rambo, *Spirit and Trauma*, 120.
21 Rambo, *Spirit and Trauma*, 123.
22 Rambo, *Spirit and Trauma*, 159–160.

Salvation as Liberation

Jesus's death and resurrection have long been interpreted as acts of liberation. According to that theological metanarrative, Jesus liberated humanity from the condemning force of inherent sinfulness or, according to the *Christus Victor* interpretation, from bondage to the devil. Theological perspectives that have emerged from the real-life struggles of marginalized and oppressed people challenge this supernatural narrative about liberation that assigns hope to an afterlife and insist that God's salvation happened and still happens in history.

Gustavo Gutiérrez introduced Latin American liberation theology as a practical, prophetic theology, defining it as critical reflection on historical praxis in light of God's revelation. Such reflection, he contends, "fulfills a prophetic function insofar as it interprets historical events with the intention of revealing and proclaiming their profound meaning."[23] The reference to history is critical. Salvation as a theological category, according to Gutiérrez, does not point toward a form of redeemed existence beyond this life but is a historical reality, just as sin is both a personal reality as well as a historical and social reality.

While sin may be personal, it is not an individual or private reality. It is not primarily a personal transgression of God's commands but is essentially a state of destructive and oppressive alienation, characterized by "the absence of fellowship and love in relationships among persons, the breach of friendship with God and with other persons, and, therefore, an interior, personal fracture."[24] Thus, sin is deeply rooted in the social and political order that defines human existence and shapes social structures and political will and actions.

Salvation, therefore, necessarily must include a transformation of that order through liberation. "This radical liberation is the gift that Christ offers us. By his death and resurrection he redeems us from sin and all its consequences."[25] Gutiérrez does not elaborate in detail about the theological

---

23 See Gustavo Gutiérrez, *A Theology of Liberation: History, Politics, and Salvation*, rev. ed., trans. and ed. Sister Caridad Inda and John Eagleson (Maryknoll, NY: Orbis Books, 1988), 10.
24 Gutiérrez, *A Theology of Liberation*, 103.
25 Gutiérrez, *A Theology of Liberation*, 103.

dynamics of Jesus's death and God's role in it but pays more attention to the incarnation and the resurrection as theological data to inform a hope-oriented, political theology. God's work of salvation through Christ restores communion with God and among human beings and provides the possibility of fulfillment for humanity in every aspect, "body and spirit, individual and society, person and cosmos, time and eternity. Christ, the image of the Father and the perfect God-Man, takes on all the dimensions of human existence."[26]

Jon Sobrino's Latin American Christology echoes Gutiérrez's emphasis on historicity. He identifies the meaning of the cross as a historical consequence of Jesus's life and prophetic public work. For Sobrino, to position the cross in history means that Jesus did not battle against supernatural powers but confronted religious authorities and political powers that manipulated God for their misuse of power and condemned Jesus as a blasphemer (Mark 4:63–64) and a political agitator (John 19:12).[27] Jesus confronted the God of ruling, oppressive powers by revealing through his life, his teachings, and his work a God of love and compassion.

By raising the question about the authentic God, Jesus confronted and challenged his contemporaries—and still confronts and challenges us—to choose "either a God wielding oppressive power or a God offering and effecting liberation. Framed in this context of a basic theological conflict, Jesus' trajectory to the cross is no accident. He himself provokes it by presenting the basic option between two deities. His course is also a trial of the deity, with Jesus appearing as a witness on one side and those in power as witnesses on the other side."[28] While Sobrino regards the cross as a central datum of the Christian faith, he argues against a magical conception of redemption that reiterates thoughtlessly that humanity is saved through Jesus's death on the cross without accounting for the theological dynamics of that event and the revolutionary concept of God that it implies. Sobrino hints at the notion of Jesus's atoning life when he suggests that the revelation of God as love was not confined to the crucifixion and resurrection but is

---

26 See Gutiérrez, *A Theology of Liberation*, 85.
27 See Jon Sobrino, *Christology at the Crossroads: A Latin American Approach*, trans. John Drury (Maryknoll, NY: Orbis Books, 1978), 202.
28 Sobrino, *Christology at the Crossroads*, 203–204.

evident throughout the life and work of the historical Jesus. The cross as a distinct and crucial aspect of the Jesus story revealed God's unconditional and suffering sympathetic love.

Sobrino's interpretation closely mirrors Moltmann's analysis in that he not only focuses on Jesus's suffering but also identifies the Father's suffering in the event of the cross. "On the cross of Jesus God himself is crucified. The Father suffers the death of the Son and takes upon himself all the pain and suffering of history. In this ultimate solidarity with humanity he reveals himself as the God of love, who opens up a hope and a future through the most negative side of history. Thus, Christian existence is nothing else but a process of participating in this same process whereby God loves the world and hence in the very life of God."[29] In other words, a Christian praxis participates in God's ongoing work of salvation and liberation through acts of care and solidarity.

Sobrino and Gutiérrez both cite the influence of theologian and philosopher Leonardo Boff and his understanding of Christ as liberator. Boff critiques traditional substitutionary atonement models and the *Christus Victor* image as schizophrenic for separating Jesus's sacrificial death as a metaphysical necessity from his life and thereby creating an abstract notion of redemption that is rooted in the past with no relevance to the problems of social sin and structural injustices. In contrast, Boff insists that redemption "is basically a praxis, a historical process, verified . . . in the turbulent reality of a concrete situation."[30] Salvation is symbolized in Jesus's liberating proclamation of the reign of God through his life and his teaching. Boff interprets the reign of God not primarily as a spiritual territory but as a new, dynamic order within the world that includes new social structures. This new order demands from followers of Jesus a personal conversion, a revolution in one's thinking and acting, and a transformation of existing structures, a revolution within society.[31]

---

29 Sobrino, *Christology at the Crossroads*, 224.
30 Leonardo Boff, *Passion of Christ, Passion of the World: The Facts, Their Interpretation, and Their Meaning Yesterday and Today*, trans. Robert R. Barr (Maryknoll, NY: Orbis Books, 1987), 89.
31 See Leonardo Boff, *Jesus Christ Liberator: A Critical Christology for Our Time*, trans. Patrick Hughes (Maryknoll, NY: Orbis Books, 1978), 64–75.

Jesus's death was the result of a conflict that he provoked with religious and political authorities over the proclamation of the new reign. Boff does not attribute any salvific significance to the crucifixion as such but only as a part of Jesus's work of liberation through his life and ministry and in conjunction with the resurrection. He holds that Jesus's death has theological relevance only within the context of his life, and Boff's argument is reminiscent of Abelard's perspective.

> *The whole life of Christ was giving, a being-for-others, an attempt to overcome all conflicts in his own existence and a realization of this goal. Jesus lived the human archetype just as God wanted, when he made him to his own image and likeness; Jesus always judged and spoke with God as his reference and starting point. Jesus thereby revealed a life of extraordinary authenticity and originality. By his preaching of the kingdom of God he lived his being-for-others to the end, experiencing the depths of despair of death (absence) of God on the cross.*[32]

Boff contends that the true meaning of Jesus's death can only be understood through the resurrection of Christ. However, resurrection is not a matter of cellular physiology or reanimation but signifies God's total and universal validation of Jesus's liberating activism, God's endorsement of Jesus's life and death paid as the price for liberation. It means "the complete and definite enthronement of human reality, spirit and body together, in the atmosphere of the divine. In other words, resurrection is complete hominization and liberation."[33] The resurrection thus is the manifestation and ultimate symbol of the reign of God, which effects persons' liberation from alienation within themselves, from others and from oppressive forces, and from God, demonstrating an ongoing revolutionary process in history.

It should not come as a surprise that Black liberation theology has emphasized similar themes in the Jesus story. Theologian James Cone, the perhaps most prominent representative of Black liberation theology,

---

32 Boff, *Jesus Christ Liberator*, 18.
33 Boff, *Passion of Christ*, 66.

defined Christian theology essentially as the exploration and formulation of God's liberating activity in the world for the empowerment of those who followed in the way of Jesus. Particularly, he saw the task of Black theology in analyzing "the nature of the gospel of Jesus Christ in the light of oppressed blacks so they will see the gospel as inseparable from their humiliated condition, and as bestowing on them the necessary power to break the chains of oppression."[34] The Black condition, according to Cone, in the concreteness of oppression is the fundamental datum of the human experience. Thus, sin is not moral impurity or the trespassing of divine laws. Rather, it is the denial of community by refusing to acknowledge God's liberating activity both on part of the oppressors and the oppressed.[35] Salvation is the restoration of community through liberation from white racism and is not something passively received or accepted but demands active participation. As Cone puts it, "God in Jesus meets us in the situation of our oppressed condition and tells us not only who *God* is and what *God* is doing about our liberation, but also who *we* are and what *we* must do about white racism."[36]

While Cone does not use the terminology of atonement much, he explores its meaning as the process of God's salvation and insists that it needs to be anchored in the historical reality of Jesus as the Oppressed One among oppressed people. The soteriological value of Jesus's life, work, and death can only lie in God's identification with the oppressed through Jesus. In order to have any relevance for descendants of slaves, Jesus must be Black, since Black Americans have been oppressed because of their blackness.[37] For Cone, this is not a statement about skin pigmentation but rather an assertion that Jesus "represents the complete opposite of the values of white culture . . . striking at white values and white religion. . . . Blackness is a manifestation of the being of God in that it reveals that neither divinity nor humanity resides in white definitions but in liberation from captivity."[38] However, Cone does not seem to suggest that Jesus's death was primarily a historical consequence of his life but rather "the revelation of the freedom of God taking upon himself the totality of human oppression; his resurrection is the disclosure

---

34 James H. Cone, *Black Theology of Liberation* (Maryknoll, NY: Orbis Books, 1986), 5.
35 See Cone, *Black Theology of Liberation*, 110–115.
36 Cone, *Black Theology of Liberation*, 90.
37 Cone, *Black Theology of Liberation*, 126.
38 Cone, *Black Theology of Liberation*, 128.

that God is not defeated by oppression but transforms it into the possibility of freedom."[39]

In *The Cross and the Lynching Tree*, Cone explores the parallels between methods of torture and execution and their theological importance as symbols of salvation and oppression that interpret each other. Theologically, he identifies Jesus as the first lynchee who was executed by the same powers that lynched Black Americans as a way of controlling them when the mechanisms of the slave system had been lost after the Civil War. The lynching tree not only created multi-generational trauma but also reflects the scandal of the cross, just as the cross reveals paradoxically God's empowering solidarity and liberating presence. Apparently referencing the *Christus Victor* atonement model and explicitly identifying his approach as a contextual theology, Cone argues that because

> God was present with Jesus on the cross and thereby refused to let Satan and death have the last word about his meaning, God was also present at every lynching in the United States. God saw what whites did and to innocent and helpless blacks and claimed their suffering as God's own. God transformed lynched black bodies into the recrucified body of Christ. Every time a white mob lynched a black person, they lynched Jesus. The lynching tree is the cross in America. When American Christians realize that they can meet Jesus only in the crucified bodies in our midst, they will encounter the real scandal of the cross.[40]

The lynching tree prevents the cross from turning into an irrelevant symbol of sentimental piety. For Cone, the cross is a symbol of hope in the face of the torture of Black bodies and the oppression of Black persons.

Building on Cone's argument from his early writings and going beyond his focus on the cross, theologian Anthony Reddie elaborates on a Black theological approach to reconciliation. He argues that traditional models of atonement have focused on the vertical dimension of reconciliation and

---

[39] Cone, *Black Theology of Liberation*, 124–125.
[40] James H. Cone, *The Cross and the Lynching Tree* (Maryknoll, NY: Orbis Books, 2011), 158.

suggests that a contextualized approach to reconciliation can integrate the vertical and horizontal dimensions. Such an approach is grounded in Jesus's life and liberating praxis and not just his death. Through Jesus's life and prophetic praxis, Reddie argues, God sides with marginalized people.

> *Jesus' praxis as demonstrated in his life demands that his presence be seen in those on the margins (Matt. 25:31–46). By seeing Christ in the "other," the divine image in the marginalized, despised and oppressed self elevates their humanity beyond the limitations placed upon them by the corrupting power of White hegemony. By concentrating upon Jesus' liberative praxis as the primary scene of effective reconciliation, one is able to detect in this injunction a commitment to see the divine image in the disparaged "other."*[41]

Rather than emphasizing the individual consciousness of sin and the possibility of personal redemption through Jesus's sacrifice, which blots out transgressions, Black theology names the sin of racism as the central factor of alienation and the possibility of repentance through reparations and the praxis of justice and equity.

Beyond a Hermeneutics of Sacrifice and Surrogacy

Womanist theology interprets the Christian tradition and its narratives from the intersectional perspective of African American women's experience in history and at present, deconstructing and reinterpreting theological constructs by paying attention to diverse contexts of social and historical experiences. JoAnne Marie Terrell defines womanist theology as "a means to explore the spiritual, ecclesial, social, political, and economic implications of the 'tridimensional phenomenon of race, class and gender oppression' in the experience of African American women."[42] The themes of sacrifice and surrogacy that have defined traditional theories of atonement name

---

41 Anthony G. Reddie, *Working against the Grain: Re-Imaging Black Theology in the 21st Century* (London & New York: Routledge, 2014), 45–46.
42 JoAnne Marie Terrell, *Power in the Blood? The Cross in the African American Experience* (Maryknoll, NY: Orbis Books, 1998), 6.

historically oppressive and abusive realities in the experience of African American women. In *Power in the Blood*, Terrell explores how Black and womanist theology have been informed by and contribute to an understanding of the cross in African American experience and how an apprehension of the doctrine of atonement in the African American community has been both empowering and disempowering. Like other womanist theologians, she advocates for a Christology from below that does not emphasize Jesus's maleness and death as much as his life and his ministry of healing and liberation. Reminiscent of Abelard's notion that Jesus's example teaches and saves humanity, Terrell holds that "anyone's death has salvific significance if we learn continuously from the life that preceded it."[43]

Terrell interprets traditional models of atonement and the persistent focus on Jesus's passion and death through the lens of the early Christian experience of oppression, persecution, and martyrdom. She argues that early Christians saw in the sacrifice of Jesus a rejection of animal sacrifices and sacred violence, an act that ended the need for sacrifice once and for all. At the same time, however, they reappropriated and reinterpreted the religious symbol of sacrifice in their understanding of the cross, which signified the theological meaning of their oppression.[44] Terrell identifies particularly the cult of martyrdom as a force that planted the idea of sacrifice deeply in the theological soil of early Christian communities, soil that was fertilized by experiences of persecution and by the expectation that Christ's triumphant return was imminent. She links the interpretation of atonement among early Christian communities to the African American experience in the wake of chattel slavery, both in terms of how this interpretation came to support slavery and helped enslaved people of African descent in North America to make meaning of their suffering. Terrell argues that the Christian doctrine of the atonement, shaped by early Christian experiences of persecution and scapegoating, subjugated enslaved people psychologically and spiritually by imposing a hermeneutics of sacrifice. "Christianizing the slaves the white slaveholder taught, 'Slaves obey your masters,' willfully disconnecting the biblical injunction from its historical context and directly connecting the hermeneutics of sacrifice to their putatively divinely sanctioned authority.

---

43 Terrell, *Power in the Blood*, 127.
44 Terrell, *Power in the Blood*, 20–21.

Thus, in effect and in kind, white people and the white power structures undergirding slavery reinvented the conditions and terms of Christian martyrdom in the slave community."[45]

Terrell posits that the message of the cross also provided meaning and a way to identify with the Jesus story of suffering because of its profound affinity with the suffering of slaves. Furthermore, by interpreting sacrificial theology in terms of sacramental existence, that is, as mediating the presence of God to white people, enslaved people claimed power and agency, which are reflected in Black liturgy, music, and confessional statements. Just as Jesus's suffering was an expression of God's love for the world, so the suffering of enslaved African Americans, according to slave religion, embodied God's love in and for their world.

Terrell's womanist theology suggests "a transformed, *sacramental* notion of sacrifice that has saving significance for the African American community and for Black women in particular."[46] Going beyond the traditional hermeneutics of sacrifice that demands enemy-love and what Terrell considers the unbiblical mandate "to love everybody," she considers a biased love for one's own as a sacramental witness to God's character.[47] Following Terrell's argument, oppressed and abused persons are under no moral obligation to love their oppressors or abusers and still can testify sacramentally to God's love without being defined by one's victimization. She concludes that "since God is love, love cannot be prescribed, circumscribed, or even defined. It can, however, be mediated through human instrumentality, a means by which God can do whatever God wills, whether God wills to forgive or 'smite' the wicked."[48] The sacramental witness that Terrell posits mediates a God who is revealed in the Jesus event as "loving and challenging, humane and sovereign, culturally engaged yet countercultural, personal, a healer and a mystic, a co-sufferer and a liberator."[49]

Terrell's argument is influenced by womanist theologian Delores Williams. Williams challenges the idea of salvific surrogacy inherent in traditional atonement models as an abusive and defiling practice that has

---

45 Terrell, *Power in the Blood*, 25.
46 Terrell, *Power in the Blood*, 139.
47 See Terrell, *Power in the Blood*, 139–140.
48 Terrell, *Power in the Blood*, 141.
49 Terrell, *Power in the Blood*, 141.

been painfully familiar to African American women and has uniquely signified their oppression. Coerced surrogacy in the antebellum period exploited women's bodies sexually, through nurturance, and as a tool for field labor. When slavery was officially abolished and white men could not demand Black women to serve them in surrogate roles, voluntary surrogacy still continued in the postbellum period and Black women substituted their labor power for that of male farm workers and in the role of the mammy.[50] The biblical story of Hagar, the African slave, as Williams interprets it, becomes an encouraging model of resistance and survival that reveals "the faith, hope and struggle with which an African slave woman worked through issues of survival, surrogacy, motherhood, rape, homelessness and economic and sexual oppression."[51] In the biblical narrative and in the historical experience of African American women, wilderness experience is religious experience. Yet, it is nevertheless a painful experience with God, who directs and saves mysteriously and makes a way where no path forward seems possible.

Williams raises the question "whether the image of a surrogate-God has salvific power for black women or whether this image supports and reinforces the exploitation that has accompanied their experience with surrogacy. If black women accept this idea of redemption, can they not also passively accept the exploitation that surrogacy brings?"[52] In a more general sense, Williams wonders if the cross as a symbol of oppression can reveal the truth about redemption. She identifies the cross not as a symbol of salvation but as the most desecrated image of human sin, destroying and defiling Jesus's body like the bodies of countless slaves and descendants of slaves. Like other liberation theologians, Williams sees redemptive and salvific power in the life of Jesus and more specifically "by Jesus' life of resistance and by the survival strategies he used to help people survive the death of identity caused by their exchange of inherited cultural meanings for the new identity shaped by the gospel ethics and world view."[53] At the heart of the Jesus event, as Williams interprets it, is Jesus's vision of reconciliation and righting relations. She concludes that humanity "is, then, redeemed through Jesus'

---

50 See Delores S. Williams, *Sisters in the Wilderness: The Challenge of Womanist God-Talk* (Maryknoll, NY: Orbis Books, 1993), 55–66.
51 Williams, *Sisters in the Wilderness*, 31.
52 Williams, *Sisters in the Wilderness*, 143.
53 Williams, *Sisters in the Wilderness*, 145.

ministerial vision of life and not through his death. There is nothing divine in the blood of the cross. God does not intend black women's surrogacy experience. Neither can Christian faith affirm such an idea. Jesus did not come to be a surrogate. Jesus came for life, to show humans a perfect vision of ministerial relation that humans had very little knowledge of."[54] Rather than following a trajectory toward an inevitably ordained surrogate death, the Jesus event revealed a vision for abundant relational life and the ethical principles and practices upon which to build such life and resist oppression.

Redemption through Interrelatedness

Feminist theologians have critiqued traditional images of the atonement as paternalistic and even sadistic, justifying and perpetuating male dominance and relationships of coercive and abusive power, and portraying God as a torturer.[55] Feminist scholar and theologian Rita Nakashima Brock focuses much of her writings on the relationship between religion and violence, in particular the violence done to Jesus, and she locates her interest biographically in childhood experiences of isolating racism that she faced as an immigrant of Japanese and Puerto Rican descent. She challenges traditional interpretation of the Jesus event, arguing that "the Christian theological tradition has interpreted Jesus's life in ways that reinforce trauma."[56] In her re-interpretation of the Jesus event and the atonement in *Journeys by Heart*, Brock agrees with liberation theologies that Jesus's death was a political event rather than part of a divine plan for salvation. More specifically, she holds that Jesus's execution was a tragedy "created by the political systems of patriarchal society and was neither inevitable nor necessary."[57] She disagrees, however, with liberationist ideas that emphasize the importance of the historical Jesus and interpret Jesus's work on behalf of the poor and oppressed as a form of heroic action that used unilateral power to actualize God's will. At the heart of Brock's feminist Christology is the claim that any power believed to have redemptive, healing, or liberating qualities necessarily needs to be shared,

---

54 Williams, *Sisters in the Wilderness*, 148.
55 See Sölle, *Suffering*, 32.
56 Brock and Parker, *Proverbs and Ashes*, 52.
57 Rita Nakashima Brock, *Journeys by Heart: A Christology of Erotic Power* (New York: Crossroad Publishing Company, 1988), 93–94.

mutual power, or what she calls erotic power. She interprets feminist Eros as a life force and explains that erotic power "is the power of our primal interrelatedness. Erotic power, as it creates and connects hearts, involves the whole person in relationships of self-awareness, vulnerability, openness, and caring."[58]

Brock critiques trinitarian formulations of atonement that are based on the Chalcedonian definition with the help of psychoanalyst Alice Miller's work on child abuse. The traditional models "reflect patriarchal family relationships between parent and child and husband and wife. In the patriarchal family, all members are regarded as possessions and extensions of the reigning authority figure. The father and son become one person."[59] Thus, the relationship between the father and the son is characterized by fusion and dependency rather than intimacy and interdependency.

Analyzing human relationships and the human condition, Brock substitutes the notion of original grace instead of a belief in original sin. For Brock, original grace acknowledges our primal interrelatedness and means that human beings are born with an openness to the presence of others, reflecting the divine reality of connection and love.[60] Such openness, on the one hand, accounts for experiences of graciousness, generosity, love, and creative interchange. On the other hand, this openness makes human beings vulnerable to abuse and destructive forces. "At the earliest part of our lives," Brock contends, "we are dependent on the loving power of others to nurture us. Their failure to do so has serious consequences. We are broken by the world of our relationships before we are able to defend ourselves."[61] Sin, then, is not a state of being nor a permeating condition somehow inherited at birth but the experience and consequence of being damaged. It is "a sign of our brokenheartedness, of how damaged we are, not of how evil, willfully disobedient, and culpable we are. Sin is not something to be punished, but something to be healed."[62]

Brock employs the metaphor of heart to describe the human condition, the human self, in a state of redemption or restoration. Heart is the

---

58 See Brock, *Journeys by Heart*, 26.
59 Brock, *Journeys by Heart*, 57.
60 See Brock, *Journeys by Heart*, 7–8.
61 Brock, *Journeys by Heart*, 16.
62 Brock, *Journeys by Heart*, 7.

true self, the seat of erotic power and capacity for intimacy, the will and ability to be connected and whole. Heart is at once fragile and vulnerable as well as powerfully creative and courageous.[63] Salvation, according to Brock, is the restoration of heart as the self in a state of original grace and cannot happen through a unilateral act of sacrificial self-giving or abusive power. It only can happen in a collaborative and co-creative relationship and community, which Brock calls "Christa/Community" in reference to the female Christ on the crucifix in the Cathedral of Saint John the Divine in New York City. While Jesus is part of that community, he is neither its center nor its measure. However, Brock sees the interactive process of erotic power of the Christa/Community primarily reflected in the healing and exorcism narratives of the gospels and particularly in the Gospel of Mark. Jesus's ability to heal and invite community, rather than his self-sacrifice, embodies the capacity for salvation through relationships of erotic power. "Jesus' heartfelt openness to the sacred reality revealed to him in the hearts of others and the willingness of those who seek help to make themselves vulnerable create the space for erotic power to emerge. Erotic power is revealed by the dialectic of the brokenhearted, who reveal the fragility of heart and the necessity for connection, and by Jesus listening to the brokenhearted, who actively seek him out."[64]

The Christa/Community that began as a healing community in Galilee maintained connections beyond Jesus's death, which was the result of a conflict with political authorities rather than of a cosmic struggle between God and the devil for human souls. According to Brock, the women, who had been witnesses to Jesus's execution and had not deserted him, became the authors of a new vision for the community that death could not destroy erotic power. Through what Brock identifies as a dangerous memory and a visionary-ecstatic image of resurrection, "the witnesses who saw him die, marked his grave in sorrow, and returned to anoint him . . . refused to let death defeat them. In taking heart they remembered his presence and affirmed divine power among them."[65] Brock's feminist, communal Christology contends that salvation is the restoration of original grace and does

---

63 See Brock, *Journeys by Heart*, xiv.
64 Brock, *Journeys by Heart*, 81.
65 Brock, *Journeys by Heart*, 100.

not come at the hand of an almighty power but through the life-giving flow of erotic power in a community that remembers both its brokenness and the possibility for healing and redemption.

Conclusion

Crucicentric models of the atonement present a theological problem. Literally, a problem is something thrown before us, causing us to stumble and possibly to fall. Traditional models of the atonement qualify as stumbling blocks to following in the way of Jesus because their focus on redemptive violence contradicts the narrative about Jesus's life-affirming public work of healing and his message about a compassionate and gracious God. More recent theological positions, which either focus on a reinterpretation of the cross or address theological dynamics of salvation, show that a violent, death-focused understanding is not only unnecessary to speak of the atonement but is indeed counter to the fullness of the Jesus event. Themes of God's solidarity in the midst of suffering, liberation, compassion, and healing replace punitive and substitutionary interpretations.

While Jesus's death on the cross is an integral and theologically meaningful part of the Jesus event, the event is much larger than what happened at Golgotha. Jesus's death needs to be understood in the context of his life. The Jesus event expanded from Bethlehem via Nazareth to the villages and the seaside of Galilee, to Bethsaida and the area of Gerasa in the Decapolis, to Samaria and finally to Jerusalem. To do justice to the extent and to the intent of the Jesus story and to construct a therapeutic theology, we must shift our focus from an atoning death to an understanding of the whole Jesus event as God's saving initiative toward humanity.

Part Two

LIFE NARRATIVES OF SHAME, SALVATION, AND REDEMPTION

A CLINICAL THEOLOGY is informed by narrative theory and by the clinical practice of spiritual care itself. Spiritual care practitioners have long used storytelling and story-listening for assessment purposes and to provide others with compassionate attention and care. Attending to a person's story and letting it resonate in the empathic space between oneself and another is a deeply meaningful act of care. Inviting and engaging another's story, specifically a story that reveals the depth of the spiritual life impacted by struggle or pain, is a sacred act and an invaluable clinical skill for spiritual care practitioners. It involves various levels of responsive communication.

In this part of the book, I examine two narratives about shame and the possibility of salvation and redemption. One is a memoir by writer and theologian Frederick Buechner. It is a recollection of Buechner's real-life events and their impact on personal development and relationships. The other is a novel, an imaginative story by Toni Morrison based on the real-life story of a formerly enslaved woman and grounded in the dreadful history of slavery, white supremacy, and racial oppression in the United States. Both speak profoundly about the invasive and destructive power of shame as well as the possibility of salvation from shame. In examining these stories, I do not claim the expertise of a literary scholar. Rather, I attend to them as a clinical theologian who practices story-listening to understand the themes and movements of the spiritual life.

Human beings are storied creatures, and in telling our stories we learn our lives and we share our lives. To know others means ultimately to become entrusted with their stories. Philosopher and theologian Stephen Crites laid a foundation for understanding narrative knowledge that is particularly relevant to spiritual care in his now classic essay about *The Narrative Quality of Experience*. Narrative knowledge, as Crites understands it, is not only interpersonal knowledge but is intrapersonal knowledge, knowledge about oneself and one's experience of the world. He further argues that narratives function to bring order to a life of experiences that might be rudimentary and in themselves not organized.[1] In other words, stories are attempts to make meaning of life experiences, and the experiences that disorient us are perhaps the ones most in need to be infused with meaning.

Crites makes a helpful distinction between sacred and mundane stories. Sacred stories, he explains, project symbolic worlds and orient the lives of people through time, while mundane stories reflect the world at hand, captured in the images of a particular culture and age. Both types of stories are distinct but not necessarily separate. They do not exclude each other; rather, one may be implicated and resonate in the other.[2] Within the theoretical framework that Crites suggests, both Buechner's memoir and Morrison's novel can be considered mundane stories, which in no way diminishes their value or power to reveal important truths. It simply means that they are not timeless but have a historical context and reflect particular cultural influences. Like sacred stories, however, they may have symbolic power. The clinical theology that I construct follows Crite's argument and proposes that mundane stories and sacred stories can interact and have the potential to interpret each other. It is the task of the clinical theologian to listen for the reciprocal resonances in both types of stories.

---

[1] See Stephen Crites, "The Narrative Quality of Experience," in *Why Narrative? Readings in Narrative Theology*, ed. Stanley Hauerwas and L. Gregory Jones (Grand Rapids: William B. Eerdmans Publishing Co., 1989), 79.

[2] See Crites, "Narrative Quality," 69–71.

3

FREDERICK BUECHNER: *TELLING SECRETS*

FREDERICK BUECHNER WAS a writer and theologian of European-American ancestry. His more than thirty publications range from novels to essay collections, autobiography, theological treatises, and sermons. In one of his sermons, he briefly describes how his early years were defined by scarcity and lacking a sense of home. "I was born in 1926 and therefore most of my childhood took place during the years of the Great Depression of the 1930s. As economic considerations kept my father continually moving from job to job, we as a family kept moving from place to place, with the result that none of the many houses we lived in ever became a home for me."[1]

The Longing for Home, as his sermon was entitled, may very well characterize Buechner's spiritual journey. For Buechner, the longing is about finding a way to be at home with one's own original self, created in the image and likeness of God, which "is the most essential part of who we are and is buried deep in all of us as a source of wisdom and strength and healing which we can draw upon or, with our terrible freedom, not draw upon as we choose."[2]

In the early 1980s, Buechner published two autobiographical works, *The Sacred Journey* in 1982 and *Now and Then* in 1983. His third autobiographical book, *Telling Secrets*, was published almost ten years later. In comparing his latest memoir to the earlier autobiographical writings, Buechner concludes that *The Sacred Journey* and *Now and Then* mainly addressed the headlines of his life, while *Telling Secrets* is a memoir of "the inner life."[3] He considers with great honesty the impact of shame in his life and the lives of those he has loved over the years while offering the reader

---

1 Frederick Buechner, *Secrets in the Dark: A Life in Sermons* (New York: HarperCollins Publishers, 1982), 222.
2 Frederick Buechner, *Telling Secrets* (San Francisco: HarperCollins Publishers, 1991), 44.
3 See Buechner, *Telling Secrets*, 2.

theological reflections that suggested meaning along the way. The memoir is in essence a description of a journey from brokenness toward wholeness, from loss and abandonment to connection with community and with the original self.

The title of the memoir does not only describe aptly Buechner's intention in writing the book but also signals one of Buechner's basic convictions about the human condition.

> *I have come to believe that by and large the human family all has the same secrets, which are both very telling and very important to tell. They are telling in the sense that they tell what is perhaps the central paradox of our condition—that what we hunger for perhaps more than anything else is to be known in our full humanness, and yet that is often just what we also fear more than anything else. It is important to tell at least from time to time the secret of who we truly and fully are . . . because otherwise we run the risk of losing track of who we truly and fully are and little by little come to accept instead the highly edited version we put forth in hope that the world will find it more acceptable than the real thing.*[4]

Buechner's characterization of the human condition expresses an essential conflict inherent in the experience of shame, namely the struggle between the "will to be known"[5] and accepted in one's full humanness and the fear of rejection. It also identifies the primary protections the self develops in response to shame, which are the *personas* it creates to mask itself.

A Traumatic Secret

Buechner begins his memoir with the account of his father's suicide when he was ten years old. This traumatic event impacted much of his growing up primarily because it became a shameful secret and had a powerful emotional

---

4 Buechner, *Telling Secrets*, 2–3.
5 For a detailed discussion of the will to be known as a driving force within the self, see Frank Woggon, "The Will to Be Known: Toward a Pastoral Anthropology of the Self," *Pastoral Psychology* 44, no. 1 (September 1995): 45–61.

ripple effect into the life of the family he created years later with his wife. On a morning in 1936, Carl Frederick Buechner Sr. made sure that Frederick Buechner and his younger brother were safe in their room where they were playing and locked himself in the garage to inhale the exhaust from the old family Chevy until the fumes overwhelmed his system and stopped his heart and breathing. Carl Buechner's choice to end his life was apparently not a rash or impulsive decision. He had prepared for it for at least a few weeks, making remarks about the car's broken exhaust system to family and friends, likely to create the impression of an accident. However, the note that he left for his wife in a secret place made it quite clear that his death was intentional.

Carl Buechner's life and death soon became a secret, mostly forgotten among his family's self-imposed silence and not even mentioned as a hushed memory. Much later, in *The Sacred Journey*, Buechner remembered his father as hard-working, even as he moved from job to job during the economic crisis of the 1930s. He also recalled how his father taught him to swim and to ride a bike by running alongside, steadying the bike and then letting go and trusting his son to manage on his own—until he ran into a hedge.[6] Those flashes of memory, as briefly as they were recorded, called to mind happy moments between young Frederick and his father, moments without shame that were as true as those that inflicted trauma and lasting pain.

Buechner remembers his family's reaction at the time as a complete and intentional lack of response to his father's death.

> *There was no funeral to mark his death and put a period at the end of the sentence that had been his life, and as far as I can remember, once he had died my mother, brother, and I rarely talked about him much ever again, either to each other or to anybody else. It made my mother too sad to talk about him, and since there was already more than enough sadness to go around, my brother and I avoided the subject with her as she avoided it for her own reasons also with us.*[7]

The grief remained unacknowledged among them, and so did the shame that came with the secret about his father's death. Yet, the shame worked

---

6 See Buechner, *Sacred Journey*, 34.
7 Buechner, *Telling Secrets*, 7–8.

its destructive path into the lives of the survivors and had started to grow its roots in Frederick's life even before the suicide. Reflecting on the causes of his father's decision to end his life and on his own secrets at a young age, Buechner identifies his father's drunken episodes at gatherings with family and friends that had left his older son embarrassed and almost unable to recognize Carl Buechner as his father. He also remembers his mother's fits of rage toward his father that "made the very earth shake beneath my feet" and sent the younger brother for weeks at time to hide in his bed, seeking a safe place away from the family conflict.[8] Even before their father's death, it appears that fear and shame had turned into a toxic mixture that led to emotional isolation for the two brothers.

In the aftermath of the trauma, the family moved far from the place of their pain to the Bermuda Islands, which Buechner remembers as idyllic and "with a greater sense of permanence than any place we had lived earlier where there had always been another job in the offering and another house to move to."[9] Buechner's mother, Katherine, assigned her older son to be the man of the family. Buechner remembers his mother's expectation as "freighted with more grief and anger and guilt and God knows what all else than it could possible bear."[10] His newly assigned role added to the grief, but Buechner could not do the necessary work of grieving. Instead, Buechner buried the grief and the pain deep inside, and "don't talk, don't trust, don't feel" became the unwritten law of the family for years to come.[11] Buechner writes: "We never talked about what had happened. We didn't trust the world with our secret, hardly trusted each other with it. And as far as my ten-year-old self was concerned anyway, the only feeling that I can remember from that distant time was the blessed relief of coming out of the dark and unmentionable sadness of my father's life and death into fragrance and greenness and light."[12]

The island magic ended for young Buechner with the news that the German army had invaded Poland and that England and France had declared war. Fear that Adolf Hitler was planning to capture Bermuda to establish a

---

8 See Buechner, *Telling Secrets*, 73.
9 Buechner, *Sacred Journey*, 47.
10 See Buechner, *Telling Secrets*, 8.
11 See Buechner, *Telling Secrets*, 8–10.
12 Buechner, *Telling Secrets*, 10.

submarine base caused a governmental order for all Americans to vacate the islands. Thus, the family moved to a small town in North Carolina where Frederick's grandparents had retired. Later, they relocated to New Jersey.

Reflecting on the season in Bermuda, Buechner wonders if he seemed to move quickly past his grief because he was not emotionally equipped as a young boy to process the impact of the traumatic loss. He refers to the myth of Oedipus to ponder about unconscious dynamics in young Frederick's response to his father's death. "You could speak in terms of Oedipal conflict and say . . . that, with his father's death, he got what subconsciously, he had of course always wanted, which was his mother for himself."[13] Buechner identifies anxiety and guilt as the dynamics behind this explanation. However, psychoanalytic theory identifies shame as the prominent dynamic in oedipal experience.[14] The fact that Buechner's mother assigned him to be the man of house after his father's death certainly could have reinforced the impression that, "at the kings death, the grief of the prince is mitigated by becoming king himself."[15]

Masking the Shame

In describing the aftermath of his father's suicide, Buechner's reflections center on his mother. Interestingly, he does not focus on her specific response to the loss, except for mentioning that she buried the memory of her husband. Rather, he introduces Katherine to his readers in a more general way.[16] That introduction, however, reveals the brokenness and shame that marked his family. Buechner remembers his mother's dressing table as "the command center" of her room until the end of her long life of almost ninety-two years.[17] He describes the utensils and tools needed to apply makeup, as his mother did, with artistry. Katherine's beauty was her priced possession, and above the dressing table hung a mirror with a French

---

13 Buechner, *Sacred Journey*, 55.
14 See, for example, Heinz Kohut, *The Analysis of the Self: A Systematic Approach to the Psychoanalytic Treatment of Narcissistic Personality Disorders* (Chicago: University of Chicago Press, 2009), 151–152.
15 Buechner, *Sacred Journey*, 55–56.
16 Buechner does not use his mother's name nor his father's name in his memoir. However, because I introduced his father by name, I also use his mother's name primarily to avoid appearances of female erasure.
17 See Buechner, *Telling Secrets*, 14.

inscription of the motto of her life. Translated into English, the inscription was: "You have to suffer to be beautiful." Buechner remembers how his mother took pains in the weeks before her death to recreate a version of the face that had made people want to be near her.[18] She never developed the loving or giving side of who she could have become through sacrificial rather than transactional relationships. Rather, when she thought that her beauty had faded, she withdrew from relationships and isolated herself in the New York City apartment, where she lived and died.

Buechner remembers that his mother would tune out the world as she wished after she decided to be deaf or perhaps actually became hard of hearing. "She developed the habit of closing her eyes when she spoke to you as if you were a dream she was dreaming. It was as if she chose not to see in your face what you might be thinking behind the simple words you were shouting, or as if, ostrich-like, closing her eyes was a way of keeping you from seeing her. With her looks gone she felt she had nothing left to offer the world, to propitiate the world."[19] When she could not meet the world anymore with a beautiful mask that she had believed to be herself, she avoided at will the gaze of the occasional visitor.

Buechner's description of his mother's dependency on facial makeup to create a *persona* reveals a deep need to mask to feel lovable and acceptable, to be sought out and admired. Ironically, a persona does not allow for true intimacy because it does not offer a genuine and mutual relationship. When the cover is blown, the person behind the mask may withdraw for fear of rejection or she may attack with rage. Buechner reports one such incident when Katherine discovered that he told a fictionalized version of his father's death in one of his novels entitled *The Return of Ansel Gibbs*. As she saw it, the book uncovered their shameful secret, violating a family rule, and she reacted with bitter fury. Buechner describes how as an adult he wanted to claim the story about his father's death as his own story. Instead, his mother's angry outburst made him regress. "I felt as much of a traitor as she charged me with being," he remembers, "and at the age of thirty-two was as horrified at what I had done as if I had been a child of ten. I was full of guilt and remorse and sure that in who-knows-what grim and lasting way I would be made to suffer

---

18 See Buechner, *Telling Secrets*, 14.
19 Buechner, *Telling Secrets*, 17.

for what I had done."[20] In her anger about having the family secret exposed, Kathrine transferred her shame to her son to lessen its impact on herself.

Buechner developed his own way of masking the brokenness or what he called the unhappiness in his life. Success and fame seemed to hold the promise of overcoming the alienation that he felt. Buechner describes himself in college at Princeton as mainly concerned with himself. In reflecting on "one of the less embarrassing poems" he wrote during those years, one that thematized how he would find himself, he remembers how he knew that he wanted to pursue a writing career.

> *I knew that I wanted to be writer, but I had no clear idea what I wanted to write about; and as to the question of why I wanted to be a writer, I believe that, apart from simply the great fun of it for me, it was as much as anything to become famous enough not to have to explain to strangers how to pronounce my difficult last name. To be famous, it seemed to me, would be no longer to have to worry about explaining who I was even to myself because what fame meant was to be so known that in a sense I would no longer be a stranger to anybody.*[21]

To be known at that point in Buechner's life meant being recognized as accomplished rather than being accepted as the person he was and with the secret he had kept for so long. Buechner indeed became well-known as a successful writer. His hope to no longer be a stranger to others and himself, however, may have echoed a spiritual yearning to be known in one's full humanness.

Becoming released from habitual secrecy took Buechner through a frightening journey reminiscent of the biblical story of Jacob's passage across the river Jabbok, where Jacob wrestled in the dark with God, with his own demon, with Esau, or perhaps with all of them (Gen 32:22–32). Years later, in a novel about the life of Jacob, Buechner wrote about the struggle.

> *For the rest of the night we battled in the reed with the Jabbok roaring down through the gorge above us. Each time I thought I was lost, I escaped somehow. There were moments when we lay*

---

20 Buechner, *Telling Secrets*, 10.
21 Buechner, *Sacred Journey*, 89–90.

> *exhausted in each other's arms the way a man and a woman lie exhausted from passion. There were moments when I seemed to be prevailing. It was as if he was letting me prevail. Then he was at me with new fury. But he did not prevail. For hours it went on that way. Our bodies were slippery with mud. We were panting like beasts. We could not see each other. We spoke no words. I did not know why we were fighting. It was like fighting in a dream.*[22]

As Buechner renders the story, it is not quite clear whether the struggle was real or imagined, and ultimately it does not matter as long as it was true. In the end, the yearning was for a blessing. As Buechner has Jacob remember, "I would not let him go for fear that the day would take him as the dark had given him. It was my life I clung to. My enemy was my life. My life was my enemy. I said, 'I will not let you go unless you bless me.' Even if his blessing meant death, I wanted it more than life."[23] The blessing was to receive a new name, to be truly known, not as a deceiver, but as one who prevailed with hope for a future. However, the blessing could only be received as a transformation of sorts through "Godwrestling," and the only way it could become transforming was through struggle, fear, and pain.[24]

A Fearsome Blessing

Buechner's struggle to be known, to connect with his true original self, extended far into the life of the family he and his wife created. He recalls how the secrets continued, combined, and multiplied, remembering that "when I married and had children, there were all the secrets of that new

---

22 Frederick Buechner, *The Son of Laughter* (San Francisco: HarperCollins Publishers, 1993), 159.
23 Buechner, *Son of Laughter*, 160.
24 The term "Godwrestling" was, to my knowledge, coined by Rabbi Arthur Waskow. Reflecting on the story of Jacob and Esau, he states that only "when Jacob struggled against that piece of Things-As-They-Must-Be, only when he knew that it was, indeed, God and not mere human wants and wishes he was wrestling with, could he turn the war against his brother into love. Recognizing that the war of brothers was rooted in the granite of the universe made it possible for him to turn that conflict into embraces." Arthur Waskow, *Godwrestling—Round 2: Ancient Wisdom, Future Paths* (Woodstock, VT: Jewish Lights Publishing, 1996), 26.

family which my wife and I had created, secrets rooted deep, of course, in the secrets of the two families that had created the two of us."[25] For years, while his family life and career as a writer seemed to flourish in the idyllic setting of the Vermont hills, the secrets and the shame bred a deep-seated fear that something terrible could happen to his children, could happen to him, and he would not be a father anymore.

From Buechner's autobiographical reflections, it appears that the father role was at the center of his identity during those years, a father who, unlike the one he had practically forgotten, was there for his children and was able to care for and protect them. However, closing himself to the secret that could not be told, he recalls that "I was looking to my children to give me more than either they had it in their power to give or could have given without somehow crippling themselves in the process."[26]

When one of Buechner's daughters developed an eating disorder and was diagnosed with anorexia nervosa, his fears become reality.[27] What seemed at first to be a harmless attempt to lose some weight turned into a life-threatening illness, which eventually required her to be hospitalized and to be fed against her will. Buechner recalls how fear and sadness defined those days, and his deep and helpless love for his daughter only intensified those feelings exponentially. As Buechner recollects the events and emotions of that time, he seems to distance himself from the painful narrative by employing the metaphor of the Cowardly Lion in the third person. Like an observer looking in from the outside, he explains that "the Cowardly Lion got more and more afraid and sad, felt more and more helpless. . . . He could not solve her problem because he was of course himself part of her problem."[28] Buechner describes the spiritual experience of that time as "hell," pointing out that he chose that term carefully. "Hell is where there is no light but only darkness," writes Buechner, "and I was so caught up in my fear for her life, which had become in a way my life too, that none of the usual sources of light worked anymore, and light was what I was starving for."[29] The metaphors

---

25 Buechner, *Telling Secrets*, 75.
26 Buechner, *Telling Secrets*, 75.
27 Buechner never mentions his daughter by name, saying that her story is hers to tell. I choose to honor his approach and did not do any detective work to find out her name.
28 Buechner, *Telling Secrets*, 23–24.
29 Buechner, *Telling Secrets*, 5.

Buechner employs to make meaning of the family crisis point to the depth of despair and the intensity of sadness, guilt, and shame that he felt.

Buechner interprets his daughter's illness as a disorder of ambivalence, likely referencing expert opinion at the time. On the one hand, the illness expresses striving for freedom and independence by refusing to do what the world is telling the adolescent person to do, even at the danger of self-destruction. On the other hand, it ironically meets the need for care and safety by affecting the body in a such way that it becomes small and childlike again and requires others to offer their care. However, Buechner also wonders about the role that secrets played in the etiology of his daughter's illness. "What, for one, was the secret that was too dark or dangerous or private or complicated to tell in any other language which our daughter could bring herself to tell about only in the symbolic language of anorexia?"[30]

While anorexia is classified as a psychiatric disorder, the notion of illness as a symbolic language to express underlying, unconscious psychological states or conflicts is reminiscent of psychosomatic disorders. Cognitive psychological models typically explain eating disorders as a result of maladaptive cognitive beliefs or schemes, and Buechner's interpretation of his daughter's illness could be considered as an example of such an explanation. Research shows, however, that emotional states also impact the development and maintenance of eating disorders, and Buechner's question about the role of secrets in the onset of his daughter's illness may very well hint at that insight.[31]

Buechner writes that this family crisis ushered a "fearsome blessing" in his life.[32] I suspect what he means by this is that his Jabbok experience was part of a passage and not a destination. The crisis strained the family for about three years. Buechner's daughter survived and reclaimed her life with medical and therapeutic help. Her recovery, however, was not just a return

---

30 Buechner, *Telling Secrets*, 75.
31 A systematic review of more than twenty research studies on the relationship that shame and guilt have with anorexia and bulimia nervosa concludes that it is plausible that shame leads to eating disorders. These findings suggest that anorexia nervosa may be understood as an attempt to regulate the painful effects of shame while also producing shame, thus creating a vicious shame-cycle. See Suzanne P. M. Blythin et al., "Experiences of Shame and Guilt in Anorexia and Bulimia Nervosa," *Psychology and Psychotherapy: Theory, Research and Practice* 93, no. 1 (March 2020): 134–159.
32 See Buechner, *Telling Secrets*, 24.

back to normalcy for the family but a call for transformation for her father. "Little by little," Buechner recalls, "the young woman I loved began to get well, emerging out of the shadows finally as strong and sane and wise as anybody I know, and little by little as I watched her healing happen, I began to see how much I was in need of healing and getting well myself."[33] In the true meaning of the word, the crisis became a turning point for Buechner, a call to attend to his own long neglected pain and to face the shameful secrets that had shaped his and his family's life.

Salvation as Healing

Buechner's call to become well was, in a way, a call to salvation. Again, the story about the crossing of the Jabbok finds resonance in Buechner's narrative, and the sacred story is implicated in the mundane. For Buechner, salvation is not a narrowly defined religious experience that is willed and orchestrated by a God who directs human affairs. "Instead, events happen under their own steam as random as rain, which means that God is present in them not as their cause but as the one who even in the hardest and most hair-raising of them offers us the possibility of that new life and healing which I believe is what salvation is."[34] Salvation comes as a God event that opens a future, but that does not mean that its call is painless. In fact, pain may be a gate to salvation, as Buechner suggests elsewhere. However, it is not pain inflicted by a punitive or offended God but, according to Buechner, pain that is horror and treasure at the same time, that tempts us to wonder if God abandoned us, and lets us speak the truth of our lives from our depth.[35]

Buechner writes about the stewardship of pain in an essay that was published one year after *Telling Secrets*. The term *stewardship* was offered to him by a retreat participant who responded to Buechner's reading from an autobiographical novel. Hearing the term haunted Buechner ever since. To be a steward of one's pain, as Buechner explains it, means not burying and

---

33 Buechner, *Telling Secrets*, 29.
34 Buechner, *Telling Secrets*, 31.
35 See Frederick Buechner, *A Crazy Holy Grace: The Healing Power of Pain and Memory* (Grand Rapids: Zondervan, 2017), 32.

forgetting it or getting trapped in it but being alive to one's pain and growing through it. "It involves taking the risk of being open, of reaching out, of keeping in touch with the pain as well as the joy of what happens because at no time more than at a painful time do we live out of the depths of who we are instead of out of the shallows."[36] For Buechner, a good steward of pain uses relationships to grow through the pain and beyond the pain. Growth happens, as he concludes in his essay, through "the unending power that can be generated by the meeting and trading of lives, which is a power to heal us and bless us and in the end maybe even to transform us into truly *human* beings at last."[37]

Healing came for Buechner through various channels. It began by acknowledging the pain and speaking about it from the depth, not just the recent pain that came with the fear about his daughter's life and illness but more importantly the pain that had been lingering for decades since that morning when his father checked on him and his brother and then closed the door to the garage. Psychotherapy became one channel for healing for Buechner and a way of exercising sacred memory, a way to recollect and claim the past, "to bless the past, even those parts of it that we have always felt cursed by, and also to be blessed by it."[38] He had to face both the shame and the guilt about keeping a secret that crippled him and his family for years. Remembering and speaking about it was a beginning to move beyond the shame. Forgiving his father for dying so young and hopeless, forgiving God for letting it happen, and forgiving himself for keeping the secret for so long meant moving beyond the guilt and toward healing. Buechner recalls a powerful therapeutic exercise when he wrote an imaginary dialogue with his father using his non-dominant hand, posing his questions to his father and listening for the answers. In this imaginary dialogue, compassionate curiosity and honest vulnerability take the place of intentional forgetfulness. Listening imaginatively to the depth of a relationship that he had ignored for a long time but that he ultimately could not forget nor lose, Buechner found an assurance about his father and their

---

36 Frederick Buechner, *The Clown in the Belfry: Writings on Faith and Fiction* (New York: HarperCollins Publishers, 1992), 99.
37 Buechner, *The Clown in the Belfry*, 104.
38 Buechner, *Telling Secrets*, 33.

relationship, and "a better way of saying so long to him than I had ever been able to say it before."[39]

Another channel of healing for Buechner was his experience of community. As long as his secrets needed to be kept, they separated him from others and sabotaged attempts to build community. Once he acknowledged and named his secrets, they lost their isolating power, and he was able to risk relationships where he could be known. The students and faculty at Wheaton College almost unexpectedly became such a community where Buechner felt a sense of belonging when he was invited to teach a course for a semester. Despite its conservative mission and restrictive code of conduct, Wheaton College was a welcoming community for Buechner, who had more liberal leanings. Buechner states that if he had turned down the invitation to teach at Wheaton on principle that his "life would have been immeasurably impoverished."[40] To be sure, Buechner does not remember Wheaton College uncritically. He acknowledges that some of the legalistic aspects of the community's life and the college's mission felt "a little suffocating."[41] However, Buechner was impressed by the authenticity of this community. For someone who had lived with secrets for decades and was learning to name them and heal from them, authentic community seemed to model the possibility for a new way of life. It appears that his term at Wheaton College amplified that promise for Buechner.

Buechner's participation in Twelve-Step Recovery groups provided him with another welcoming community and with resources for healing. Buechner found healing community particularly in groups for Adult Children of Alcoholics. Members in those groups modeled for him how to face and tell one's secrets. "They do not give each other advice. They simply give each other stories about the good and the bad of what has happened to them over the years. . . . In other words, they tell each other their secrets, and as you listen to them, you hear among other things your own secrets on their lips."[42] Buechner describes the power within those groups as a power of solidarity in brokenness and of commitment to support each other in the

---

39 Buechner, *Telling Secrets*, 100.
40 Buechner, *Telling Secrets*, 79.
41 Buechner, *Telling Secrets*, 80.
42 Buechner, *Telling Secrets*, 90.

effort of a new life, one that is lived honestly and with dedication to one's own health and integrity and to others who share that journey. The group's opening ritual reflects how shame that stems from secrecy can be overcome through acceptance and community. After group participants share their names and sources of brokenness by way of introduction, they offer a simple, communal welcome to each participant and thus extend acceptance to each person. Buechner identifies the power of Twelve-Step Groups in a way as the power of second chances. He holds that these groups "are more like what families at their best can be than most families are, certainly more than the family that I grew up in myself ever was. They are more like families because in them something which is often extraordinarily like truth is spoken in something that is extraordinarily like love."[43] The healing principle at the heart of recovery support group is acceptance, which is perhaps what everyone hopes to receive in family relationships. For many, however, as for Buechner, the family of origin lacks the emotional capacity to provide empathic nurture and acceptance. Rather, a family of choice at a later stage in life does.

While Buechner found outside resources for his healing journey through psychotherapy and various communities, he concludes that the source of healing is not outside the self but rather at the core of one's original self. In exploring the possibility for healing from a theological perspective, he refers to the creation story in Genesis and the statement that humans were created "in the image of God" (Gen 1:26–27). "Life batters and shapes us in all sorts of ways before it's done," he states, "but those original selves which we were born with and which I believe we continue in some measure to be no matter what are selves which still echo with the holiness of their origin."[44] By suggesting that the original self can be a source of healing from spiritual and emotional pain, Buechner does not simply espouse a philosophy of self-healing. Rather, the original self is the source of healing because it is the place where God can connect to save and restore wholeness.[45]

---

43 Buechner, *Telling Secrets*, 94.
44 Buechner, *Telling Secrets*, 44.
45 See Buechner, *Telling Secrets*, 105. In a sermon about Deuteronomy 6:4–7 and Matthew 27:45–46, Buechner describes that connection as God's love "in the wilderness" of persons' lives, which invites love of God as a force that creates community with others. See Buechner, *Secrets in the Dark*, 103–104.

Conclusion

Buechner's autobiographical story vividly illustrates his conviction about the conflict that he believes defines the human condition, namely that the desire to be known and the fear of being known co-exist as psychological and spiritual dilemmas. His narrative highlights the lasting relationship between personal trauma and shame, and how shameful, isolating secrecy can shape family systems and impact a family across generations.

The meaning of traumatic experience varies from person to person, and there is no one interpretation or set of symptoms that follows trauma. Research has shown, however, that the effect of personal trauma, which is a category that applies to the suicide of Buechner's father, can last longer than other types of trauma, such as war or environmental disaster. Since personal trauma is often suffered in isolation from others, feelings of shame, depression, and anxiety often occur in the aftermath.[46] Buechner clearly describes the isolating effects that resulted from his father's death and the long-lasting impact of trauma. Among them, shame became a powerful emotional dynamic that affected not only him and his family of origin but also the family he and his wife created.

Attempts to mitigate the effects of trauma by developing a persona to mask the shame only intensify the alienation between self and others. However, Buechner's autobiographical reflections not only detail the destructive, self-defeating, and alienating effects of shame but also point to the possibility of growth and healing through a stewardship of pain that seeks community. Stewardship is an active and intentional practice of caretaking. The stewardship of pain that Buechner identifies as essential to the healing process attends to one's pain with self-awareness, self-disclosure, and self-care.

---

46 See Amanda Evans and Patricia Coccoma, *Trauma-Informed Care: How Neuroscience Influences Practice* (London & New York: Routledge, 2014), 11.

4

TONI MORRISON: *BELOVED*

TONI MORRISON WAS an American writer of African descent, a book editor, university professor, and visiting lecturer. Her novels chronicle the experience of enslaved African American people and their descendants and the impact of the history of slavery and racism on the African American psyche. Her novel *Beloved* won the Pulitzer Prize in 1987 and became perhaps her best-known book. In a brief essay "On Beloved," Morrison explained that her wary alertness to history, as it had been written with absences, silences, and censure by those who oppressed people of African descent, provided the impetus for writing the novel. Racial history and marginal experience, Morrison concluded, had been understood at best as "a supplemental record, unassociated with the mainstream of history; an expanded footnote, as it were, that is interesting but hardly central to the nation's past."[1]

True Fiction

While *Beloved* is a fictitious narrative, the novel was inspired by the historical account of Margaret Garner's killing of one of her children. A woman who had escaped slavery with her family from Kentucky to Ohio in 1856, Garner attempted to kill all of her children and then herself when a slave-catcher with the help of federal marshals tried to apprehend her and her family under the Fugitive Slave Act of 1850 while they were staying with family in Cincinnati. She would rather have seen her children dead than be returned to a life of slavery but was not able to complete her plan before she was overpowered and arrested. She killed her two-year old daughter, though, and stabbed herself and her other children, but only to wound them and herself. The issue of infanticide made her story both sensational and

---

1 Toni Morrison, *The Source of Self-Regard: Selected Essays, Speeches, and Meditations* (2019; repr., New York: Vintage Books, 2020), 281.

scandalous at the time and afterward.[2] However, Morrison found the historical account too confining for a creative writer. In the foreword to the novel, she explained that it offered too "little imaginative space for my purposes. So I would invent her thoughts, plumb them for the subtext that was historically true in essence, but not strictly factual in order to relate her history to contemporary issues about freedom, responsibility and 'women's place.'"[3]

Literary scholar Jonathan Gottschall notes that fiction can function as a mirror of life and show life as it is actually lived. More specifically, he makes the point that fiction is typically about trouble and about the conflicts and predicaments of the human condition. He notes that a universal grammar in storytelling is about confronting adversities and the struggle to overcome them.[4] Morrison's novel certainly fits his description of a universal grammar. It is a story about adversities and about struggles that reflect the history of slavery and racial oppression in North America and their impact on individuals, families, and communities.

Morrison's novel is likely a product of both explicit and implicit memory that constitute storytelling. It translates those memories into a narrative about the human condition affected by the oppressive forces of slavery, racial violence, and injustice. The novel conveys important truths about salvation and liberation, lived experiences of suffering and redemption, and the need for reconciliation and acceptance.

Approaching the Story

I approach Morrison's novel with a history of white, male privilege in my background. In other words, I look like the oppressors and abusers in her narrative. I am therefore cautiously interpreting Morrison's true fiction. My hope is that in naming and attending to privilege and the fact that I am formed, in part, by northern European descent, I will be less likely to be

---

2 For a historical account and discussion of the incident, see Samuel J. May, "Margaret Garner and Seven Others," in *Toni Morrison's Beloved: A Casebook*, ed. William L. Andrews and Nellie Y. McKay (New York & Oxford: Oxford University Press, 1999), 25–36.
3 Toni Morrison, *Beloved* (New York: Vintage Books, 2020), xvii.
4 See Jonathan Gottschall, *The Storytelling Animal: How Stories Make Us Human* Boston & New York: Houghton Mifflin Harcourt Publishing Company, 2012), 55.

blindsided by my own background and story so that I am better able to experience and understand Morrison's novel in an empathic manner. After all, Sethe, who has the leading role in the novel, cannot correct me or clarify her story for me if my listening skills fail me. Should my attempts to listen empathically to her story fail, I must leave it to readers who are familiar with Sethe's story to correct me in their minds and to trust their understandings rather than mine.

The narrative that Morrison weaved in *Beloved* does not develop neatly in a linear fashion but emerges through flashbacks and recovered memories. It is a messy and terrifying story of violence and abuse, humiliation and pride, and attempts to love and overcome within an oppressive and inhumane social system. The story increasingly confronts evidence of trauma and shame in the lives of Sethe and those around her. The fragmented lives of the novel's characters come to light and come together slowly to signal the possibility of wholeness and healing, painful as the memories are. However, there is also a constant threat of disintegration, of being swallowed or consumed by the memories. The story is multi-layered. It moves between the present and the past, between some dreamlike passages and stream-of-consciousness narration, between striking symbolism and harrowing descriptions of abuse. *Beloved* could be considered a gothic ghost story that opens with a reference to a spiteful and poltergeist-like presence in the house on 124 Bluestone Road in Cincinnati where Sethe lives with her daughter Denver. The house "was palsied by the baby's fury at having its throat cut," a house like so many houses "packed to its rafters with some dead Negro's grief."[5] However, as Sethe's individual story of violent trauma is inevitably linked to the larger narrative about the suffering of countless enslaved persons, Morrison's novel may be more accurately understood as a story about a haunting and violent past. The story suggests the possibility of healing and freedom beyond escape, a freedom that summons the strength to love in a way that is both dangerous and life-giving.

Sethe and her youngest daughter, Denver, are isolated and ostracized by the Black community in the house on Blue Stone Road that used to belong to Sethe's mother-in-law, Baby Suggs, who died almost nine years

---

5 Morrison, *Beloved*, 6.

earlier. Sethe's two sons used to live with them, but they left, scared away by the spirit of their infant sister, whom Sethe had killed years earlier for the same reason that Garner killed her daughter. The infant spirit has terrorized the family and the house like a poltergeist ever since Sethe moved back after she was released from prison.

Paul D. appears on the scene as the last surviving enslaved male person from the enslavement camp in Kentucky from which Sethe had escaped after violent abuse by a new overseer and his nephews. Paul D. immediately senses the haunting presence in the house as evil. Sethe, however, tries to correct him and almost affectionately identifies the terrorizing spirit as "just sad."[6] Nevertheless, during Paul D.'s first visit to the house, he stands up to a violent display of terror by the infant's spirit, threatening to fight it and commanding it to leave, which it does. The departure of the spirit leaves Denver even more lonely, isolated, and miserable because her older sister's spirit, scary as it was, was her only company.

At Sethe's invitation, Paul D. moves in with her and Denver and becomes Sethe's lover. However, their relationship almost immediately becomes contaminated by the past and the history of abuse they both share. After they are sexually intimate the same day that the spirit leaves the house, they are both disillusioned, resentful, and almost disgusted by each other. "His dreaming of her," Morrison writes, "had been too long and too long ago. Her deprivation had been not having any dreams of her own at all. Now they were sorry and too shy to make talk."[7] However, their initial sexual encounter will not define their relationship, and Paul D. comes to love Sethe "a little bit more every day."[8]

The haunting past is not easily gotten rid of, though, even as Paul D.'s exorcism seemed successful. As a terrorizing infant spirit, the past presented itself with a fury while still meeting the younger sister's need for companionship. In the ghostly presence of a young woman who suddenly appears at the house one day after Sethe and Paul D. return from visiting the carnival, the past reappears, needy, demanding, and craving love and attention. The exhausted stranger introduces herself by the name Beloved, which is the

---

6 See Morrison, *Beloved*, 10.
7 Morrison, *Beloved*, 25.
8 Morrison, *Beloved*, 136.

inscription on the headstone on the grave of the daughter that Sethe killed. Sethe and Paul D. take her in, and it becomes clear that the young woman is the embodied spirit of Sethe's oldest daughter.

However, as it turns out, Beloved represents many things. She acts and interacts at times almost in a childlike fashion and, at other times, can exhibit a shining and alluring presence. One autumn night, Beloved comes to Paul D. and demands that he call her name and to be touched by him, a demand that Paul D. resists at first but then gives in to.[9] From Sethe, Beloved craves her love and attention and almost literally her life in the form of stories. She incessantly prompts Sethe to tell her stories, many of which are painful, shame inducing, and previously unspoken. Sethe gives in to the spirit's bidding and feeds Beloved's cravings, and in the process her life emerges in memories as one shattered by trauma and grief. While she faces her past, Sethe is overcome and drained by the stories she recalls and withdraws from others. However, the community that once shunned her gathers in a solidarity of trauma, and a group of women come to the house to expel the spirit with their chants. After Beloved disintegrates into nothingness, Paul D. tries to intervene and pleads in an attempt to instill hope that might carry them beyond the painful memories. "'Sethe,' he says, 'me and you we got more yesterday than anybody. We need some kind of tomorrow.'"[10]

Abuse, Trauma, and Shame

Sethe's story emerges as one about a heavy burden of multiple and significant traumata. The killing of her infant daughter must be considered traumatic, even as it was not a desperate, impulsive, or insane deed but a calculated and deeply paradoxical act of mother love to spare the child the fate of slavery and death at the hand of abusers. "How if I hadn't killed her," ruminates Sethe as she imagines a conversation with Beloved, "she would have died and that is something I could not bear to happen to her."[11] It was a brutal act nevertheless as she cut the child's throat with a hacksaw, almost severing her head. Sethe's own experience of trauma, engraved as elaborate scars into her body

---

9 See Morrison, *Beloved*, 137–138.
10 Morrison, *Beloved*, 322.
11 Morrison, *Beloved*, 236.

and always with her, seems to both numb her emotionally in that moment and, at the same time, fuel her resolve to commit a violent and scandalous act of love that would condemn and haunt her. The violent symbolism of the murderous act is reminiscent of the marks left by the shackles used to control enslaved persons. "Beloved's scarred neck—the mark made by the handsaw Sethe used to slit her daughter's throat—signifies not only the shaming mark or stigma of slavery," explains literary scholar Brooks Bouson, "but also the maternal and intergenerational transmission of black shame and trauma."[12] Even in an unthinkable attempt to save her daughter from slavery, Sethe marks her ironically in the way that enslaved individuals would bear the signs of oppression and of "the shame of being collared like a beast."[13]

Although Sethe's history of trauma, humiliation, and shame started long before that day, it is the haunting memory of that day embodied in Beloved's presence and her insistent questions that slowly extract many of Sethe's stories and weave them into the larger picture of the scarred life of a woman who survived horrific abuse. Sethe's recollections represent many others that could be told about the oppression and abuse of enslaved women. Sethe hardly knew her mother, who had to work in the fields and had her daughter wet-nursed by another enslaved woman. Sethe's mother was lynched in front of her, likely for attempting to run away and as a warning to others who might have thought about doing the same. The memory of the hanging disturbs Sethe deeply as "something she had forgotten she knew. Something privately shameful that had seeped into a slit in her mind."[14] If her mother indeed attempted to run away, the implication is that she was willing to abandon her daughter, that Sethe was not worth as much as the promise of freedom or enough to make a plan to escape the abuse on the farm together.

Literary scholar Linda Koolish discusses the power of trauma and shame in Sethe's story and how Sethe tried to beat back the terrible knowledge of abandonment by dissociating from it.[15] To allow herself to live with

---

12 J. Brooks Bouson, *Quiet as It's Kept: Shame, Trauma, and Race in the Novels of Toni Morrison* (Albany: State University of New York Press, 2000), 147.
13 Morrison, *Beloved*, 322.
14 Morrison, *Beloved*, 73.
15 See Lynda Koolish, "'To Be Loved Is to Cry Shame: A Psychological Reading of Toni Morrison's *Beloved*," *MELUS* 23, no. 4 (Winter 2001): 183.

the memories and feel the shame without redemption would have meant to relive the trauma of abandonment and her mother's violent death on a daily basis. Beloved's presence offers the promise of redemption by being able to love and care for her, to "feed" her ravenous cravings for Sethe's stories and for her life, and to be the mother that she herself never had. Sethe allows herself to remember but does not yet find redemption in the process.

Before Beloved appears at the house, Sethe's memories about life in Kentucky from where she fled seem disorganized, her brain almost working deviously as if to convince herself that despite the abuse there was good and beauty in her life. She remembers that

> *although there was not a leaf on that farm that did not make her want to scream, it rolled itself out before her in shameless beauty. It never looked as terrible as it was and it made her wonder, if hell was a pretty place too. Fire and brimstone all right, but hidden in lacy gloves. Boys hanging from the most beautiful sycamores in the world. It shamed her—remembering the wonderful soughing trees rather than the boys. Try as she might to make it otherwise, the sycamores beat out the children every time and she could not forgive her memory for that.*[16]

Rather than remembering the lynching and the victims, Sethe's recollection focuses on a detail that helps her not to acknowledge the horror of that scene, protecting her at least in the moment from the emotional pain of traumatic memory. Such distractions in her memory could be understood as expressions of dissociation, a self-protective process and "defensive strategy that enables aspects of the event to be disconnected or not remembered, and makes the situation momentarily bearable."[17] In a similar way, Sethe explains to Paul D. the scars on her back from the brutal flogging that caused her to escape in an almost picturesque way as the image of a tree that is still growing. However, when Paul D. leans in on her and rubs his cheek on her

---

16 Morrison, *Beloved*, 7.
17 Carrie Clark, Catherine C. Classen, Anne Fourt, and Maithili Shetty, *Treating the Trauma Survivor: An Essential Guide to Trauma-Informed Care* (London & New York: Routledge, 2015), 74.

back, the symbolism of the scars becomes revealing. He "learned that way her sorrow, the roots of it; its wide trunk and intricate branches."[18] Sethe's explanation that the tree of scars on her back was still growing makes it clear that the experience of trauma, if not cared for, is an ever-present reality, not a thing from the past but something that leaves a brutal and lasting imprint on her life.

As Sethe wanders into her past enticed by Beloved, most painful among her memories seems to be the recollection of being raped by two white boys, who also held her down and took her breastmilk. Being robbed of that precious substance that she herself was deprived of as an infant due to her mother's work in the rice fields was the worst aspect of the abuse. It shook her at her core, leaving her incapable of giving what her baby needed.[19] Barbara Shapiro uses intersubjective theory to interpret the experience in conjunction with Sethe's own deprivation as an infant who was robbed of essential nourishment. "Sethe was not physically starved as a baby—she did receive milk from another nursing slave woman—but she was emotionally starved of a significant nurturing relationship, of which the nursing milk is symbolic. That relationship is associated with one's core being or essence; if she has no nursing milk to call her own, she feels without a self to call her own. Thus, even before she was raped by the white farm boys, Sethe was ravaged as an infant, robbed of her milk/essence by the white social structure."[20]

Primary and secondary abuse intertwine in Sethe's memory, and both feed her shame. She powerfully laments that "anybody white could take your whole self for anything that came to mind. Not just work, kill, or maim you, but dirty you so bad you couldn't like yourself anymore. Dirty you so bad you forgot who you were and couldn't think it up."[21]

Sethe's story shows that traumatic and racial shame can be contagious and may be transmitted intergenerationally. Denver, Sethe's younger daughter, claims Beloved as her sister, remembering that she "swallowed her blood right along with my mother's milk."[22] Thus, Denver is intimately

---

18 Morrison, *Beloved*, 20.
19 See Morrison, *Beloved*, 236.
20 Barbara Shapiro, "The Bonds of Love and the Boundaries of Self in Toni Morrison's *Beloved*," *Contemporary Literature* 32, no. 2 (Summer 1991): 198.
21 Morrison, *Beloved*, 295.
22 Morrison, *Beloved*, 242.

linked to Beloved and to the act that took her sister's life. The knowledge of her mother's murderous act of love creates a chronic state of anxiety for Denver. "All the time, I'm afraid the thing that happened that made it all right for my mother to kill my sister could happen again. I don't know what it is, I don't know who it is, but maybe there is something else terrible enough to make her do it again. I need to know what that thing might be, but I don't want to."[23] Born on the river between the land of freedom and the territory of slavery, Denver carries both the legacy of slavery and the promise of freedom. However, that promise is not realized anytime soon, since she is taken to prison with her mother. When she is later asked to remember that time, she wills herself deaf for two years, thus being able to ignore possible reminders of the killing and its aftermath. Her hearing returns only when she identifies with the spiteful rage of the infant ghost that haunts the house where they live and, as Koolish points out, "when she acknowledges the self she has silenced, the shadow self who has knowledge of her mother's violent act."[24] Sethe isolates Denver from others after being released from prison, keeps her inside, presumably to protect her from negative attention by the community, But Sethe hurts Denver nevertheless through her protective measures. To be kept apart means to be different and not to belong. In the midst of isolation from the community, Denver's grandmother, Baby Suggs, became a nurturing presence in her life and managed despite her own shame to affirm Denver's worth, bless her, telling her that she was "charmed" and needed to love herself and her body.[25]

As the characters' memories emerge and center on physical oppression, sexual assault, and humiliation, Bouson points out that the narrative "underscores the link between trauma and shame in *Beloved*, showing that, as trauma investigators have concluded, the deliberate and sadistic infliction of injury can induce unbearable and chronic feelings of shame."[26] Bouson draws upon psychiatrist Judith Herman's research on trauma and recovery, which found that people who have been repeatedly and violently traumatized in captivity can suffer from a "contaminated identity" and be "preoccupied

---

23 Morrison, *Beloved*, 242.
24 Koolish, "Psychological Reading," 187.
25 See Morrison, *Beloved*, 247.
26 Bouson, *Quiet as It's Kept*, 135.

with shame, self-loathing, and a sense of failure."[27] Indeed, Sethe's story is not the only one marked by the trauma and shame of enslavement. Paul D. recalls the abuse he experienced when he was transported to a prison camp after he had been sold at Sweet Home and threatening his new owner.[28] Shackled to ten other slaves, Paul D. and the men were driven like a herd of animals across Kentucky to the Virginia prison camp where they were housed in cages. In the mornings, guards would force prisoners onto their knees and have them perform oral sex. Men who fought the abuse were shot in the head on the spot. After Paul D. and others fled the camp during a natural disaster, he tried repress his memories "one by one, into the tobacco tin lodged in his chest. By the time he got to 124 nothing in this world could pry it open."[29] Shortly thereafter, though, the ghost of slavery emerged from the waters, moved into the house on 124 Bluestone Road, and pried open more than just the tobacco tin in Paul D.'s chest.

The Ghost of Slavery

Even as Beloved embodies the adult spirit of the infant daughter whom Sethe killed, she also strangely remembers her torment on a slave ship during the Middle Passage. Although she was born in the United States, Beloved seems to represent a slave ship survivor.[30] The symbolism of her emerging from the water to appear at Sethe's house may reflect that aspect of her story. Based on theories of multiple personality disorder and other dissociative psychological states, Koolish has argued that Beloved represents aspects of various characters in the novel that have been disowned by those respective characters because of the impact of trauma and shame.[31] Additionally, Bouson highlights that Beloved also signifies the sexually exploited enslaved woman who embodies the shaming stereotypes of the dominant culture and is "'beloved in the dark and bitch in the light.'"[32] Given these various interpretations,

---

27 Judith L. Herman, *Trauma and Recovery: The Aftermath of Violence—From Domestic Abuse to Political Terror* (New York: Basic Books, 1992), 94.
28 See Morrison, *Beloved*, 125–129.
29 Morrison, *Beloved*, 133.
30 See Morrison, *Beloved*, 248–252.
31 See Koolish, "Psychological Reading," 177.
32 See Bouson, *Quiet as It's Kept*, 152–153.

Beloved seems to represent the traumatic memory of slavery in its many aspects—individually for Sethe and those around her, collectively for African-American people, and collectively for a forgetful nation that was built on the institution of slavery.

In reflecting on the origin and meaning of *Beloved*, Morrison asserts that not only the oppressors and their descendants enforced silence in the way that history was written but that enslaved people and their descendants also chose silence for a long time. The characters in Morrison's novel act out the attempt to keep silent. "The shared effort to avoid imagining slave life as lived from their own point of view became the subtheme, the structure of the work. Forgetting the past was the engine, and the characters (except for one) are intent on forgetting. That one exception being the one hungry for a past, desperate for not being just remembered, but being dealt with, confronted."[33]

Beloved indeed confronts Sethe with her-story of slave life and makes her "re-memory." Beloved becomes the ghost of slavery who craves the stories of those who were enslaved, who escaped but are not yet free. In having slave stories told to her, the truth about the past emerges. It becomes clear how everyone's life is entangled in the past, which can be denied and ignored but cannot be erased. Psychiatrist and trauma therapist Bessel van der Kolk points out that people "cannot put traumatic events behind until they are able to acknowledge what has happened and start to recognize the invisible demons they're struggling with. . . . Telling the story is important; without stories, memories become frozen; and without memory you cannot imagine how things can be different."[34] Recovering the stories of the past, painful and shameful as they may be, therein lies for Sethe the promise of recovery.

However, van der Kolk also makes clear that "telling a story about the event does not guarantee that the traumatic memories will be laid to rest."[35] Recovery may come when one feels safe enough to recall the trauma and integrate it as part of the past without being retraumatized by it. To do so, van

---

[33] Morrison, *Source of Self-Regard*, 283.
[34] Bessel van der Kolk, *The Body Keeps the Score: Brain, Mind, and Body in the Healing of Trauma* (New York: Viking, 2014), 221.
[35] van der Kolk, *The Body Keeps the Score*, 221.

der Kolk explains, one needs to keep in balance the emotional brain and the rational brain in recalling and telling the story because traumatic memory is fundamentally different from regular memory. Regular memory recalls the past in stories that have a beginning, an end, and a story line, however brief it may be. Traumatic memories are fragmented and disorganized in flashbacks and sensations, often with some details remembered all too clearly.[36] Some of Sethe's memories before Beloved's arrival resemble more closely typical traumatic memories, such as her memory about the lynching, which focused on the appearance of the trees rather than the horror of the bodies hanging from the trees. Stamp Paid, a formerly enslaved person who helped Sethe cross the river after she had escaped from the enslavement camp, on the other hand, remembers with disturbing sensations how he witnessed lynchings and the burning of colored schools. "He smelled skin, skin and hot blood. The skin was one thing, but human blood cooked in a lynch fire was a whole other thing. The stench stank."[37]

Beloved bids Sethe to re-memory and to assemble fragmented memories into stories about the past. Since Beloved returned to her "of her own free will," Sethe now "can look at things again because she's here to see them too."[38] Beloved is at the same time a manipulative and unyieldingly demanding force in the house on 124 Bluestone Road as well as a voice that, almost therapeutically, invites looking at the past and that seems to offer Sethe the possibility of redemption. "I'll tend her as no mother ever tended a child, a daughter," resolves Sethe and assures Beloved in her mind of her caring attention.[39] "Think what spring will be for us! I plant carrots just so she can see them, and turnips. Have you ever seen one, baby? . . . We'll smell them together. Beloved. Beloved. Because you mine and I have to show you these things, and teach you what a mother should."[40] While Sethe begins to recall the past and to tell her stories, imagining the possibility of a nurturing relationship with the daughter she killed and who came back to her, healing and salvation are yet to come. In fact, Paul D. finds her eventually disoriented, confused, and tired, not getting out of bed, exhausted from

---

36 See van der Kolk, *The Body Keeps the Score*, 195.
37 Morrison, *Beloved*, 212.
38 Morrison, *Beloved*, 237.
39 Morrison, *Beloved*, 236.
40 Morrison, *Beloved*, 237.

feeding Beloved's cravings for her memories.[41] As Sethe becomes increasingly distressed and is being taken over by the past, her story points to the possible danger of engaging traumatic memories and facing shame without the safety of an accepting and supportive relational environment.

Beloved is a contradictory and perhaps even grotesque figure. Craving attention and love, she wants to be cared for but also acts as a skilled and manipulative instigator. She appears to offer the possibility of redemption but leads Sethe into an emotional and dangerous impasse. She has a striking presence yet appears otherworldly at the same time. She represents the past and promises to open the door to a future, literally pregnant with possibilities.

In analyzing Beloved's seeming contradictions, literary scholar Linda Krumholz places Beloved in the trickster tradition, which has long been a part of African and African American storytelling, and she sees Beloved as both healing and disturbing. "Beloved is both the pain and the cure. As an embodiment of the repressed past, she acts as an unconscious imp, stealing away the volition of the characters, and as a psychoanalytic urge, she pries open suppressed memories and emotions."[42] If the trickster tradition indeed influenced the development of Beloved's character and considering the shape-shifting abilities that trickster figures typically have in folklore and mythology, Beloved's vanishing at the end of the narrative may not just be the result of an exorcism but the beginning of yet another transition, just as she transformed from spiteful poltergeist into a young woman.

Salvation through Re-Memorying and Re-Membering

Sethe's process of salvation and healing is a process of integrating the past into her life story and of becoming re-connected. A significant and eventually life-sustaining re-connection happens when Paul D. appears at her house. Having been humiliated and brutalized, Paul D. seeks at first companionship and perhaps shelter but learns to love Sethe and offers her

---

41 See Morrison, *Beloved*, 320.
42 Linda Krumholz, "The Ghosts of Slavery: A Historical Recovery in Toni Morrison's *Beloved*," in *Toni Morrison's Beloved: A Casebook*, ed. William L. Andrews and Nellie Y. McKay (New York & Oxford: Oxford University Press, 199), 114.

an empathic relationship, much to the dismay of Beloved, who is jealous of him. Even after he departs the house scared by the knowledge of Sethe's violent act of love, he stays devoted to her and becomes in the end the one who affirms her best self, hoping for a future with her.[43] The central re-connection, however, is between Sethe and the embodied spirit of the daughter she killed. Their relationship is both redemptive in nature and ambiguous. Krumholz suggests that Beloved represents a therapeutic element of unease and disruption. "As an eruption of the past and the repressed unconscious," she explains, "Beloved catalyzes the healing process for the characters and for the reader; thus, she is a disruption necessary for healing."[44] Her daughter's embodied spirit re-connects Sethe with the past and with the meaning it holds, and she ultimately also becomes the catalyst for re-connecting Sethe with her community.

The reconnection with her community and inclusion by her community happens for Sethe through a healing ritual of solidarity when thirty women gather in a chanting circle in front of her house to drive away the spirit they consider evil. Morrison makes an explicit reference to a religious notion of salvation when she describes the effect of the women's singing. "For Sethe it was as though the Clearing had come to her with all its heat and simmering leaves, where the voices of women searched for the right combination, the key, the code, the sound that broke the back of words. Building voice upon voice until they found it, and when they did it was a wave of sound wide enough to sound deep water and knock the pods off chestnut trees. It broke over Sethe and she trembled like the baptized in its wash."[45] The women share the experience of enslavement and of suffering from oppression and abuse, and Sethe is literally drawn into their chanting circle. Even as she wants to resist losing the connection with Beloved, Sethe joins the women of her community and is accepted into their community.

Pastoral theologian John Patton has argued that memory brings together care and community, that re-membering is not just an individual process of recalling the past but rather a communal process of coming together or being reunited. "Care and community," he states, drawing upon

---

43 See Morrison, *Beloved*, 322.
44 Krumholz, "The Ghosts of Slavery," 110.
45 Morrison, *Beloved*, 308.

an argument by educator and activist Parker Palmer, "are obviously related to each other, but it is memory that brings them fully into relationship. Community 'is lost knowledge that must be remembered and recovered. Remembered means to re-member. It means to put the body back together. The opposite of remember is not to forget, but to dismember.'"[46] As Sethe remembers, she also is being re-membered. That is, she is being re-connected with her past and her community. Salvation becomes not an act of individual call and response but a communal experience of being drawn and received into a circle of women who know Sethe's suffering. Because of this knowledge, they chant their prayers.

At the heart of Sethe's journey toward healing is her process of re-memorying as she painfully recollects her past and faces her shame and guilt. In speaking her memories, her shame begins to lose its isolating power. But her attempt to gain Beloved's forgiveness proves to be futile and almost self-destructive. Krumholz explains that "Beloved is the murdered child, the repressed past, Sethe's own guilt and loss, and so Beloved can never forgive. But the former slave women understand the context within which Sethe acted; they share in many of her miseries. And so her fellow sufferers come to her aid to exorcise the ghost of her past preying on her life, because Beloved is in some sense their ghost, too."[47] Krumholz suggests that Sethe's journey of re-memorying culminates in the ritual of re-membering that the women of the community provide to her. Unbeknownst to them, Denver's employer, Edward Bodwin, a generous Quaker who has supported the Underground Railroad, arrives. However, Sethe is caught up in her past and confuses him with the white man who came to take her children back into slavery. She relives the trauma of that fateful moment and tries to attack him with an ice pick rather than hurt her children, but she is held back by Denver. However, her connection to the past in that moment becomes redemptive as she chooses a different course of action out of love for her children. "As a freed woman with a group of peers surrounding her," states Krumholz, "Sethe can act on her motherlove as she would have chosen originally. . . . The reconstruction of the scene of the trauma completes the psychological

---

46 John Patton, *Pastoral Care in Context: An Introduction to Pastoral Care* (Louisville: Westminster John Knox Press, 1993), 27–28.
47 Krumholz, "The Ghosts of Slavery," 117–118.

cleansing of the ritual and exorcises Beloved from Sethe's life."[48] Through the ritual of re-memorying, Sethe both recovers her story and recovers *from* her story. The exorcism of the ghost of slavery does not imply forgetfulness about the past but liberation from the past by acknowledging the pain and by integrating the stories of trauma and abuse, symbolized by the attempt of the community of formerly enslaved women to include Sethe in their circle.

While Krumholz and others offer insightful literary-psychological analyses of Sethe's healing ritual, Morrison's reference to the ritual of baptism gives a hint of a theological perspective of redemption in Sethe's story. An understanding of baptism as an acted, effectual sign of salvation implies that a symbolic act can bring about actual, redemptive change. In the ritual that the women enact in front of the house on 124 Bluestone Road, Sethe is drawn in and participates as a candidate for healing. She is surrounded and supported by the voices of her community and re-enacts the moment of trauma and condemnation. While God's presence in Morrison's novel is elusive, the ritual releases the shaming and restraining power of the past and opens up a future, symbolized in Denver, who has become the African American woman teacher "who has taken on the task of carrying the story through the generations."[49]

Conclusion

Sethe's story thematizes trauma and shame that originate in conditions of systemic and dehumanizing oppression and social abuse over generations. While Sethe's experiences of trauma may be categorized as interpersonal, Morrison's novel provides a historical, political, and social system's perspective exemplified in the fictional account of one woman's life and those closely connected to her. Sethe's story describes the human condition, violated and yearning for healing, as marked by deep-seated and isolating shame along with feelings of guilt.

Sethe's story is multi-layered. Intergenerational trauma intersects with personal trauma, memories of the past with present hopes for redemption and for a future, guilt with shame. Moral theologian Matthew Ichihashi Potts

---

48 Krumholz, "The Ghosts of Slavery," 119.
49 Krumholz, "The Ghosts of Slavery," 119.

recent interpretation of *Beloved* focuses on guilt and forgiveness as central themes in Sethe's story, "The gift Beloved brings to Sethe," Potts explains, "is the possibility that the past can be forgotten. But this forgetting invites other gifts: first, the knowledge that Beloved is no longer angry, that some anger has been appeased. And second, a wish to see the wound."[50] Sethe has guarded her wound carefully; opening it up to Beloved's craving inquiries drains her body and her soul. Potts argues that forgiveness is ultimately not about forgetting but about remembering and acknowledging the past and the losses that have occurred. For Sethe, the process of remembering is at once dangerous and redemptive.

While forgiveness is certainly an important theme in Sethe's story, Morrison describes even more clearly the self-defeating and fragmenting effect of shame that sabotages the integration of the past and wholeness within one's self. Sethe tries to protect herself and her remaining family from shame through hiding, isolating her family in the house on Bluestone Road and hiding from memories of the past until Beloved appears and forces her to connect to her past. Facing the memories of the past becomes a draining process and a liberating process, symbolized in the end by driving away the spirit that is obsessed with Sethe's past. That process is completed through a ritual of acceptance and inclusion, a practical act of solidarity and support that draws Sethe out of her hiding place and into a circle of women who know her suffering.

---

50 Matthew Ichihashi Potts, *Forgiveness: An Alternative Account* (New Haven & London: Yale University Press, 2022), 198.

Part Three

SHAME

ALL CARING OR healing interventions begin with an assessment. The traditional theological assessment of the human condition in the Western Christian tradition has been based in an interpretation of Genesis 3, the so-called story of the fall of humanity into sin. This assessment was first introduced by Paul, who juxtaposed "one man's" trespassing that caused death for all with "one man's" gift of life and righteousness (Rom 5:1–21; 1 Cor 15:21–22). Whether this traditional reading identifies the truth of the story depends on what sin is believed to mean and if the notion of fall accurately describes the human experience in the Genesis narrative. An alternative reading may find that it is not a tale of moral failure or a story about falling from innocence into sin but rather an origin story that describes humanity's existential loss of wholeness. Eden was the place of undivided life. The first humans recognized each other in their likeness as "bones of my bones and flesh of my flesh" (Gen 2:23). The garden of creation was a mythical place of wholeness where everyone and everything belonged together.

Traditional Christian interpretations of Genesis 3 reference the story as a scriptural basis for the doctrine of sin, sin being understood as transgression against God's command, a moral offense, and a state of guilty disobedience. Ironically, the narrative in Genesis 3 is about picking and eating the fruit of ethical knowledge. It is an origin story about humanity's rise to self-consciousness and learning good and evil, even as that development marks a painful transition that involves loss and grief, resulting in fear and shame. According to the narrative, eating the fruit of knowledge about good and evil did not lead to a guilty conscience but rather to an alienating sense of shame that sent the humans hiding among the trees of a mythical garden. The narrative does not mention guilt at all but describes behavior that is congruent with shameful self-consciousness. Genesis 2 ends with the observation that "the man and his wife were both naked, and they were not ashamed" (Gen 2:25). As the story proceeds, "the eyes of both were opened, and they knew that they were naked; and they sewed fig leaves together and made loincloths for themselves" (Gen 3:7). They hid from each other and from the Creator (Gen 3:10). As if in a shock of discovery, the humans realize that they are exposed and unlike each other, and they painfully and fearfully come to know a world of distinction, separation, and alienation.[1] The narrative, however, does not just highlight the effects of shame but also the effects of God's care once shame entered the story as an inevitable reality, fashioning clothing and thus offering protection from shameful exposure.

Contrary to popular misunderstanding of myths as falsehoods, they are in fact stories about events of primal importance that want to reveal truth about the beginning of times, life, community, and the relationship between the divine realm and the human realm. The creation myths in Hebrew scripture are no exception, aside from purging polytheistic motives from the narrative. In their context, they provided a theological perspective about the beginnings of life, nature, humanity and its relationship to God, and why life was the way it was. They assess the human condition both in a state of original blessing and wholeness and in a state of lost wholeness marked by shame, fragmentation, and alienation. The sacred narrative in Genesis 2–3 resonates with mundane narratives, and some similar themes emerge at the intersection between the sacred and the mundane: loss of community, fear or shock of exposure, shame as the emotional impulse to hide from others and from God. Expanding on these themes and the concept of shame as a master emotion in dialogue with psychological perspectives and theological reflections about the human condition will help us in turn to attend to the human condition with compassion and care.

---

[1] See Arthur Waskow, *Godwrestling—Round 2: Ancient Wisdom, Future Paths* (Woodstock, VT: Jewish Lights Publishing, 1996), 81.

5

PSYCHOLOGICAL PERSPECTIVES

FROM A PSYCHOLOGICAL perspective, shame is something of a paradox. On the one hand, it has been the "ignored emotion" for much of the history of psychiatry and, on the other hand, it "is the hidden power behind much of what occupies us in everyday life."[1] Developmental psychologist Michael Lewis holds that shame is ubiquitous with a chameleon nature, showing up as anger or "humiliated fury," withdrawal, procrastination and avoidance, or helplessness.[2] It transcends personal histories and cultural boundaries. Researchers have found that shame can be socially interactive and spread in relationships and can also be "contagious" to produce vicarious shame.[3] Given the ubiquity of shame and its powerful effect on human experience and behavior, psychologist and therapist Carl Goldberg and others have identified shame as a master emotion.[4] This classification takes into account the psychological and social influence that shame exerts in the formation of the self, societies, and cultures. Clinical psychologist Gershen Kaufman's description of the far-reaching impact of shame into various dimensions encapsulates the notion of shame as a master emotion.

> *Shame is the principal impediment in all relationships, whether parent-child, teacher-student, or therapist-client. It violates both inner security and interpersonal trust. Shame wounds not only the self, but also a family, an ethnic and minority group within a dominant culture, or even an entire nation. Any disenfranchised,*

---

1 Donald L. Nathanson, *Shame and Pride: Affect, Sex, and the Birth of the Self* (New York & London: W. W. Norton & Co., 1992), 21.
2 See Michael Lewis, *Shame: The Exposed Self* (New York: The Free Press, 1992), 2–5.
3 See Stephanie C. M. Welten, Marcel Zeelenberg, and Seger M. Breugelmans, "Vicarious Shame," *Cognition and Emotions* 26, no. 5 (2012): 836–846.
4 See Carl Goldberg, *Understanding Shame* (Northvale, NJ & London: Jason Aronson Inc., 1991), 43–79.

> discriminated-against, or persecuted minority group will experience the shame of inferiority, the humiliation of being outcast. Racial, ethnic, and religious group tensions are inevitable consequences of that shame. Just as personal identity becomes molded by shame, ethnic-religious identity and national character are similarly shaped. . . . Shame is a universal dynamic in child rearing, education, interpersonal relations, psychotherapy, ethnic group relations, national culture and politics, and international relations.[5]

As a master emotion, shame relates to other emotions, generating and orchestrating them, or interacting with them in various ways. An emotion that is often identified as closely related to shame or in its place is guilt. However, while both emotions are related, they are distinct from each other and have different roles in human development and experience.

Shame and Guilt

Guilt and shame are two self-conscious emotions that are frequently confused or conflated. Both can be deeply painful and distressing. Guilt has certainly dominated the psychological and theological landscape in interpreting the human experience. Ironically, as pastoral theologian Stephanie Arel points out, the focus on guilt only feeds the shame experience. "Confusing shame and guilt in language and practice around sin," contends Arel, "compounds the paradoxical character, while exclusive focus on guilt ignores the experience of shame and prohibits healing from shame's detrimental effects. The continual eclipsing of shame, buried by language of guilt and sin, leads in effect to the perpetuation of shame itself and its damaging evolution into withdrawal and/or violence, since shame inhabits the self yet is generally disregarded."[6] Although shame and guilt can intertwine and coexist in response to the same experience, they are distinct responses that function and impact the self and its relationships in their own ways. Both shame

---

5 Gershen Kaufman, *The Psychology of Shame: Theory and Treatment of Shame-Based Syndromes*, 2nd ed. (New York: Springer Publishing Company, 1996), 7.
6 Stephanie N. Arel, *Affect Theory, Shame, and Christian Formation* London & Cham, Switzerland: Palgrave Macmillan, 2016), 4.

and guilt may be experienced either as affect, feeling, or emotion. Psychiatrist Donald Nathanson distinguishes between those three emotional states in terms of biology, self-awareness, and biography.[7] Affect is the biological aspect of the emotional life, a known or predictable biological response to a trigger event. In the case of shame, affect may be involuntary blushing triggered by a moment of embarrassment. Guilt may manifest affectively as a knot in the stomach or as hypervigilance. A feeling includes awareness that an affect has been triggered and moves the experience from biology to the realm of psychology. An emotion combines affective awareness with memories of previous experiences of the affect and places the current affective experience in the context of biography, adding the dimension of meaning within the context of a personal life story.

Shame and guilt are both considered innate affects. However, shame precedes guilt as an affect developmentally and can be observed as early as infancy, while a rudimentary sense of right and wrong that may eventually result in a sense of guilt can be seen in the social interactions of toddlers but does not begin to solidify until the preschool years.[8] The main distinction between shame and guilt, though, does not lie in the sequence of developmental processes but in the role that the self occupies in the emotional experience. Clinical psychologist Helen Block Lewis was a pioneer studying the difference between shame and guilt based on psychoanalytic theory and insights from ego psychology along with field studies in cognitive styles. She demonstrated in her now classic study *Shame and Guilt in Neurosis* that shame and guilt referenced the self in different ways. Lewis found that the "experience of shame is directly about the *self*, which is the focus of evaluation. In guilt, the self is not the central object of negative evaluation, but rather the *thing* done or undone is the focus. In guilt, the self is negatively evaluated in connection with something but is not itself the focus of the experience."[9] In other words, guilt is about what I have done, might do,

---

7 See Nathanson, *Shame and Pride*, 49–51.
8 See June Price Tangney and Ronda L. Dearing, *Shame and Guilt* (New York & London: The Guilford Press, 2002), 142. Donald Nathanson discusses how infants are attuned to the presence or absence of affective resonance in caregivers and how the absence of such resonance can trigger shame responses. See *Shame and Pride*, 113.
9 Helen Block Lewis, *Shame and Guilt in Neurosis* (New York: International Universities Press, 1971), 30.

or have not done while shame is about who I am. Guilt marks the self as responsible; shame marks the self as vulnerable.

Social psychologists Maria Miceli and Cristiano Castelfranchi refer to Lewis's work and suggest reconsidering the differences between shame and guilt in terms of the kind of self-evaluation involved in the emotional experiences. Both experiences are self-critical, but the criticism takes different forms. While guilt implies a moral evaluation that assigns responsibility to the self, shame involves a nonmoral self-evaluation based on the perceived discrepancy between the actual self and one's ideal self.[10] Guilt evaluates the self with regard to a particular behavior in a specific instance. It is about what has been done or not done at a certain point in time. Shame, on the other hand, is a general, wide-ranging, negative self-judgment about one's identity, a deep-seated sense of inherent defectiveness and lack of worth as a person. Guilt judges an action or behavior and concludes that I have *done* wrong; shame judges the self and presumes that I *am* wrong. This entrenched sense of shame is not a short-lived experience in response to an experience of momentary humiliation or embarrassment from which one may recover relatively quickly through self-regulation or caring assistance. Rather, the experience has been identified in various ways as chronic shame, shame-proneness, or the shame-bound self. This shame experience is not a fleeting affect, feeling, or emotion but is an existential dilemma and identifies the self over time as unworthy, defective, or unacceptable.

Shame and guilt reference the self in self-conscious ways, but they do so within different relational contexts. Guilt evaluates the relationship between self and others, the *interpersonal* meaning and impact of an action. Shame, on the other hand, examines the self primarily in an *intrapersonal* context and defines a person's most intimate relationship with one's self. Although the origins of shame may be interpersonal, and even though it is being characterized as an alienating affect and may powerfully damage interpersonal relationships, its first and primary relational context is the self's relationship with itself. Through the process of internalization, shame appoints the self as the judge of the self. Thus, interpersonal experiences that generate shame

---

10 See Maria Miceli and Cristiano Castelfranchi, "Reconsidering the Differences between Shame and Guilt," *Europe's Journal of Psychology* 13, no. 3 (2018): 711.

become part of one's identity. Kaufman explains that even though "it is a complex and multifaceted process, *internalization* is actually a simple idea. It is through *imagery* (encompassing visual, auditory, and kinesthetic dimensions) that the self internalizes experiences. What is internalized are images and scenes that have become imprinted with affect."[11] Internalized experiences turn into self-beliefs and, in the case of shame, often into self-defeating beliefs. Affects become emotions and thus part of one's biography.

Emotions are critical to human experience because they serve important intrapersonal, interpersonal, and social functions. They influence behavior and perception, motivate action, and shape thought processes and social interactions. Guilt and shame are no different in that they have distinct functions. It is beyond the scope of this chapter to discuss in detail the different roles that guilt and shame play psychologically and in psychopathology. At the risk of oversimplifying the distinction between them, constructive guilt primarily is an emotion that protects relationships while constructive shame is primarily an emotion that protects the self. Guilt signals a threat to relationships through actual or contemplated transgressions or through the violation of social norms. It may prevent contemplated action, or it may right wrongs by asking forgiveness and making amends. For that reason, psychologists June Tangney and Ronda Dearing describe constructive guilt as "a hopeful, future-oriented moral-emotional experience" that can induce behavioral change and restore relationships.[12] Such understanding indicates that guilt is ideally psychologically adaptive in that it serves a constructive and restorative function in interpersonal relationships and social contexts. However, Tangney and Dearing point out that guilt can also be maladaptive, particularly when it becomes fused with shame, which leads to unresolvable guilt experiences. While "pure" guilt can lead to apologies, amends, and reparations, "a self that is defective at its core is much more difficult to transform or amend. Attempts at reparation or atonement are apt to be seen as inadequate as the self remains unworthy. Thus, shame—and, in turn, shame-fused guilt—offers little opportunity for redemption."[13] Tangney and Dearing conclude that "guilt with *an overlay of shame*" leads to

---

11 Kaufman, *The Psychology of Shame*, 57.
12 See Tangney and Dearing, *Shame and Guilt*, 118–119.
13 Tangney and Dearing, 122.

chronic feelings of guilt and incessant rumination that are often discussed as psychopathology in the clinical literature.

As far as the functions of shame are concerned, psychologist and theologian Carl Schneider distinguishes between "two faces of shame." He identifies *disgrace-shame* as "a painful experience of the disintegration of one's world. . . . The self is no longer whole but divided. It feels less than it wants to be, less than at its best it knows itself to be."[14] *Discretion-shame*, on the other hand, he describes as an emotion that reflects an order of things. It "not only reflects, but sustains, our personal and social ordering of the world."[15] Discretion-shame signals to the self its vulnerability and potential for exposure. It is the protective covering of the vulnerable self that perceives a threat of violation or is in danger of pushing its limits and failing at the attempt. Schneider suggests that even disgrace-shame may serve a needed function in the life of the self. He holds that each element of the emotional process involved in the experience of shame—disruption, disorientation, and painful self-consciousness—have *revelatory* capacity. Schneider links shame with self-discovery and concludes that shame has "a singular capacity to disclose the self to the self. 'In contrast to all other affects, shame is an experience of the self by the self.'"[16] Even the deeply painful and humiliating experience of disgrace-shame thus may serve a function of self-discovery that motivates future-directed action and change within the self and its relationships.

Practical theologian Stephen Pattison adds to the discussion about the function of shame by highlighting that shame plays an important role in the process of socialization. "Shame," according to Pattison, "and the capacity for shame is a necessary part of being human. Shame marks the boundaries of self with others and the human community."[17] From the perspective of social psychology, experiences of shame assist the emerging self to internalize the norms and expectations of one's ingroup. Short-lived experiences of disapproval and rejection as responses to undesirable or unacceptable

---

14 Carl D. Schneider, *Shame, Exposure, and Privacy* (New York & London: W. W. Norton & Co., 1977), 22.
15 Schneider, Shame, *Exposure, and Privacy*, 20.
16 Schneider, *Shame, Exposure, and Privacy*, 25.
17 Stephen Pattison, *Saving Face: Enfacement, Shame, Theology* (Farnham & Burlington: Ashgate Publishing, 2013), 58.

behavior can serve a corrective function, if they are followed by caregiving that effectively aids the recovery from shame. If, however, recovery does not happen, the developing self is left in a state of alienation and rejection that becomes internalized and pronounces oneself as unacceptable.

The Phenomenology of Shame

While Schneider identifies two faces of shame in reference to categories or types of shame, the phenomenon of shame actually has many faces or facets. The human face is the affective mirror of the emotional life and may display shame outwardly as blushing with embarrassment, averting one's gaze from contact with other faces, or turning it to the ground. Pattison discusses in detail the relationship between face, identity, and shame from a pastoral theological perspective. He points out that "loss of face" is a metaphor for the loss of honor, dignity, and respect, "for shamed, defaced, or defective identity. . . . It implies diminishment, exclusion, alienation, uncleanness and unwantedness."[18] The loss of face may be displayed literally and outwardly, or it may remain hidden and invisible to others but nevertheless excruciatingly painful to the self.

> *The charge nurse on the palliative care unit made the referral. "Mrs. Greene is a new arrival. End-stage liver cancer. I think she and her husband can use some support." After the palliative care chaplain knocked on their door and entered the room, he saw a couple in their late seventies holding hands, like lovers of fifty-three years would do when they were scared or anxious. Mr. Greene had pulled an oversized recliner next to the bed. His wife was sitting up in the bed, looking frail and emaciated, so thin that it appeared as if only her bones were tightly covered with jaundiced skin like parchment. When her eyes met the chaplain's gaze, Mrs. Greene quickly pulled the sheet up to her face and slowly slid down in the bed to cover herself completely, like a girl that hid at bedtime from a scary dream that had not even happened. The chaplain hardly*

---

18 Pattison, *Saving Face*, 51.

could introduce himself, when her husband got up, grabbed his hand and shook it firmly, pulling him towards himself. He guided the visitor to sit down in a chair next to the recliner, while his wife remained hidden under the bed sheet, and he began to tell their story with the illness and the difficult journey it had taken them. Suddenly, Mr. Greene pulled out of his pocket a stack of photos held together by a rubber band. "Have I shown you the pictures from our anniversary cruise?" he asked. No, he had not, and why should he, thought the chaplain. Mr. Greene did not wait for a response and put the pictures in a stranger's hand, like one would share precious memories with a friend or a close relative, who was visiting from out of town. "This was two years ago," he said, "just before Betty got sick." In the photo, a happy couple smiled back at the chaplain, anticipating the ship's departure at a Miami pier, watching a sunset at an idyllic beach, and posing with the ship's captain in the dining room with red velvet curtains draping down the edges of the pictures. The woman in the pictures was tanned, smiled and did not look her age. She obviously paid attention to her appearance, and she did not yet know about an illness that would severely damage her body and send her hiding under the covers of a hospital bed one day. Thus, the chaplain met Elisabeth Greene for the second time and witnessed the beauty and the pain of a long-term love captured on high-gloss photo paper, threatened but still alive in a room on the palliative care unit.

The encounter between the chaplain and the couple on the palliative care unit illustrates Buechner's claim that we yearn to be fully known and, at the same time, also fear to be known. It shows how an acute sense of shame, in this situation likely body-shame, can make a person feel small, wanting to hide and disappear.[19] Self-concealment, the desire and act to hide parts or all of one's self, generally is a response to shame-proneness or chronic shame. Research shows that shame in response to physical changes in cancer

---

19 Tangney and Dearing discuss how the internal attribution of inadequacies, transgressions, and flaws create a feeling of being disgraced and the desire to hide. See Tangney and Dearing, *Shame and Guilt*, 54.

patients can engender self-concealing behavior both in patients and in their spouses.[20] Such behavior may take various forms, from keeping secrets, to concealing physical symptoms and feelings, to not communicating medical facts. For Mrs. Greene, it was a full cover-up under the sheets of a hospital bed and the refusal to reappear in the presence of a stranger. Her husband, on the other hand, wanted her and them as a couple to be known beyond their identity as a patient and a caregiver when their life was different—at a time of celebration and when they were not confined to medical facilities and treatments.

Shame seeks covering or hiding, whether it is between the trees of a mythical garden or under the covers of a hospital bed on a palliative care unit. It may be through withdrawal from relationships and scrutinizing looks or by constructing a personal mask, a persona, behind which one can hide the defective self. Such masks may project academic or professional success, grandiose claims, aggressiveness, or so-called selfless service, to mention just a few varieties. In his study about *The Mask of Shame*, psychoanalyst Léon Wurmser interprets the desire for self-concealment and a hiding place both as an internalized form of punishment and as an archaic type of self-protection. "The humiliated one," he explains, "is shunned. He is sent into solitude, outside of human intercourse, discarded from the communality of civilized society, driven into the wilderness like the prophets of the Old Testament or voted into exile."[21] At the same time, shame anxiety functions to set in motion behavior that isolates the person from the danger of unwanted exposure. Wurmser argues that, ironically, the persona that serves to cover up shame is indeed a metaphor for the depersonalization of the self.[22] The mask projects a false self and creates a pseudo identity in hopes that it is acceptable or may take the hurt that would seriously injure the self. Behind the mask, however, the turmoil within the self continues. Psychotherapist Patricia DeYoung explains the inner turmoil that shame creates and that it is a form of desolate emotional pain. While shame seems like a

---

20 See Reut Wertheim et al., "Hide and 'Sick': Self-Concealment, Shame and Distress in the Setting of Psycho-Oncology," *Palliative and Supportive Care* 16, no. 4 (August 2018): 467.
21 Léon Wurmser, *The Mask of Shame* (1981; repr., Northvale, NJ & London: Jason Aronson Inc., 1994), 82.
22 See Wurmser, *The Mask of Shame*, 236–240.

personal failure, it is relational in all its variations. "Shame is the experience of self-in-relation when 'in-relation' is ruptured or disconnected. A chronic sense of disconnection becomes a profound sense of isolation, which in turn leads to feelings of despair and unworthiness."[23]

Even though shame can alienate us from others and from our own self, it is also a mark of our common humanity and characterizes human persons as self-conscious beings. Shame discloses our vulnerability and our dependence on relationships, on the need of the self to emerge and thrive within a relational matrix of love and support. Psychologist and psychotherapist Carl Goldberg emphasizes the existential role of shame in that it reveals our common human experience and vulnerability and the impulse to protect the self. "During moments of shame," explains Goldberg, "we become acutely aware of how fragile are the conditions upon which our hopes and aspirations depend. At these moments we realize how easily and quickly our desires may be taken from us. We may even painfully recognize that our wants will be empty, even if they are satisfied. The customary response to heightened self-consciousness is that of trying to hide our valued and vulnerable self from everyone, including ourselves."[24] The paradoxical nature of shame as an alienating affect and a common denominator of our humanity makes it not only a multifaceted psychological phenomenon but also a potentially change-producing and transforming force, if one can hold the tension contained in the seeming contradictions of paradox and live with and within the paradox. Living with and within the paradox means to accept the polarity, translate it into meaningful perspectives and behavior, and allow it to become a catalyst for change.

Narcissism, Shame, and the Self-Object God

No discussion about shame and the self can ignore the connection between shame and narcissism. Psychoanalytic therapists, in particular, have highlighted and explored that relationship. Wurmser identifies shame as "the veiled companion of narcissism."[25] Shame propensity has been linked in

---

23 Patricia A. DeYoung, *Understanding and Treating Chronic Shame: A Relational/Neurobiological Approach* (New York & London: Routledge, 2015), 18.
24 Goldberg, *Understanding Shame*, 158–159.
25 Wurmser, *The Mask of Shame*, 16.

clinical observations and in psychoanalytical theories to narcissistic vulnerability, which results from traumatic disturbances and disappointment within the developing self. When relationships lack essential nurturing functions, they render the developing self vulnerable to future experiences of perceived or actual rejection, humiliation, and failure.[26] These narcissistic injuries past and present mark the self as defective and generate defenses against the emotional pain that shame inflicts. The shamelessness attributed to persons with narcissistic traits is in fact not a lack of shame but rather a desperate defense to keep it at bay.

Drawing on psychiatrist Heinz Kohut's self psychology, psychoanalyst Andrew Morrison concludes that individuals who have suffered chronically narcissistic injuries live by archaic grandiose fantasies that have not been modified by empathic and realistic responses from caregivers or, in self psychology terms, from self-objects.[27] Inevitably, they face repeated failure to achieve their unrealistic ambitions. Therefore, Morrison explains,

> *their shame is experienced in relation to repeated failure to realize their exhibitionistic, grandiose ambitions: to the emptiness (depletion) of their self with regard to their ideals; and failure too in their attempt to establish close, meaningful interpersonal relationships. . . . In essence, these are individuals who cannot attain even a modicum of self-acceptance, who cannot believe that anyone else could possibly accept them, for all their emptiness and failure at their own, self-appointed, grandiose life tasks. This lack of acceptance by self and others is, I suggest, a central narcissistic dilemma.*[28]

---

26 Heinz Kohut developed self psychology and a unique theory of the self from a psychoanalytical approach to therapy and explained narcissistic vulnerability as a condition in persons' suffering from narcissistic personality disorder. See Kohut, *The Analysis of the Self: A Systematic Approach to the Psychoanalytic Treatment of Narcissistic Personality Disorders* (1971; repr., Chicago: University of Chicago Press, 2009), 46–47.

27 Kohut uses the term both hyphenated and as one word without hyphen. In my discussion, I am hyphenating the term, except where it appears without hyphen in direct quotes.

28 Andrew P. Morrison, "Shame, Ideal Self, and Narcissism," in *Essential Papers on Narcissism*, ed. Andrew P. Morrison (New York: New York University Press, 1986), 368.

Narcissistic personalities do not have too much of a sense of self but rather too little. Persons who are prone to experience shame due to narcissistic injuries may very well appear to be successful, gifted, and sensitive. Their attempts to perform well in certain areas and their achievements, however, are likely to be reflections of their search for the self, desperate attempts to heal a fragile and fragmented self and to gain acceptance and responsiveness from self-objects, which are persons whom they see as an extension of and in service of the self. Having suffered deep narcissistic injuries, they have adjusted their behavior to expectations, and their creativity and achievements are adaptive rather than unique self-expressions. Despite excellent grades, promotions, and honors, they still fall short of their own grandiose ideals, even as they may display a grandiose narcissism. While their performance may find applause and recognition from others, their self remains unrecognized and isolated.

The relationship between shame and narcissism is typically discussed in the context of the diagnosis of narcissistic personality disorder.[29] However, Kohut laid the groundwork for a wider perspective on narcissism. He disagreed with the traditional psychoanalytic single-axis interpretation that assumed a continuum of development from narcissism to object love. Instead, Kohut's self psychology postulates that narcissism represents an "independent line of development, from the primitive to the most mature, adaptive, and culturally valuable."[30] This understanding of narcissism is perhaps the most important contribution and revision that self psychology offered to the field of psychoanalytic studies, namely that narcissism and object love are not in opposition but rather develop alongside each other. The self, according to Kohut, invests both in others and in itself. It cannot be described or evaluated in absolute terms but needs to be understood as a narcissistic continuum. Narcissism, like

---

[29] The DSM-5 lists nine diagnostic criteria, including grandiosity; preoccupation with fantasies of unlimited success, power, brilliance, or beauty; belief that one is special; a requirement for excessive admiration; a sense of entitlement; a tendency to exploit others; an absence of empathy; a preoccupation with envy; and an attitude of arrogance. American Psychiatric Association, *Diagnostic and Statistical Manual of Mental Disorders*, 5th ed. (Washington, DC: American Psychiatric Publishing, 2015), para. 301.81.

[30] Heinz Kohut, "Thoughts on Narcissism and Narcissistic Rage," in *The Search for the Self: Selected Writings of Heinz Kohut 1950–1978*, vol. 2, ed. Paul H. Ornstein (New York: International Universities Press, 1978), 617.

object love, moves from primitive modes to mature states of self-focus and self-investment.[31]

To grow into a mature narcissistic state of self-investment, the self needs to develop within a relational matrix of reliable, nurturing relationships that support the developing self. Kohut identified those relationships as self-object relationships. They provide certain functions that are necessary for the development of a cohesively structured self, such as responsive mirroring through acknowledgement and acceptance, receptiveness to idealization, admiration. Self-object relationships meet the self's need to, at least temporarily, merge with someone or with something powerful and allow for twinship experiences, which respond to the need to feel a degree of alikeness with others. Kohut explains that "self-selfobject relationships form the essence of psychological life from birth to death, that a move from dependence (symbiosis) to independence (autonomy) in the psychological sphere is no more possible, let alone desirable, than a corresponding move from a life dependent on oxygen to a life independent of it in the biological sphere. The developments that characterize normal psychological life must, in our view, be seen in the changing nature of the relationship between the self and its selfobjects, but not in the relinquishments of its selfobjects."[32]

While self-object functions ideally become gradually internalized to create a cohesive self and allow for self-regulation, the need for self-object relationships never completely ceases. In the crucial developmental stage of infancy, the primary caregiver fills that role. Later in adolescence, the peer group becomes an important self-object. Throughout adulthood, friends, spouses, and even careers may become at least temporarily self-objects, particularly in states of regression, while also retaining their status as subjects or love objects in relationships. Growth happens both through the experience of reliable empathic attunement and through experiences of empathic failure by self-objects. If empathic failures emerge from a baseline of consistent and accurate caring attunement, they can lead from dependence on self-object functions to the gradual development of a solidified and independent self.

---

31 See Heinz Kohut, *The Kohut Seminars on Self Psychology and Psychotherapy with Adolescents and Young Adults,* ed. Miriam Elson (New York: W. W. Norton and Co., 1987), 20.

32 Heinz Kohut, *How Does Analysis Cure?*, ed. Arnold Goldberg (Chicago & London: University of Chicago Press, 1984), 47.

Within the theoretical framework of self psychology, religious beliefs can function narcissistically and God may become a self-object for part of one's spiritual formation or, if the self remains fragile, even permanently. Kohut hints at times that religious experience "in which the figure of the perfect and omnipotent God, with whom the powerless and humble believer wants to merge, corresponds to the ancient omnipotent self-object, the idealized parent imago."[33] The notion of God as self-object does not negate or exclude the existence of an I-Thou relationship of faith. Just as self-love and object love are independent lines of development, I-Thou relations and self-object relations exist parallel to each other. Some religious practices and conventions are reminiscent of self-object needs and functions, such as mirroring, merger, and admiration. The Aaronic blessing, for example, that is regularly recited liturgically in Christian worship, brings to mind the early self-object experience of infancy when the delight in the face of a parent, who bends over the crib and looks down at the child, mirrors acceptance and love. "May the Lord bless you and guard you. May the Lord light up His face to you and grant grace to you. May the Lord lift up His face to you and give you peace" (Num 6:24–26). The face of blessing nurtures healthy growth, whereas a consistent lack of parental or divine responsiveness over time communicates unworthiness and generates shame responses that become ingrained and habitual in the life of the self. Consequently, a religious faith that experiences God as a shaming power may likely struggle to integrate experiences of acceptance, grace, and belonging in the life of the self and to extend those experiences to others.

Clinical psychologist and theologian Robert Randall has pointed to the potential of Kohut's self psychology for both psychology and religion and for the dialogue between the disciplines, particularly in reference to the concept of self-objects and self-object functions. He highlights the value and possible meaning of supportive self-object functions for the religious imagination and experience, such as merger experiences, as well as mirroring and idealizing self-object relations.[34] Family and child therapist Zev Ganz has expanded this perspective and suggests that the notion of self-object failure,

---

33 Kohut, *The Analysis of the Self*, 106, n. 1.
34 See Robert L. Randall, "The Legacy of Kohut for Religion and Psychology," *Journal of Religion and Health* 23, no. 2 (June 1984): 108.

which is central to the development of an independent self, also applies to God as a self-object. "The selfobject link with the divine provides opportunities for both mirroring and idealizing functions, but inevitably in the course of this relationship failures in the provision of these functions will transpire. For example, this may occur when the believer feels like God has forsaken him, or during a moment when God's influence does not seem great or powerful."[35] Even though God's failure as a self-object may involve a transient experience of shame much like an optimal empathic failure by a parental self-object, Ganz holds that it can become a catalyst for the growth of the self and for spiritual development if it is experienced within an otherwise safe relationship with the divine and, if needed, with the assistance of spiritually integrated psychotherapy.

Cultures of Narcissism and Shame and the Problem of Violence

The narcissistic continuum does not only characterize the individual self but also describes a social reality. Social theorist and cultural critic Christopher Lash identified narcissism not only as an individual psychiatric diagnosis but as a cultural diagnosis. His premise was that every "society reproduces its culture—its norms, its underlying assumptions, its modes of organizing experience—in the individual, in the form of personality."[36] Lasch does not equate narcissism simply with selfishness or self-centeredness to give a moralistic indictment of U.S. culture in the 1970s. Rather, he recognizes and elaborates on the fact that the narcissistic personality is a deeply wounded and deprived personality, and that the expressions commonly identified with narcissistic behavior are indeed the defenses of a fragile self. What may sound like a label in Lasch's discussion about the etiology, development, and expressions of narcissism points to an important discrepancy between the existential, inner narcissistic experience and the public, social experience and presentation.

---

35 Zev Ganz, "God as Selfobject and the Therapeutic Potential of Divine Failure," *Clinical Social Work Journal* 45, no. 4 (December 2017): 336.
36 Christopher Lasch, *The Culture of Narcissism: American Life in an Age of Diminishing Expectations* (New York & London: W. W. Norton & Co., 1979), 46.

Lasch does not apply the notion of a narcissistic continuum in his discussion and does not recognize mature forms of narcissism. Rather, he views narcissism exclusively from a pathological point of view. "For all his inner suffering," Lasch contends, "the narcissist has many traits that make for success in bureaucratic institutions, which put a premium on the manipulation of interpersonal relations, discourage the formation of deep personal attachments, and at the same time provide the narcissist with the approval he needs to validate his self-esteem."[37] Lasch contends that narcissism is not merely rooted in early childhood development and the reliability of formative relationships but also in social conditions and influences that support the development of narcissistic traits. Among the conditions and influences he discusses are hyper-competitiveness in work environments, hero worship, the narcissistic idealization of celebrities, theatrics and spectacle in politics, and the bureaucratic institutions that feed narcissistic expression.

Interestingly, Lasch does not mention shame as an underlying dynamic in narcissistic culture, which may be due to the fact that, for the most part, shame had been a widely ignored emotion in scholarly discussions until the late 1980s.[38] However, if shame plays a defining role in individual narcissistic development and experience, it also shapes narcissistic culture. Psychiatrist and psychoanalyst Andrew Morrison has pointed to the central role that society plays "in setting the stage for shame through poverty, racism, sexual abuse and harassment, alcoholism, and the stigmas of illness, homosexuality, and old age."[39] In addition to exploring individual factors in the etiology of shame, such as lack of parental attunement along with grandiose, unrealistic, and unreachable ideals and aspirations, he also identifies a "culture of shame" that he finds readily exposed through media attention to shameful incidents and tales of degradation. The following clinical vignette illustrates how a secretive culture can instill and perpetuate shame.

---

37 Lasch, *The Culture of Narcissism*, 56.
38 Ignoring the crippling effects of shame, Lasch addressed the topic in the early 1990s, when shame had received much scholarly and popular attention. He published an article in favor of shame, arguing that in a shameless society, shame had lost its "moral resonance" and meaning as decent respect for privacy. See Christopher Lasch, "For Shame: Why Americans Should Be Weary of Self-Esteem," *The New Republic* (August 10, 1992): 29–34.
39 Andrew P. Morrison, *The Culture of Shame* (1996; repr., Northvale, NJ & London: Jason Aronson Inc., 1998), 195–196.

James had known that he was attracted to other boys since middle school. Growing up in a religiously observant Protestant family, he was taught in church that his attraction was sinful, and he never felt safe to confide in anybody about his sexual orientation, except for a gay high school friend with whom he had his first sexual encounter. After high school, he enlisted in the U.S. Navy, was nominated to attend the Naval Academy, and became a highly decorated officer. However, his successes and honors did not outweigh the "Don't ask, don't tell rule" of military culture that kept him from letting himself be known and continued to instill shame. Over the years, he had a few, secretive relationships with men but was never in a committed relationship. After he retired from the Navy, he perceived a calling to professional ministry, enrolled at a seminary of his denomination, and, as a requirement of his educational program, took a unit of Clinical Pastoral Education. The rule of military culture exercised its power far beyond James's retirement, and he did not dare to reveal his full identity to his peer group and remained hidden. During a peer's seemingly judgmental case presentation about an encounter with a lesbian couple, James became unusually reactive, hostile, and judgmental toward the presenter. When the CPE educator engaged him in supervision to explore his response, he deflected initially and then became very emotional, saying with tears in his eyes that it may as well have been him who was "judged as destined for eternal condemnation." During that session, the educator learned about his life-long struggle to hide his true self. When he thanked James for trusting him with his long-kept secret and wondered what it might be like for him to share his identity with his peer group, James responded, "I could never do that. I don't even know how to do that. You just don't tell." "I understand," his supervisor said, "it's been a rule in your life for such a long time, and it's scary to go against it. And yet, you just did, and as a result I know you better and feel closer to you. How does it feel to you?"

As cultures function, a shame culture shapes patterns of behavior and ways to interpret the world. While a culture of shame may encourage emotionally exhibitionistic behavior on stage, it discourages true vulnerability and intimacy within relationships. The world, that is, the reality outside of the self, becomes a measure of a person's sense of inadequacy and unworthiness.

Morrison also points to the relationship between shame and violence in societies shaped by shame culture. Unremitted shame, oppression, and humiliation, he explains, may well lead to aggression and retaliation.[40] The relationship between narcissism, shame, and violence has been highlighted particularly in psychoanalytic studies. Kohut, for example, identified narcissistic rage along with shame as a response to actual or anticipated narcissistic injuries. Kohut explained that, while narcissistic rage occurs in many forms, it can be distinguished from other forms of aggression. "The need for revenge, for righting a wrong, for undoing hurt by whatever means, and a deeply anchored, unrelenting compulsion in pursuit of all these aims, which gives no rest to those who have suffered narcissistic injury—these are the characteristic features of narcissistic rage in all its forms and which sets it apart from other kinds of aggression."[41] Within a culture of narcissism and shame, narcissistic rage, unlike other forms of aggression, does not cease after action against a perceived aggressor. The rage cannot be satisfied but lingers as a seething force within the self, just as the narcissistic injuries and shame linger within a fragmented self.

Shame and humiliation are considered root causes of violent behavior, and a culture of shame is likely to generate violence in various forms—from emotional to physical violence and from individual aggression to collective violence. "The emotion of shame," forensic psychiatrist James Gilligan explains, "is the primary or ultimate cause of all violence whether toward others or toward the self."[42] Gilligan's statement, of course, must not be taken to mean that all who experience intense and painful shame will act out with violence. Gilligan clarifies that, "while shame is a *necessary* condition for the causation of violence, it is not a *sufficient* condition."[43] He points out that several other preconditions need to be present for violence to erupt,

---

40 Morrison, *The Culture of Shame*, 198.
41 Kohut, "Narcissistic Rage," 637–638.
42 James Gilligan, *Violence: Reflections on a National Epidemic* (New York: G. P. Putnam's Sons, 1996), 110.
43 James Gilligan, "Shame, Guilt, and Violence," *Social Research* 70, no. 4 (Winter 2003): 1165.

such as a lack of capacity for guilt and remorse, an overwhelming intensity of shame, and the absence of sufficient nonviolent means for coping. The violent offenders whom Gilligan treated lacked all of these inhibitions against violence. Gilligan identifies as a fourth precondition the socialization into a male gender role that is shaped by patriarchal culture and teaches violence as a way to maintain one's masculinity. Gilligan bases his findings on his work with violent inmates as well as on research in forensic and experimental psychology and sociology. He concludes that the "consensus that has emerged from this work is that the most potent stimulus of aggression and violence, and the one that is most reliable in eliciting this response is not frustration per se (as the 'frustration-aggression' hypothesis had claimed), but rather insult and humiliation."[44]

Myth and science at times do agree. Gilligan references the Hebrew origin story in Genesis 4 about the first murderous act in human history as an example of violence resulting from humiliation and shame.[45] The narrative of Cain and Abel arrives at the same psychological insight that scientific research suggests, namely that intolerable shame can lead to violent aggression and even murder. In the story, both brothers brought offerings to the Lord, one fruits of the soil and the other a choice animal sacrifice. However, the Lord was partial to animal sacrifice and "had regard for Abel and his offering, but for Cain and his offering he had no regard. So Cain was very angry, and his countenance fell" (Gen 4:4b–5a). The lack of regard by an all-powerful force, a divine empathic self-object failure, resulted in a painful experience of humiliation, felt rejection, and shame. God became a shaming agent, and Cain lost face, which led to an angry and calculated act of fratricide. Shame entered the life of humans in the previous chapter in Genesis and now caused the first act of violence against humans recorded in Hebrew scripture. Notable in the story is that, just as in the Yahwist creation account, God attends to the human creature in travail and, while pointing out the consequences of Cain's act, God offers Cain a mark of protection. Divine empathic failure does not negate God's compassion for Cain, who is overcome with a sense of alienation and the urge to flee and hide from God and others.

---

44 Gilligan, "Shame, Guilt, and Violence," 1159.
45 See Gilligan, "Shame, Guilt, and Violence," 1156.

Trauma and Shame

Buechner's and Sethe's case studies clearly showed the relationship between trauma and shame. Sethe's story in *Beloved* demonstrates both the connection between personal trauma and shame as well as intergenerational trauma and shame. Toni Morrison's fictional narrative is consistent with research that shows that interpersonal trauma with repeated experiences of betrayal predict increased shame and dissociation.[46] Personal or interpersonal trauma such as various forms of betrayal, abuse, or violence can result in feelings of existential shame, partly because it is often experienced in isolation. Tragically, victims of trauma may blame themselves for what happened to them. Exploring trauma from a pastoral theological perspective, Shelly Rambo concludes that "we are confronted with the fragility and vulnerability of human persons and the degree to which we can wound and be wounded by others."[47] Shame is the mark of the fragile and vulnerable self in danger of disintegration in the aftermath of trauma. Especially if trauma is suffered at the hands of someone in a close relationship or a person one depends on, it can create a shameful dilemma about staying connected with one who inflicted wounds and pain. The self is left disoriented within a relational matrix that is supposed to provide stability, care, and support but has also caused injury to the self.

However, not every experience of adversity should be considered traumatic in a clinical sense. Traumatic experiences are to a large extent defined by the perception of those who suffer the experience. Trauma theory identifies a traumatic event "as one that leaves an individual feeling overwhelmed. The situation is perceived as threatening; it leaves the person feeling out of control or helpless and unable to assimilate or integrate the event."[48] A key element of trauma is the inability to cope effectively with the experience and, particularly in the event of multiple exposures to trauma, have one's identity

---

46 See Melissa G. Platt and Jennifer J. Freyd, "Betray My Trust, Shame on Me: Shame, Dissociation, Fear, and Betrayal Trauma," *Psychological Trauma: Theory, Research, Practice, and Policy* 7, no. 4 (July 2015): 401–402.
47 Shelly Rambo, *Spirit and Trauma: A Theology of Remaining* (Louisville: Westminster John Knox Press, 2010), 145 n. 2.
48 Carrie Clark, Catherine C. Classen, Anne Fourt, and Maithili Shetty, *Treating the Trauma Survivor: An Essential Guide to Trauma-Informed Care* (New York & London: Routledge, 2015), 6.

organized around traumatic experiences. Interpersonal trauma, especially at a young age, can create distortions in a person's sense of self and being in the world that impact their ability to invest themselves in relationships. Distortions may affect survivors' understanding of safety, their sense of self-worth and esteem, their ability to trust, and their sense of power and control. Feelings of shame and self-blame that what happened to them was a consequence of their flawed being can inhibit initiative and openness in relationships and hinder empathic connections. "Survivors frequently have difficulties maintaining relationships or feeling close to others. They lack certainty about the reliability of others, which often leads to feelings of distrust, suspicion, fear, and problems with intimacy. They may feel ambivalent about relationships, longing for connection and attachment and simultaneously fearing vulnerability and intimacy."[49] The existential dilemma that Buechner names at the beginning of his memoir is all the more true for survivors of interpersonal trauma. The desire to be known and to have one's wounds known and attended to is in conflict with the fear of being exposed, found out, hurt, and rejected.

Several studies have examined the role of shame in post-traumatic stress disorder (PTSD) and veterans when shame was not a result of being victimized but rather a consequence of ethically ambiguous experiences in combat or conflicts between deeply held moral convictions and actions or inaction in the line of duty. These ethically ambiguous experiences are identified as moral injuries.[50] Research with veterans diagnosed with PTSD suggests that shame and guilt are closely intertwined. While psychologists June Tangney and Ronda Dearing found that guilt became maladaptive when fused with shame, pure, shame-free, trauma-related guilt did not exist for these veterans. The results of that research indicate "that trauma-related guilt is possibly always fused with shame."[51] However, the study also showed that shame is more strongly associated with trauma rather than with guilt in PTSD, which

---

49 Clark et al., *Treating the Trauma Survivor*, 28.
50 See Brett T. Litz et al., "Moral Injury and Moral Repair in War Veterans: A Preliminary Model and Intervention Strategy," *Clinical Psychology Review* 29, no. 8 (December 2009): 695–706.
51 Jenny A. Bannister et al., "Differential Relationships of Guilt and Shame on Posttraumatic Stress Disorder Among Veterans," *Psychological Trauma: Theory, Research, Practice, and Policy* 11, no. 1 (January 2019): 39.

is supported by studies with civilians.[52] The implication is that self-identified guilt in trauma that is related to moral injuries may be secondary to shame, even if guilt is identified as a primary emotional response, and that treatment needs to focus on shame rather than guilt.

Both common and traumatic experiences shape brain development. The impact of trauma and the dynamics of shame are not merely emotional or transmitted through thought processes but also create neuronal pathways and influence hemispheric development within the brain. Psychiatrist Daniel Siegel explains how psychological trauma and resulting flooding by stress hormones may produce toxic effects on brain development that affect a person's ability to adapt to future stress or self-regulate emotional experiences, including shame.[53] However, trauma and shame do not only influence individual development but can have even more wide-reaching impact. Siegel holds that "the disorganizing effects of trauma and its lack of resolution can be passed from generation to generation. The emotional suffering, the stress-induced damage to cognitive functioning, the internal chaos of intrusive, implicit memories, and the potential interpersonal violence created as a result of trauma produce a ripple effect of devastation across the boundaries of time and human lives."[54] Traumatic shame is not just a matter of psychology or spirituality but also a matter of biology, both in terms of the physical experience of shame and in terms of the development of chronic and intergenerational shame.

Psychotherapist Patricia DeYoung builds upon Siegel's research about interpersonal neurobiology in her approach to treating chronic and traumatic shame. Shame that develops in response to relational trauma requires a relational or intersubjective approach to caring and healing that replaces empathic failure with compassionate empathic attunement and reprograms the brain by fostering emotional self-regulation and neural integration. DeYoung defines chronic shame relationally as "the experience of one's felt sense of self disintegrating in relation to a dysregulating other" and as "the experience of self-in-relation when 'in-relation' is ruptured and disconnected.

---

52 See Bannister et al., "Guilt and Shame," 38.
53 See Daniel J. Siegel, *The Developing Mind: How Relationships and the Brain Interact to Shape Who We Are* (New York: The Guilford Press, 1999), 294–295.
54 Siegel, *The Developing Mind*, 60.

A chronic sense of self-in-disconnection becomes a profound sense of isolation, which in turn leads to despair and unworthiness."[55] Buechner's memoir reflects that the effects of interpersonal trauma are often suffered under the veil of secrecy. The result means that trauma has a strong potential to create an isolated self and the shame that accompanies such development. Interpersonal trauma, particularly if it is experienced repetitively and is not attended to with care, can form lifelong, chronic patterns of self-judgment and self-diminishing awareness.

Addiction and the Vicious Cycle of Shame

In the aftermath of trauma, addiction can become part of the continuing passage of suffering. Not everyone or even a majority of those who suffer trauma becomes addicted. However, one way to try to alleviate the internal pain of trauma and possibly the shame is by medicating it. Self-medication theories show that uncomfortable and intolerable affect may become an etiological factor in substance abuse and addiction.[56] While addictions may numb the pain, they do not provide healing and likely create new suffering and a vicious cycle of shame. The shame cycle in addiction may start with a chronic sense of unworthiness, inferiority, and separation from others. Drugs, alcohol, or other addictive behaviors are used to distract from the shame, to numb the emotional pain, and possibly to lower inhibitions to social interactions. When the use of chemicals or addictive behavior lead to the loss of control, self-defeating decisions and actions, or to the violation of one's values, self-judgment results in shame, which requires more medicating. The shame cycle is complete and continues to spiral downward. Addiction and shame are intimately linked in a self-destructive process of seeking control while losing control. Multiple addictions may co-exist so that one addiction can numb the shame about the other.

Clinical psychologist Philip Flores rightly points out that the etiology of addiction is not a clear-cut, one-dimensional phenomenon. Persons become

---

55 DeYoung, *Chronic Shame*, 18.
56 For a discussion of research about the interaction between psychopathology and chemical addiction, see Roger D. Weiss and Steven M. Mirin, "Substance Abuse as an Attempt at Self-Medication," in *Essential Papers on Addiction*, ed. Daniel L. Yalisove (New York & London: New York University Press, 1997), 441–452.

addicted for many different reasons, and biological, psychological, and spiritual causes each may be a primary etiological factor by itself or intertwined with the others. From the perspective of self psychology, Flores understands addiction as an attachment disorder and explains that "individuals who have difficulty establishing emotionally regulating attachments are more inclined to substitute drugs and alcohol for their deficiency in intimacy."[57] He implies a variation of self-medication theories, asserting that "dysfunctional attachment styles interfere with the ability to derive satisfaction from interpersonal relationships. . . . Experiences related to early developmental failures leave certain individuals with vulnerabilities that enhance addictive-type behaviors and these behaviors are misguided attempts at self-repair."[58] The failures that Flores refers to are not the optimal empathic self-object failures that help to form an independent and cohesive self, but they are traumatic failures in the provision of care that lead to developmental arrests and an inability to regulate emotions. Addiction substitutes as an attachment to an external mechanism of emotional regulation by numbing painful and intolerable feelings.

Flores views addiction as "an epiphenomenon of narcissistic defenses against shame, fear, and other painful affects."[59] For some vulnerable persons with unmet developmental needs and deficits in self, addiction, like narcissism, produces a false self that retreats from intimate relationships in a continuing response to rejecting and shaming relationships in their past. However, the cycle of remorse and shame prevents them from repairing the past by requiring continuous addictive behavior. Thus, the cycle of shame, substance abuse, and self-loathing continues. Healing ultimately depends on engaging in a relationship, which addiction attempts to avoid, of therapeutic intimacy where persons allow themselves to be vulnerable and known. "Repair and restoration of the self can be accomplished only within a healing and healthy relationship. The patient needs a consistent, nurturing, mirroring and holding environment that can contain and manage negative, destructive impulses."[60] Flores emphasizes that the healing relationship that creates a safe space to face and integrate shame is ideally a relationship with a

---

57 Philip J. Flores, *Addiction as an Attachment Disorder* (Lanham & Oxford: Jason Aronson Inc., 2004), 7.
58 Flores, *Addiction as an Attachment Disorder*, 7.
59 Flores, *Addiction as an Attachment Disorder*, 83.
60 Flores, *Addiction as an Attachment Disorder*, 83.

group as an attachment object that gives addicted persons a larger and more diverse number of self-object relations.[61] The promise of healing from addiction comes through community that offers solidarity in suffering, acceptance, corrective experiences, and support in one's efforts to change.

Social Oppression and Shame

Shame manifests not just in response to individual interactions or self-object failures but also as a result of social conditions and inequalities. Social oppression marginalizes and devalues groups of people by categorizing them as inferior to a dominant group that holds power. Systemic and institutionalized mistreatment, exploitation, violence, and denial of equal rights are means of inflicting emotional, spiritual, and physical wounds that leave lasting pain or scars on individuals and communities. Consistent shaming messages, public policies and actions that convey a lack of value, denial of rights and resources, and demeaning stereotypes can instill identity-based and culture-centered shame. Clinical social worker Brené Brown, for example, identifies a shame web of layered and conflicting expectations as a central and common denominator in women's experiences of gender-based oppression and related shame. "Once entangled in this web," she contends, "women feel flooded with feelings of fear, blame and disconnection.... But if we understand fear, blame and disconnection as intricately woven together to create shame, it becomes very clear why shame is so powerful, complex and difficult to overcome."[62] She continues to explain that, beyond gender, the expectations "that form the web are often based on characteristics like our race, class, sexual orientation, age or religious identity."[63]

The metaphor of a shame web powerfully captures feeling helplessly trapped in a self-defeating cycle that often accompanies toxic, social shame. Consider, for example, the following clinical vignette from the supervision of hospital chaplaincy.

---

61 See Flores, *Addiction as an Attachment Disorder*, 233–236.
62 Brené Brown, *I Thought It Was Just Me (But It Isn't): Making the Journey from "What People Think" to "I Am Enough"* (2007; repr., New York: Avery, 2008), 18.
63 Brown, *I Thought It Was Just Me (But It Isn't)*, 18.

> Kristin was a gifted young woman, who had come to the United States from Sweden to attend Bible college. She had grown up in a conservative Protestant family in the Free Church tradition that did not recognize women in any leadership positions and only allowed women to do certain missionary work. Male family members had the unquestionable right to inquire about all aspects of Kristin's life and demand compliance with their "guidance." Kristin came to the United States to prepare herself for ministry in foreign missions. Later she wondered how much of her decision was an attempt to get away from an oppressive religious culture and family environment. After graduating from Bible college, she attended seminary, initially due to the fact that she was dating a fellow student, who had been accepted into seminary. While their relationship did not last, academic theology quickly captivated Kristin's attention and energy, and she excelled in her classes. She was particularly interested in liberationist theories and became involved in ministry with refugees and found much satisfaction and affirmation in her volunteer work. However, her family continually questioned her educational endeavors, demanded that she return to Sweden and provided no support for her evolving vision for professional ministry. During a required internship in hospital chaplaincy, Kristin began to examine her personal story through clinical supervision and how it shaped her identity and vision for ministry. In her clinical work, she found herself reactive in self-sabotaging ways, particularly when she encountered male authority figures. Rather than claiming her authority collegially and voicing her often astute insights, Kristin would typically withdraw and act in isolation without consulting with other team members, which led to several complaints about her by nursing staff. When she processed the feedback in supervision, she was initially sad about how she was perceived by others and felt deeply inadequate. Gradually, however, she gained an understanding of how her shame impacted her relationships in the clinic.

Kristin was caught in a shame-web that had been intricately woven in a complex collaboration between religious authorities, her family, and herself.

It spanned thousands of miles across an ocean and caused her to feel stuck and repeat self-sabotaging behavior. Her confessed theology of liberationist theories and her embedded theology of restrictions and judgment were as far apart as her native country and the country of her studies. Deeply ingrained gender-based expectations and controls and the fear of being disowned by her family and disconnected from her roots threatened to sabotage Kristin's courageous work toward self-affirmation and professional growth.

Toni Morrison's writings confront both the oppression of women and oppression through racism. Like sexism, racism perpetuates structural injustice and inequality. Morrison's novel reflects how personal and interpersonal shame as well as intergenerational shame have been linked to the experience of slavery and racism. Morrison draws a distinction between both experiences, stating that the "origins of slavery are not necessarily (or ordinarily) racist."[64] Slavery, she explains, was primarily a commercial and economic endeavor, while racism is a dehumanizing system of beliefs and structures that sustains the vilification, demonization, and crucifixion of people of color. Even if racism did not create the transatlantic slave trade, it provided the justification that was needed to sustain a dehumanizing institution within a widely Christian society. Several of Morrison's stories portray individuals for whom enslavement and racist oppression are closely linked to the experience of shame. Morrison holds that the experience of slavery, the "slavebody," was associated with dishonor and that the freed "blackbody" was subsequently held in contempt and met with disgust, "morphed into a synonym for poor people, a synonym for criminalism and a flash point for public policy."[65] Whiteness was associated with superiority and purity, while blackness was identified with inferiority and impurity. Interpersonally, contempt and disgust are distinct shame-inducing effects that can generate in their objects self-contempt and self-disgust through a process of internalization. Through a deliberate process that combined social, political, and psychological dynamics, the institution of slavery and systemic racism in the United States have created and perpetuated racialized shame and self-loathing in individuals and communities.

---

64 Toni Morrison, *The Source of Self-Regard: Selected Essays, Speeches, and Meditations* (2019; repr., New York: Vintage Books, 2020), 75.
65 Morrison, *The Source of Self-Regard*, 76–77.

Racialized shame is not just a psycho-social reality but is also a theological reality. Social justice activist Michael Crumpler identifies a theology of Black shame that has been constructed on the foundation of a theology of white supremacy that has infused Black religious life.[66] Ephesians 6:5–6 is one of the biblical texts that has shaped both theologies over centuries. "Slaves, obey your earthly masters with fear and trembling, in singleness of heart, as you obey Christ; not only while being watched, and to please them, but as slaves of Christ, doing the will of God from the heart." Crumpler argues that by equating the relationship between slave and slave owner with the relationship that a believer has with Christ and by preaching this so-called gospel, proponents of slavery attempted to control Black people and support their abuse theologically.

> *Such obedience was incumbent upon the oppressed in order to achieve salvation on earth and in the hereafter. Furthermore, one's obedience to his master correlated directly to one's obedience to Christ. The inevitable outcome of such a compact is failure, in that slavery is inherently dehumanizing—the oppressor never sees the oppressed as fully human. This dehumanization leaves the slave suspended in a self-defeating quest for survival and believing that 'if I am the model slave I will be rewarded by my God and my master, but if I fail I will be condemned.' This results in a perpetual state of Black shame.*[67]

Black liberation theology, according to Crumpler, is a transformative response that deconstructs a theology of white supremacy and empowers persons of African descent to claim their heritage and equal rights within society and the church.

While Morrison, Crumpler, and others highlight the toxic effects of shame as a result of social and theological oppression, another perspective views shame as a potentially corrective response to social injustice and

---

66 See Michael J. Crumpler, "Give us What Magic Johnson Got! Spiritual Care for Black Lives, Living with HIV and Aids in the Era of #Black Lives Matter" in *Spiritual Care in an Age of #Black Lives Matter*, ed. Danielle J. Buhuro (Eugene, OR: Cascade Books, 2019), 108–109.

67 Crumpler, "Spiritual Care for Black Lives Living with HIV and Aids," 108.

violence that may serve a reforming function. Political philosopher Christopher Lebron makes a moral argument that confronts racial inequality and considers shame as a potential catalyst for social change. Lebron builds on the thesis that most people find the notion of inequality based on race morally unacceptable and contend that moral outrage by itself is an incomplete and inadequate response. Lebron states that shame "seems appropriate with respect to social inequality. Shame is commonly understood as a moral reaction of a certain kind. It is one in which a person becomes aware of a discrepancy between the person one takes oneself to be and the person one is at a given moment. . . . The reaction of shame is one of disappointment and dismay over a perceived failing or a falling away from one's ideals."[68] Lebron points to three distinct features of shame as part of a moral response to racial injustice. Shame signals a lack of integrity or moral wholeness and a need to attend to the felt disjuncture between ideal self and actual self. In addition, shame prepares persons to act differently in future situations by shining a spotlight on cognitive-affective failures after the relevant moment. Finally, shame signals our failure to flourish because it confronts us falling short of our ideals, which are instrumental, if not intrinsically valuable, for the flourishing life. Thus, shame may help reclaim and realize a flourishing life that extends to others.

Conclusion

The notion of shame as a master emotion suggests, on the one hand, that shame occupies a primary place and has a generative function within the hierarchy of emotions. On the other hand, shame as a master emotion implies that shame can be a dominant and oppressive force in persons' lives. The term *shame-bound*, which has been used to describe persons who are prone to experience intense shame, describes the force of shame fittingly. Maladaptive or toxic shame is literally self-defeating. Gilligan aptly refers to the impact of shame and humiliation as "the death of the self."[69] Considering the effects of consistent early self-object failures, one may even conclude that

---

68 Christopher J. Lebron, *The Color of Our Shame: Race and Justice in Our Time* (Oxford & New York: Oxford University Press, 2013), 21.
69 See Gilligan, "Shame, Guilt, and Violence," 1153.

shame aborts the self before the self is born as a cohesive entity. In thinking about the restoration of the self, the Johannine notion of "being born from above" or "being born anew" (John 3:7) takes on new meaning. Rather than being a distinguishing mark of true Jesus believers, being born again can be understood as a metaphor for the restoration or the rebirth of the self through faith, that is, by responding to the calling of the God event upon us.

However, shame is multifactorial, and one-dimensional explanations will likely not suffice to explain shame's impact in the life of individuals nor to fashion therapeutic responses. While shame has been explored primarily in the context of individual psychological development and attachments, Lasch and Andrew Morrison have shown that cultural, societal, and systemic forces have significant impact on personality development and the etiology of shame. As Toni Morrison's novel reflects, the socio-political system of slavery and racist ideology have produced a deep-seated sense of shame in individuals as well as intergenerational shame that spans across decades and even centuries. Neither racism nor the shame that results from racist ideology and structures are matters of the past. They continue to exercise their oppressive power and continue to challenge us to seek therapeutic responses that do not focus only on individuals but also on the transformation of systemic causes of racialized shame. Similarly, sexism and the inferiorization and oppression of women have motivated sexual violence and generated female shame. While individual therapeutic responses are needed to effect healing, sexism as much as racism calls for just responses and systemic initiatives to heal and prevent shame.

6

THEOLOGICAL APPROACHES

WHILE CHRISTIAN THEOLOGY has been reluctant to make shame an explicit subject of discourse, Christian piety, proclamation, and practice have contributed to a culture of shame collectively and individually with personal stories marked by shame. My clinical practice and my experience in clinical pastoral supervision point to the power of shame in faith stories. When shame is in the blind spot, it wields its power even more forcefully and damagingly. At the same time, the master story about the Jesus event that shaped Christianity is a genuinely restorative response to the human condition marked by shame, albeit rarely interpreted in that way. Pattison highlights the complex and ambivalent relationship between Christian faith and shame. He argues that "Christianity can create, exploit, and deny shame in groups and individuals. However, it can also diminish and alleviate shame, enhancing worth, efficacy, and esteem."[1]

In an autoethnographic reflection, Pattison illustrates how Christian theology and ideology can intersect with personal experience to engender shame. Pointing to the fact that "Christian ideas and images are polyvocal, pluralistic, and susceptible to many interpretations,"[2] he explains how themes of domination, submission, and denial of self in Christian teaching can instill or confirm shame, depending on a person's psychological state. Pattison identifies religiously engendered shame, surmising that "the God of the majority orthodox tradition, with whose images I was confronted as a child, is a shame-generating monster. . . . To live in the presence of this kind of God is to exist in a state of almost permanent chronic shame and abjection. It is to feel at all times acutely self-conscious and inadequate, that one is perpetually weighed in the balance and found desperately wanting."[3]

---

1 Stephen Pattison, *Shame: Theory, Therapy, Theology* (Cambridge, UK & New York: Cambridge University Press, 2000), 229.
2 Pattison, *Shame: Theory, Therapy, Theology*, 230.
3 Pattison, *Shame: Theory, Therapy, Theology*, 241.

The predominance of guilt and need for forgiveness in Christian teaching along with the implicit religious shaming that Pattison describes creates at best confusion and at worst spiritual suffering. A theological exploration of shame that considers a biblical perspective and constructive theological responses to shame can lay a foundation for re-visioning atonement.

Shame and Guilt Revisited: "A Man Had Two Sons"

The so-called parable of the prodigal son (Luke 15:11–32) offers some noteworthy insight into the dynamics and differences between guilt and shame, forgiveness and acceptance, separation and belonging. It is perhaps one of the best-known stories in Christian scripture. The fact that this story primarily is known under this name, which focuses on the younger son, shows that Christianity favors guilt over shame in interpreting the human condition. In the history of interpretation, the elder brother received mainly attention as the presumptive representative of an unrepentant Israel.[4] The Greek text, however, does not indicate a focus on either one of the sons. In fact, the story begins with a statement that a "certain man had two sons," thus, directing the attention of the listeners to both sons.

> And the young one said to the father: "Father, give (me) the part of your property that falls to me." And he divided his livelihood between them. And after gathering for many days everything, the younger son left for a country far away, and there he wasted his assets through reckless living. When he had spent everything, there came a severe famine over that country, and he was in need. And moving forward, he clung to one of the citizens of that country, and he sent him into his fields to tend to pigs, and he had the desire to fill himself up from the carob pods which the pigs were eating, but no one gave him (any). Coming thus to himself, he said, "How

---

4 See Amy-Jill Levine, *Short Stories by Jesus: The Enigmatic Parables of a Controversial Rabbi* (New York: HarperCollins, 2014), 30. Levine quotes church father Jerome's verdict that the older son, Israel, was "far from the grace of the Holy Spirit, banished from his father's counsel," pointing out that the first reference to the "prodigal son" was in Jerome's writings.

many of my father's day laborers have an abundance of bread, but here I am lost in a famine. Rising up, I will go to my father and will say to him, 'Father, I have sinned against the heaven and before you, it is no longer fitting for me to be called your son. Make me like one of your day laborers.'" And rising up, he came close to his father. While he was still far in the distance, his father saw him and felt compassion and running he threw himself around his neck and kissed him. But the son said to him, "Father, I have sinned against the heaven and before you, it is no longer fitting for me to be called your son." Yet, the father said to his servants, "Right now, bring the best robe and put it on him, and give a ring on his hand and sandals on his feet, and bring the fattened calf, slaughter (it), and celebrate eating (it), because this son of mine was dead and came back to life, was lost and is found. And they began to rejoice.

Yet, there was his son, the older one, in a field. And while he was coming, approaching the house, he heard music and dancing, and summoning to himself one of the servants, he asked what this might be. He told him, "Your brother has come, and your father slaughtered the fattened calf, because he received him back being healthy." Now he was angry and did not want to go in, but his father, coming out, urged him. Yet, responding he said to his father, "See, for so many years I am serving you (like a slave) and never did I disobey your order, and never did you give me a goat, so that I might celebrate with my friends. When, however, this son of yours, who wasted your livelihood with prostitutes, came, you slaughtered for him the fattened calf." But he said to him, "Child, you are always with me, and everything of mine is yours. To celebrate and be glad was necessary, because your brother, this one, was dead and became alive, and having been lost he was found."[5]

The parable is set in the Gospel of Luke as part of Jesus's discourse with the Pharisees about their critique of Jesus associating with sinners. The parable is not just a story about a family reunion that almost happened, but a story about salvation and the possibility of restoration. However, it

---

5 Author's translation.

is not a salvation story in the way that we have traditionally learned about the meaning of this parable. Rather, it is an assessment of the human condition in the experiences of guilt and shame and an announcement about the possibility of restoration. The participle *anastas* is used twice to introduce the younger son's plan and his implementation to get up, return, and request from his father a place among the day laborers. The word is closely related to the Greek term for resurrection, *anastasis*, and resembles it phonetically. Similarly, the father's metaphorical use of the verb for "coming to life again," *anazao*, suggests a process that leads from death to resurrection. The question is: Whose salvation is the focus of the story? The opening sentence tells the listener that it is a story in two acts, each devoted to one of the sons. As the story goes, the first act about the younger brother is complete with a beginning, a story line, and an ending. The second act, involving the elder brother, however, remains open-ended.[6] The listeners do not find out whether he will join the celebration. The father's invitation to celebrate and be glad about the return of the younger brother remains unanswered in the story. The invitation is for the listeners to identify with the older son and to decide how to respond.

At first glance, the point of the story seems to illustrate the interplay of human repentance and God's forgiveness. A secondary purpose may be an attempt to get the Pharisees to identify with the older son. However, the parable operates on several different levels. Biblical scholar Bernard Brandon Scott suggests that the primary narrative level is part of the larger story in Luke and is about vindicating Jesus's relationships with sinners.[7] The second and third levels, he explains, connect the story about a father with two sons to the other two parables in Luke 15 that emphasize the theme of joy over the lost being found. The three parables together make a narrative unit.

I propose that there is a further narrative level that describes the human condition in terms of guilt and shame and, thus, adds an element of theological surprise. Luke seems to have Jesus identify guilt in the first act and highlight shame in the second act as the more problematic condition to overcome. At the same time, the narrative invites the listeners to identify with

---

6 See Bernard Brandon Scott, *Hear Then the Parable: A Commentary of the Parables of Jesus* (Minneapolis: Fortress Press, 1989), 108–109.
7 See Scott, *Hear Then the Parable*, 101–102.

the elder brother, to move to a place of empathy and compassion toward the one who returned to the family, and to enter into community. To move into an empathic and compassionate space that allows for community, the elder brother—and those who listen to the parable—need a conversion, *metanoia*, a change of heart and mind.

In traditional interpretations of the story, the younger brother typically is identified as the one who has a change of heart and repents. By asking for his part of the inheritance before his father's death, he not only went against the customs of his time and culture but, in effect, wished or declared his father dead. He became guilty of violating customary inheritance arrangements and dishonoring his father. It would have been utterly surprising to the parable's original listeners that the father actually dispensed part of his estate. The father's action suggests that he is not the typical Middle Eastern patriarch of his time and culture. Indeed, he makes himself vulnerable and risks his honor and economic consequences by giving his younger son not only the right of possession of part of his estate but also the right of disposition.[8] The son, in turn, sells his assets and leaves for another country where he settles into a reckless and self-destructive life that eventually leaves him destitute and facing starvation.

The decision of the younger son to return to his homestead to join his father's workforce seems calculated. Taking a legalistic perspective, he realistically assumes that he lost his status in the family when he requested his inheritance prematurely and squandered it. Yet having experienced his father's uncharacteristic response to his request for his inheritance, he may be cautiously hopeful about requesting a place among the laborers at his father's estate. He is not looking for grace but for an opportunity to earn enough to survive and perhaps even to make a living. The Greek text describes his decision not simply as turning around but first of all as an inward turn, an introspective process, and a self-assessment. The son takes a measure of himself, acknowledges his violation of cultural and religious rules and his personal offense against his father, and imagines that he could return, confess to his failure, and belong again to his father's household, even if not as a son. While he may have engaged in shameful behavior by working as a Jew for a hog

---

[8] See Scott, *Hear Then the Parable*, 110–111.

farmer, the narrative does not suggest shame being a dynamic in his decision. Shame would not allow him to face himself squarely, nor would it allow him to face his father and admit his offense. Rather, his decision to return to his father's estate seems to be motivated, on the one hand, by a possibility for survival and, on the other hand, by a self-assessment and an acknowledgement that he was guilty of offending his father's honor by breaking the rules that govern inheritance.

When the younger son puts his imagination into action and makes the journey home, he is in for a surprise, and so are those who listen to the story. Again, the story presents the father as a rather uncharacteristic patriarch. The father's affectionate response suggests that he may have been looking out for his son, perhaps hoping for his return. Meeting his son with overwhelming affection, his response could be interpreted again as violating his honor.[9] The parable certainly does not illustrate an atonement as a resolution to an offense by offering satisfaction or sacrifice. Rather, the father's actions risk his honor again and suggest that he forgives his son without even being asked to do so. Even more, he reinstates against all expectations the younger son to his familiar status with robe and ring. Thereby, he also restores his son's standing in the community in a possibly scandalous move.[10] Finally, the father orders a lavish celebration, likely for the whole community, to share the joy about the return of his son.

Not everyone, however, is ready, willing, and eager to join the party. The elder son is suspicious as he hears noise of celebration. Rather than finding out himself, he summons someone to provide the information he requires. In anger, the elder son refuses to join the celebration even though custom would require him to take a role. His anger implies another underlying emotional response because anger is most often a secondary emotion. Frequently, the primary emotion is fear, which reacts to an actual or perceived threat to the self and arouses anger.[11]

His father's unexpected response to his brother's return takes the elder son by surprise. It also ushers a threat to his status within the family and

---

9 See Scott, *Hear Then the Parable*, 117.
10 See Kenneth E. Bailey, *Poet and Peasant* (1976; repr., Grand Rapids: William B. Eerdmans Publishing Company, 1990), 185.
11 See Andrew D. Lester, *The Angry Christian: A Theology of Care and Counseling* (Louisville: Westminster John Knox Press, 2003), 82–83.

to his plans for succession. However, a more deep-seated sense of shame likely determines the elder son's response, and his anger masks his shame. While his brother has been motivated by survival instinct and guilt to return home, the elder son is driven by shame to withdraw from the community that celebrates salvation. His words reflect his fragile self, comparing himself both to a slave and to his brother, who, in his judgment, is being celebrated undeservedly.

The elder son clearly views himself as the rejected one, the one whose efforts are not acknowledged nor rewarded. While his brother, who squandered his inheritance and made immoral choices, is celebrated with a feast of a fattened calf, he has not even felt permission to share a goat with his friends. While his brother assumed that he did not belong with the family anymore, the elder brother does not feel that he belongs either and counts himself among the slaves. The father, however, responds as affectionately to the elder one as he did to the younger one. Just as he welcomed the returning son, he moves toward the elder son, meets him outside to invite him inside, and affirms his place with him in the family and in his heart.[12]

The parable seems to illustrate a distinction within human experience and a duality of human struggles and strivings. Biblical scholar Kenneth Bailey argues that Jesus discusses two basic human types. "One is lawless without the law, and the other is lawless within the law. Both rebel. Both break the father's heart. Both end up in a faraway country, one physically, the other spiritually."[13] While Bailey takes a legal perspective, there also is a difference between the sons' psychological dispositions to explore. Kohut identified the duality of human experience in a symbolic way, using gender-exclusive language, as the difference between "guilty man" and "tragic man." Guilty man, according to Kohut, is best understood as being caught in conflict between destructive drives and inhibiting or prohibiting forces.[14] As the terminology suggests, the primary emotional experience is

---

12 Addressing the elder son as "child" (*teknon*) affirms the son's status in relationship to the father and is an affectionate expression, given that the elder son is likely an adult or a young adult. A parallel in addressing an adult in that way is Mark 2:5 (par. Matt 9:2), where Jesus uses that term in talking to a paralyzed person seeking healing.
13 Bailey, *Poet and Peasant*, 203.
14 See Heinz Kohut, *The Restoration of the Self* (1977; repr., Chicago & London: The University Press of Chicago, 2009), 243.

guilt. Although people typically do not fit neatly into categories, the parable's younger brother resembles a guilty man because he is, on the one hand, driven by desires that turn out to be self-destructive, and, on the other hand, feels inhibited to act on some desires. No one allows him to eat from the pigs' feed. He declares his guilt in relation to his father and in violation of cultural and religious norms. The elder brother, who is the heir but feels like a slave and does not want to join the joyous celebration, resembles the tragic man in search for the self. The tragic man is defined by shame and the psychological experience of a fragmented or depleted self.[15] Shame is a driving and inhibiting force in his life. For Kohut, tragic man is the symbol for the primary and dominant human condition. Healing for guilty man comes as conflict resolution through the expansion of consciousness. Healing for tragic man comes as the ability to experience deeply the joy of existence and life as worthwhile.[16]

Finally, there is a conspicuously missing element in Jesus's parable about a family. The complete absence of a female character is striking. Where is the mother in this family's story? Given the time and context of the parable, it is likely that the listeners imagined a traditional family structure with a male and female parent. Perhaps we are to assume that the mother died. But if her death was indeed part of the back story, why would it not be mentioned explicitly? Or is it that women were present but not counted as is the case in other gospel narratives (Matt 14:21)? Given that other parables in the Gospel of Luke portray women as protagonists (Luke 15:8–10; Luke 18:2–5), that explanation seems unlikely for this parable.

Based on the uncharacteristic depiction of the father's behavior in the story, Scott suggests that he represents the maternal theme within the parable.[17] While the father may appear more affectionate than one would expect, it seems curious that Jesus would substitute him as a mother figure without any explanation. Rather, it is likely that the missing female presence in the parable is intentional and symbolic. The absence represents a lack of empathic presence and nurture, both of which have been traditionally assigned to the

---

15 See Kohut, *The Restoration of the Self*, 243.
16 See Robert L. Randall, "Soteriological Dimensions in the Work of Heinz Kohut," *Journal of Religion and Health* 19, no. 2 (Summer 1980): 88–89.
17 See Scott, *Hear Then the Parable*, 117.

role of the mother. Although the father responds affectionately to both sons in a time of crisis, the elder brother's shame-response suggests that empathic failures have been part of his backstory. Thus, rather than being an allegory that represents God as a forgiving father, the parable of a man who had two sons is a subversive story about the human condition, about human struggles with guilt and shame in the absence of empathic nurture, and about the possibilities for healing. The man with two sons is a human father who can and does respond with affection, and who likely has failed his sons in the past just as any other parent fails. The parable's subversive message lies in the father's surprising response to both sons and in the audience's identification with the elder son, not to convict the story's listeners but to provide a healing perspective on shame through acceptance. The parable invites the listeners, just as the father invites his elder son, to accept that they are accepted and belong in the family together with the younger brother.

Shame in Recent Theological Analysis

Friedrich Schleiermacher is perhaps the principal Protestant theologian who viewed emotions as central to the Christian faith and made them a focus of theological analysis. Along with the feeling of absolute or utter dependence that essentially defined for Schleiermacher religious faith, he identified reverence, humility, love, gratitude, compassion, and remorse as religious feelings that connected human beings to the divine.[18] Not surprisingly, shame did not make the list of religious feelings, even though it is the first human emotion in relationship to God described in Christianity's canon of sacred scriptures.

While shame has been mainly ignored as a topic of theological analysis for most of the history of Christian theology, some more recent, modern theological treatises have explored dynamics of shame as they explain the human condition. Among them, theologian Dietrich Bonhoeffer's attention to shame in several of his writings is perhaps the most extensive treatment of the topic by a systematic theologian. Paul Tillich addressed the reality

---

18 Friedrich Schleiermacher, *On Religion: Speeches to Its Cultured Despisers*, 2nd ed., trans. and ed. Richard Crouter (Cambridge, UK: Cambridge University Press, 1996), 45–46.

and impact of shame, albeit without naming it explicitly, in one of his most recognized sermons. Most of the expositions, however, have emanated since the 1980s in the North American context from pastoral theological research and dialogue with increasing psychological research and publications about shame. These theological attempts to engage shame deserve critical consideration to reconstruct a Christian understanding of the atonement and salvation.

Shame as the Memory of Lost Wholeness: Dietrich Bonhoeffer

In *Creation and Fall*, Bonhoeffer explores aspects of a theological anthropology, what it means to be created in the image of God, and what the so-called corruption of that image implies. In Bonhoeffer's interpretation, shame defines fallen humanity. Bonhoeffer finds that the notion that human beings were made in the image of God cannot be determined as *analogia entis* in which human existence as such reflects the likeness of God's being. Rather, the image of God must be understood as *analogia relationis*, interpreting it in relational rather than ontological terms because God's being through the work of Christ is qualified as "being for humankind."[19] Thus, the nature of the self is intrinsically relational and necessarily embodied. Bonhoeffer's argument clearly reflects his incarnational theology. Humankind is created in the image of God "not in spite but precisely in its bodily nature. For in their bodily nature human beings are related to the earth and to other bodies; they are there for others and are dependent on others. In their bodily existence human beings find their brothers and sisters and find the earth."[20]

Furthermore, for Bonhoeffer, to be created in the image of God means to have freedom and responsibility. Freedom in the image of God cannot be construed as a form of individualistic freedom, as a right or a possession, but is paradoxically freedom to be bound in relationship to the creator and to fellow creatures. "Because freedom is not a quality that can be uncovered; it is not a possession, something to hand, an object; . . . instead it is a relation and nothing else. To be more precise, freedom is a relation between two

---

19 See Dietrich Bonhoeffer, *Creation and Fall: A Theological Exposition of Genesis 1–3*, trans. Douglas Stephen Bax, *Dietrich Bonhoeffer Works*, vol. 3, ed. John W. DeGruchy (Minneapolis: Fortress Press, 1997), 65.
20 Bonhoeffer, *Creation and Fall*, 79.

persons. Being free means 'being-free-for-the-other,' because I am bound to the other. Only in relation to the other I am free."[21] In other words, freedom, for Bonhoeffer, is not freedom of will but freedom of will-to-be-in-relationship. The notion of freedom is qualified through the relational nature of the self and is closely linked to responsibility. Bonhoeffer's theological anthropology does not conceive of freedom without responsibility. "The structure of responsible life," states Bonhoeffer, "is determined in a twofold manner, namely, by life's bond to human beings and to God, and by the freedom of one's own life. It is the bond of life to human beings and to God that constitutes the freedom of our own life."[22] Responsibility is in the true sense of the word the ability to respond to the call of the God event in Christ and to fellow human creatures.

As Bonhoeffer understands it, the loss and denial of relationship is at the heart of the corruption of the image of God in human beings. Sin is not manifest in broken laws but rather in broken relationships. It is not the loss of morality but the loss of boundaries and, therefore, of community. Bonhoeffer uses the language of addiction to describe the human condition and gives an explanation that resembles a description of narcissistic reality when he points out that "the boundless obsessive desire to be without any limits" characterizes the self after the fall into sin.[23] Rather than existing in a life-sustaining matrix of relationships, the self attempts to understand and define itself in isolation and becomes its own sole referent. Bonhoeffer holds that shame is the manifestation of broken community between the self and the other; shame indicates the loss of belonging with others. "Shame arises only out of the knowledge of humankind's dividedness of the world's dividedness in general, and thus also of one's own dividedness. Shame expresses the fact that we no longer accept the other as God's gift but instead are consumed with an obsessive desire for the other; . . . Shame is a cover in which I hide myself from the other because of my own evil and the other person's evil, that is, because of the dividedness that has come between us."[24]

---

21 Bonhoeffer, *Creation and Fall*, 63.
22 Dietrich Bonhoeffer, *Ethics*, trans. Reinhard Krauss, Charles C. West, and Douglas W. Scott, *Dietrich Bonhoeffer Works*, vol. 6., ed. Clifford J. Green (Minneapolis: Fortress Press, 2005), 257.
23 See Bonhoeffer, *Creation and Fall*, 123.
24 Bonhoeffer, *Creation and Fall*, 101.

Decades before psychological research came to distinguish between shame and guilt and before developmental psychology established the primacy of shame, Bonhoeffer's theological analysis discerned the difference and proposed that shame was more elemental than guilt. In his *Ethics* fragment, Bonhoeffer argues that

> *human beings are ashamed because of the lost unity with God and one another. Shame and remorse must not be confused with each other. Human beings feel remorse when they have done something wrong, shame when they are missing something. Shame is more elemental than remorse. It is a peculiar fact that we lower our eyes whenever we meet the eyes of another. This is not an expression of remorse about having done something wrong, but of shame; in being looked at, we are reminded of our own nakedness, of something that is missing, of the lost wholeness of life.*[25]

Bonhoeffer points to the vicious cycle of shame, finding that the origins of shame lie in the disunion between God, self, and others and that shame, at the same time, perpetuates that disunion. However, he sees a redeeming function of shame in its inherent memory about lost unity and, thus, also about the possibility of restoration. As such, shame is not just an inevitable mark of the human condition but also a "natural" mark of humanity.[26]

Schneider echoes Bonhoeffer's argument when he identifies shame as both characteristic of human brokenness and of human beings' inherent sociality. "Shame symbolizes our mutual involvement. It also reminds us of the dividedness and estrangement that characterize that involvement. To refuse to acknowledge this broken character of our lives leaves us open to that which is demonic and destructive. Because we know ourselves incapable of living together in a community of complete trust and openness more than momentarily, shame is and will be always in order as a mark of our vulnerability as selves both separate from and belonging to a larger

---

25 Bonhoeffer, *Ethics*, 303.
26 See Bonhoeffer, *Ethics*, 173. Bonhoeffer holds that through the fall of humankind, "creation" became "nature," which is the form of life that is directed toward justification, redemption, and justification through Christ.

Whole."²⁷ Similar to Bonhoeffer, Schneider describes shame as a paradox. It is an isolating phenomenon and an alienating emotion. At the same time, shame is a reminder that we belong in community, even as we fear exposure in front of others.

Bonhoeffer reflects theologically on the possibility and practice of restoring community in *Life Together*, which summarizes his thoughts about Christian community based upon the spiritual practices of the seminary community in Finkenwalde, where he taught. He explores the practice of mutual confession as a means of grace and a "breakthrough to community."²⁸ For Bonhoeffer, the restoration of community happens precisely through an act of exposure and humiliation that is at the same time an act of acceptance and inclusion. Shame loses its power when the self moves out of hiding into community. However, such movement is painful and challenging. "In confession, we break through to the genuine community of the cross of Jesus Christ; in confession we confirm our cross. In the profound spiritual and physical pain of humiliation before another believer, which means before God, we experience the cross of Jesus as our deliverance and salvation."²⁹ For Bonhoeffer, the act of confession is not an anonymous encounter where confessor and penitent are separated but is the enacted identification with Jesus's humiliation at the cross and the experience that another is made to be grace for us.

While Bonhoeffer discusses the corruption of the image of God in traditional terms, he does not seem to suggest that the image of God is lost after the so-called fall.³⁰ Although his interpretation of the human condition resonates with modern psychological insight into human development and redefines sin, his vision about the restoration of the image through the Jesus event follows largely a traditional, crucicentric interpretation. Bonhoeffer

---

27 Carl D. Schneider, "The End of Shame," in *The Challenge of Psychology to Faith*, ed. Steven Kepnes and David Tracy (Edinburgh: T & T Clark; New York: Seabury Press, 1982), 38.
28 See Dietrich Bonhoeffer, *Life Together and Prayerbook of the Bible*, trans. Daniel W. Bloesch and James H. Burtness, *Dietrich Bonhoeffer Works*, vol. 5, ed. Geffrey B. Kelly (Minneapolis: Fortress Press, 1996), 109–110.
29 Bonhoeffer, *Life Together*, 111–112.
30 The same terminology that is used in Gen 1:26 to identify human beings as created in the image of God is also used in Gen 9:6 to affirm the value of human life and prohibit the shedding of human blood.

clearly distinguishes between guilt and shame in exploring the human condition, but he almost exclusively uses the language of forgiveness to talk about the restoration of the image of God in human beings and about salvation. While his discussion about confession explicitly uses the language of forgiveness, it implies that shame is overcome by acceptance. The importance of Bonhoeffer's theological response to shame lies in its pioneering role in modern theology and in its transformational and relational approach to understanding the human self, broken community, and the process of restoration.

Shame as the Contradiction of Grace: Paul Tillich

The inability to forgive oneself typically reflects a deep-seated sense of shame rather than guilt. In a widely recognized sermon about Romans 5:20 entitled "You Are Accepted," Tillich explores this experience as a struggle with self-acceptance that involves the denial of grace. Even though Tillich does not name shame explicitly as a psycho-spiritual dynamic in human experience, his sermon is a powerful response to the human condition in general and to shame in particular. He lays the groundwork for his message when he identifies sin not as an action or a series of actions but as a state of existence.

More specifically, as Tillich understands it, sin is a universal state of separation between individuals, from oneself, and from the Ground of Being.[31] He explains the nature of the separation as "the power of estrangement from our true being."[32] Tillich's discussion of sin as separation and the struggle to belong with others, with oneself, and with God points to shame rather than guilt as a defining reality in human experience. In his *Systematic Theology*, he uses the plural "sins" to identify immoral behavior and offenses but reserves the singular "sin" to talk about the human condition in existential terms.[33] In the sermon about Romans 5, Tillich wonders if the meaning of the word is still known and suggests "that 'sin' should never be used in the plural, and that not our sins but rather our *sin* is the great, all-pervading problem of

---

31 See Paul Tillich, *The Shaking of the Foundations* (New York: Charles Scribner's Sons, 1948), 154–155.
32 Paul Tillich, *Systematic Theology*, vol. 3 (Chicago: The University of Chicago Press, 1963), 225.
33 Tillich, *Systematic Theology*, vol. 3, 225.

our life."³⁴ While Tillich uses the terminology of guilt and forgiveness in his sermon, his existential description of human experience in the state of sin reflects the loneliness and the hiddenness of shame. "Who has not, at some time, been lonely in the midst of a social event? The separation from the rest of life is most acute when we are surrounded by it in noise and talk. We realize then much more than in moments of solitude how strange we are to each other, how estranged life is from life. Each one of us draws back into himself. We cannot penetrate the hidden center of another individual; nor can that individual pass through the shroud that covers our own being."³⁵ Furthermore, Tillich's portrayal of the "self without self," being separated from oneself, brings to mind Kohut's description of the narcissistic self, the fragmented self, unable to truly love self or others and moving "against itself through aggression, hate, and despair."³⁶ However, Tillich not only identifies the destructive power of estrangement in individual human experience but suggests that it has also shaped oppressive and destructive systems, such as the Nazi ideology and movement in Germany and racist violence in the United States. Sin, as Tillich describes it, is as much a social and political reality as it is an individual predicament.

Tillich argues against an acceptance of Christian doctrines that are devoid of grace. For redemption to take effect, God's salvation needs to be experienced as the reality of grace which, for Tillich, is the experience of being accepted in spite of who we are and what we have done. Tillich proclaims discerningly the possibility that grace "strikes us when we are in great pain and restlessness. It strikes us when we walk through the dark valley of a meaningless and empty life. It strikes us when we feel that our separation is deeper than usual, because we have violated another life, a life which we loved, or from which we were estranged. It strikes us when our disgust for our own being, our indifference, our weakness, our hostility, and our lack of direction and composure have become intolerable to us."³⁷

Tillich's mention of self-disgust is perhaps the closest he comes to naming shame and self-judgment. God in Christ overcomes the deep

---

34 Tillich, *The Shaking of the Foundations*, 154.
35 Tillich, *The Shaking of the Foundations*, 156–157.
36 Tillich, *The Shaking of the Foundations*, 158.
37 Tillich, *The Shaking of the Foundations*, 161.

separation and, through acceptance, the shame that characterizes the state of sin. Grace, as Tillich proclaims it, occurs in spite of something and "is the *re*union of life with life, the *re*conciliation of the self with itself. Grace is the acceptance of that which is rejected."[38] As Tillich sees it, the healing response to self-contempt is God's gracious acceptance, which in turn enables self-acceptance. When divine grace makes self-acceptance possible, persons do not have to avert their eyes in shame from the gaze of others anymore but "experience the grace of being able to look frankly into the eyes of another, the miraculous grace of reunion of life with life."[39]

Tillich's sermon is an important pastoral theological statement. Although Tillich uses the language of guilt to address the reality of shame, his distinction between forgiveness and acceptance in the context of God's salvific work foreshadows later developments in pastoral theology. Within the theological framework that Tillich suggests, forgiveness addresses "sins," but acceptance addresses "sin" and is the means by which the God event in the Jesus story overcomes separation. Forgiveness is the father's response to the returning son; acceptance is the reality that the elder son is challenged to accept.

Shame and the Struggle to Forgive: John Patton

Pastoral theologian John Patton has examined the effect of shame on the practice of forgiveness. His particular focus is on the struggle or inability to forgive. Patton notes that clients who talk about their own or another person's guilt often struggle profoundly with shame rather than with guilt. While the title of his book *Is Human Forgiveness Possible?* could suggest a focus on guilt, Patton's distinguishes between guilt and shame in the context of forgiveness.

He explains that the "act which calls for forgiveness usually causes guilt in the injuring person and shame in the person injured by that act."[40] To defend themselves from shame, injured persons may use various psychological

---

38 Tillich, *The Shaking of the Foundations*, 156.
39 Tillich, *The Shaking of the Foundations*, 162.
40 John Patton, *Is Human Forgiveness Possible? A Pastoral Care Perspective* (Nashville: Abingdon Press, 1985), 13. Patton's finding is supported by Solomon Schimmel's later study of repentance and forgiveness, which cites research that "found that people who are forgiving of others tend to be more guilt-prone, whereas unforgiving people tend to

defenses. The power to forgive and righteousness are two primary defenses that are supported by religious imperatives. Patton argues that in order to resolve their struggle with forgiveness, injured persons need to surrender their power to forgive or to withhold forgiveness and their righteousness. He identifies pastoral counseling as a praxis of spiritual care that can facilitate the healing process.

Patton holds that power and rage are two closely related defenses against shame. Rage can overtly feel powerful as it takes a threatening stance against another. Other uses of power may be more subtle and even disguise themselves as doubt or a stated lack of ability. Specifically, Patton finds that the expressed inability to forgive is a self-protective use of power. He holds that "striving for power is, perhaps, most frequently a direct attempt to compensate for the sense of inferiority in relation to another and the shame it produces. To the extent one is successful in gaining power over others, one becomes increasingly less vulnerable to future shame."[41] The power to forgive or to withhold forgiveness, in particular, can be an unconscious attempt to maintain a relationship, even if that relationship has been hurtful or abusive. It also defends against shame by elevating the injured person to a position of being able to grant something to or withhold from the perpetrator. As long as forgiveness is withheld, shame may be kept at bay.

Patton makes it clear that these responses are not deliberate decisions; rather, they are unconscious processes within a fragile and injured self. "The essential element in the defensive use of power in relationships between persons," he explains, "is the necessity of one person's being under or over the other. When power is used, there is some attempt to assert or take advantage, and this may be done from the position of power or powerlessness."[42] Such use of power, as Patton understands it, is an expression of sin that denies "our likeness to other persons without having to claim advantages of either power or powerlessness in relation to them."[43]

Patton also identifies righteousness as another defense against shame that is religiously supported. The Greek term for righteousness, *dikaiosynē*,

---

be more shame-prone." Solomon Schimmel, *Wounds Not Healed by Time: The Power of Repentance and Forgiveness* (Oxford & New York: Oxfords University Press, 2002), 59.
41 Patton, *Is Human Forgiveness Possible?*, 75.
42 Patton, *Is Human Forgiveness Possible?*, 87.
43 Patton, *Is Human Forgiveness Possible?*, 87.

appears almost one hundred times in Christian scriptures, primarily in Pauline literature.[44] It can mean "righteousness" or "justice." The imperative to be righteous and to practice righteousness is also ushered in Jesus's teachings, particularly in Matthew's gospel (e.g., Matt 3:15; 5:6; 6:33; 21:32). Patton points out that the biblical concept of righteousness can be misconstrued and employed as a defensive misinterpretation of the biblical concept. Righteousness as a defense lifts a person morally above another, the injured person above the perpetrator. Righteousness may find various expressions. Patton views perfectionism, a frequent response to shame, as one expression of righteousness. Searching and pointing out the guilt of the person who injured oneself is another way to be right. This may be combined with an assertion of innocence or with placing blame on others. What may sound like self-righteousness, Patton emphasizes, "is intended not as a dismissal. Rather it is a call for investigation of a profound human phenomenon—the need to be right in order to protect oneself from what is experienced as a threat of destruction."[45] Just as power and rage can be close allies in defense of a threat, self-righteous rage in the extreme may dehumanize the other and become explosive.

Power, rage, and righteousness when used to defend against shame are significant barriers to human forgiveness. The story about the elder son in Luke 15 may serve as a case study for all three of these defenses. He uses his power to summon information that enrages him and causes him to deny a relationship with his brother. His anger is combined with a righteous attitude that elevates him above the other who made dishonorable and immoral choices while he instead always served his father's interests. Patton concludes what the parable seems to suggest, namely that the "primary pastoral task is bringing the shamed person back into relationship," to rebuild the interpersonal bridge by offering a caring relationship to the one who is estranged and feels separated.[46] Facilitated by an empathic, pastoral-therapeutic connection that helps to establish a secure enough sense of self, surrendering one's power and righteousness and accepting one's shame can create the possibility

---

44 See Karl Kertelge, *"dikaiosynē,"* in *Exegetical Dictionary of the New Testament*, vol. 1, ed. Horst Balz and Gerhard Schneider (Grand Rapids: William B. Eerdmans Publishing Company, 1990), 326.
45 Patton, *Is Human Forgiveness Possible?*, 94.
46 Patton, *Is Human Forgiveness Possible?*, 181.

to re-establish community and discover likeness rather than insisting on separation.

According to Patton, forgiveness is not something to be done or to be encouraged but something to be discovered. Paradoxically, when one surrenders the power to forgive, forgiveness becomes a possibility. "The implication of forgiveness understood as discovery rather than act is that pastoral caring is helping persons not with forgiveness but with the pain of being themselves."[47] Still, Patton's analysis leads to the question of whether forgiveness always means that estrangement is overcome. Can a person discover forgiveness and still choose separation from the one who inflicted the injury? While a person may accept and integrate into her life-narrative traumatic shame resulting from abuse and discover forgiveness, she may still choose for good reasons to stay separated from the perpetrator, remain a stranger rather than offer a relationship. The denial of community may not anymore be a defense against shame but rather a choice in the process of healing from shame. The discovery of forgiveness, thus, may manifest as an interpersonal process that leads to the restoration of a relationship, or it may manifest as an intrapersonal process of releasing power without re-establishing connection with the one who injured the self.

Beyond the Exploitation of Shame in Christian Practice: Stephen Pattison

Pastoral theologian Stephen Pattison has explored the phenomenon of shame with attention to psychological theories, therapeutic responses, and theological perspectives. His primary motivation was to better understand his own experience with shame in relation to religion.[48] Pattison acknowledges that no social organization can avoid shame and that the elimination of shame within Christian communities is not a realistic goal. However, shame is not merely a social reality within the church but also a theological reality because Christian ideas and practices, as Pattison asserts, have instilled shame and exploited shame, perhaps not always deliberately but nevertheless in effect. Going beyond Pattison's analysis, one can argue that Christian ideas and practices have not only shamed individuals and groups

---

47 Patton, *Is Human Forgiveness Possible?*, 185–186.
48 See Pattison, *Shame: Theory, Therapy, Theology*, 310.

within Christian communities but also in society at large and continue to do so. As I am writing these paragraphs, for instance, several Christian religious liberty organizations are promoting legislation aimed at reversing LGBTQ rights in several U.S. states, particularly regulations that stigmatize transgender youth. The shaming impact of such marginalizing initiatives on developing selves cannot be underestimated, and affirming initiatives need to be strengthened, broadened, or developed to provide a healing response.

Pattison points to three aspects of Christian practice that are particularly prone to exploiting shame. First, traditional church discipline can be understood as the threat or infliction of shame in order to enforce religious norms, discourage deviant behavior, and "to maintain obedience together with organizational unity, conformity, and purity."[49] Since shame creates a need for approval and recognition, shamed persons likely want to prove themselves to the community and to God as good followers. Second, evangelism and church maintenance are means for membership recruitment and retention. In deploying the language of shame, Pattison explains, evangelistic efforts may attract those who hope for deliverance from their sense of badness. "The idealized Christian God who can rescue the passive shamed and provide them with a sense of cleanliness and worth in the context of a community that values and wants them is a powerful attraction to the narcissistically wounded and unwanted, the loveless who would be lovely."[50] A third practice, Pattison suggests, is ministerial recruitment of persons who are drawn to become clergy because of a deep-seated sense of shame. The idealized ministerial role of one who is "closely identified with God and set apart may be appealing to people who have an inadequate sense of their own worth and value."[51] The mantle of ministry with all of its significance may promise to cover a depleted and wounded self in search of recognition and eager to compensate for a fundamental sense of shame.

Pattison calls upon theologians to take responsibility for the effects of ideas and symbols that they generate or perpetuate, particularly those that create or intensify shame. He argues for a therapeutic theology, proposing that theological images, symbols, and approaches that encourage

---

49 See Pattison, *Shame: Theory, Therapy, Theology*, 277.
50 Pattison, *Shame: Theory, Therapy, Theology*, 279–280.
51 Pattison, *Shame: Theory, Therapy, Theology*, 280–281.

reconciliation, responsibility, and worth should be amplified, advanced, and broadly disseminated. In order to do this work, Pattison suggests that theology needs to reclaim its function as a subversive practice by creating new metaphors and symbols and by rebalancing the symbolic ecology. Such rebalancing may be accomplished by rediscovering ideas, metaphors, or symbols that have been forgotten or disregarded in Christian teaching or by reinterpreting traditional symbols and stories. "With some courage and imagination," Pattison insists, "theology has the possibility of engaging with human hurt and healing in new and creative ways, enabling rather than imposing meanings, symbols and images that enlighten rather than imprison."[52] Pattison offers six fragmentary images, motifs, and themes to respond theologically to shame.

Pattison juxtaposes an emphasis on fallenness and sinfulness in Western theology with the fundamental goodness and value of humanity and creation. The theme of goodness and value emphasizes God's blessing and ongoing creative engagement with the world. As people "join in the work of creation," Pattison points out, "they manifest aspects of the image and likeness of the creator."[53] Pattison argues against the glorification of a single saving death. Rather, Jesus's death must be understood in the context of his life, which "consisted in creating a living concrete community of 'saving' relationships in which people find themselves and each other."[54] Thus, salvation and redemption happen in a living community as an ongoing, creative, and reconciling process.

Pattison's third motif is closely related. Sin is not personal disobedience but is damage to persons, and salvation is the compassionate engagement with alienated and shamed persons and communities. Fourthly, God is not a despot or super-father who demands obedience and submission. Rather, God should be imagined in metaphors that can hold God's immanence and transcendence and reflect divine loving presence. At the same time, theology needs to be able to name God's absence, that God's face is hidden from humanity and does not gaze upon the self with scrutinizing, divine super-vision. Even though this might seem like a contradiction to the

---

52 Pattison, *Shame: Theory, Therapy, Theology*, 300.
53 Pattison, *Shame: Theory, Therapy, Theology*, 301.
54 Pattison, *Shame: Theory, Therapy, Theology*, 302.

previous theme, Pattison argues that fragmentary and "fragmented images of God might contribute more to the healing of the fragmented than the unitary God of orthodoxy. They may enable us to move more effectively toward divinity by recognizing and giving face to each other."[55] Finally, Pattison highlights Jesus's ministry of acceptance and inclusion that created a new community while cautioning against idealizing Jesus and ignoring the ambivalent effects of his teachings and acts. This new community, the dominion of God that Jesus announced, welcomed "socially marginalized and stigmatized—that is, objectively defiled, shamed—people such as lepers and demoniacs, being healed by Jesus."[56] Recognizing their personhood and responding to their suffering and need to belong, Jesus effectively countered shame by integrating shamed and excluded individuals into a religious community (cf. Luke 17:12–21).

Pattison does not arrive at a comprehensive or conclusive approach to shame but presents a tentative, interdisciplinary, working understanding of shame as "toxic unwantedness" that results in social and personal alienation.[57] Pattison argues that the Church has contributed to the toxic unwantedness of individuals and groups through various practices, and that Christian communities have an important role in the restoration of wounded and marginalized individuals and groups because the healing of the self comes in and through human community. Pattison views the tentative nature of theological knowledge about shame as an opportunity rather than a liability. "The way lies open," he concludes, "for Christians to develop new and more sophisticated, complex theories of theology and action around shame."[58]

Shame and the Conversion to Genuine Presence: Neil Pembroke

In conversation with the dialogical philosophies of Martin Buber and Gabriel Marcel, pastoral counselor Neil Pembroke offers a theory of pastoral presence to examine how failure to be genuinely present in pastoral counseling along with defective modes of caring can generate shame both within

---

55 Pattison, *Shame: Theory, Therapy, Theology*, 306.
56 Pattison, *Shame: Theory, Therapy, Theology*, 306.
57 See Pattison, *Shame: Theory, Therapy, Theology*, 182–183.
58 Pattison, *Shame: Theory, Therapy, Theology*, 228.

the counselee and the counselor. Pembroke proposes that shame can serve a redemptive function, however, when it induces a movement of critical introspection in spiritual care providers to contemplate not merely the actual self that failed in being present but also the potential self that has a capacity for genuine presence and is prepared to make decisive changes.[59] Theologically speaking, such redemptive introspection is the work of the Holy Spirit, which, according to the story of Pentecost (Acts 2:1–2), is the symbol for the God event that creates connection in spite of barriers. God's spirit works through failure and shame to connect the self with its possibility and, if that possibility is realized, with other persons through genuine presence. The notion of the potential self is distinguished from the concept of an ideal self, which is often discussed when exploring shame dynamics. The ideal self is a false, pretentious, and possibly grandiose sense of self that covers a defective self-image. The potential self, on the other hand, is the self a person is willing and able to become through self-investment and intentional efforts to change.

Pembroke's theory of pastoral presence is at the heart of his model of pastoral counseling. The notion of pastoral presence by itself is a rather vague concept that can mean various things to different practitioners. Without specification, it is an almost meaningless description of a spiritual care intervention. However, if it is examined and defined functionally, the notion of pastoral presence can conceptualize spiritual care interventions in a meaningful way. Pembroke holds that genuine, caring presence is an authentic encounter in which I and Thou share "in being, in life, in the life of the other."[60] More specifically, he identifies availability and confirmation as key functions in the practice of pastoral presence.

Compassionate availability, according to Pembroke, "involves receiving the other and her hopes and fears, her joys and sorrows, *chez soi*. In the case of compassionate understanding, one draws the pain and distress of the other into one's innermost sphere."[61] Drawing on Marcel's philosophy, Pembroke explains that availability is an openness to the claims of another,

---

59 See Neil Pembroke, *The Art of Listening: Dialogue, Shame, and Pastoral Care* (Edinburgh & New York: T. T. Clark/Handsel Press; Grand Rapids: William B. Eerdmans Publishing Company, 2002), 8–9.
60 Pembroke, *The Art of Listening*, 11.
61 Pembroke, *The Art of Listening*, 52.

a hospitable receptivity that "involves a readiness to make available one's personal centre [sic], one's innermost domain. . . . Receptivity means that I invite the other to 'be at home' with me."[62] Availability is not an invitation to share everything about oneself with another in a caregiving situation because such exchanges would demonstrate a lack of professional boundaries rather than an ability to be present with another. Rather, Pembroke identifies availability as a process that clinical pastoral education has long identified as the use of self that allows another's being and experience to resonate deeply within oneself. Pembroke identifies two other qualities of availability: fidelity and belonging. Fidelity is a faithful commitment to another over time. It is a promise to join another that will not be questioned nor revoked. Belonging to another is the act of giving myself in service to the other. While the concept of belonging could suggest a state of servility or servitude, it is ideally a shared experience and should be considered an expression of freedom rather than of disenfranchisement.[63]

The concept of confirmation is rooted in Buber's philosophy and refers to a process of assisting another in realizing her potential. Confirmation is a key element in dialogical relationships and "is grounded in an acknowledgment of otherness. As I enter into dialogue with the other, I accept her uniqueness and particularity and struggle with her in the release of her potential as a person."[64] Confirmation as a function of pastoral presence facilitates personal growth and wholeness in the other person against the forces of fragmentation and division. In Buber's philosophy, confirmation is a relationship that involves both acceptance and confrontation. "Confirmation begins with acceptance," Pembroke explains, "but it also includes wrestling with the other against himself as he grows into his potential."[65] Even as the process may be confrontational, it must not impose a direction upon another person's growth. Rather, it is a dialogical movement toward psychological wholeness and facilitates the release and realization of what has been present all along but restrained within another. Confirmation as a therapeutic intervention aids the discovery of one's potential self.

---

62 Pembroke, *The Art of Listening*, 21
63 See Pembroke, *The Art of Listening*, 23–27.
64 Pembroke, *The Art of Listening*, 31.
65 Pembroke, *The Art of Listening*, 79.

For Pembroke, pastoral presence as the practice of availability and confirmation holds the promise to counter shame. At the same time, failure to be genuinely present to a care seeker can perpetuate or induce shame. "Where there is a distorted presence," holds Pembroke, "a failure to be available, there is a potential for a high level of embarrassment and shame. When a shame-prone personality experiences a lack of attention, a failure in self-giving, she is confirmed in her sense of inferiority and worthlessness."[66] Inherent in the experience of shame is disconfirmation, a sense of being reduced and not known.

The failure to be present to a care seeker, however, not only has the potential to induce shame in that person but also in the spiritual caregiver as well. For the caregiver, the shame experience may communicate a lack of competence or may be due to a more general sense of having failed another person or violated one's professional values. Drawing upon theologian James Fowler's work, Pembroke suggests that such pastoral shame ultimately might not cause a lasting disruption in the relationship but can motivate a change, a conversion, toward genuine presence and, thus, toward establishing an effective, compassionate, and caring relationship. Shame, he explains, can activate the reforming function of the conscience.[67] Through contemplation, a self-examination that does not get trapped in self-judgment, the spiritual care provider can lean into God's reforming power and initiate a course correction in relationship with the other person to share in their being, their life, and their pain.

Pembroke's discussion is somewhat unique in that it addresses shame within spiritual care encounters as it affects both participants in the relationship. Furthermore, it focuses on the damaging effects of shame as

---

66 Pembroke, *The Art of Listening*, 161.
67 See Pembroke, *The Art of Listening*, 205. Using the notion of conversion, Pembroke draws upon Karl Barth's moral interpretation of the role of shame in human experience, albeit without Barth's Christological orientation. According to Barth, the example of humanity that Christ provides through his life shames us and signals the need for a saving conversion. "The terrible paradox of his sin in this form is," writes Barth about the human experience confronted by the Jesus event, "that if he refuses the man Jesus, he does not refuse only this man and His (and therefore his own God) but he also refuses to be himself, breaking free from his own reality, losing himself in the attempt to assert himself, and thus becoming his own pitiful shadow." Karl Barth, *Church Dogmatics*, vol. IV.2, trans. G.W. Bromiley, ed. G.W. Bromiley and T. F. Torrance (London & New York: T. & T. Clark, 1958), 408.

well as on what Pembroke identifies as the redemptive or reforming function of shame. Pembroke's main conclusion is that a therapeutic effect in spiritual care encounters is not achieved as much through skillful counseling techniques and expert psychological assistance as it is through the quality of a relationship that is characterized by self-giving, emotional availability, and fidelity that genuinely values and invests in another. A question that must be asked, however, and remains unanswered in Pembroke's analysis is why shame might function differently in the one who seeks care and the one who responds to that need. While shame may increase psychological and spiritual pain in the care seeker, according to Pembroke, it may serve a redemptive function that motivates change toward genuine presence in the care provider. The question is why it would not have the potential to serve a redeeming function for the care seeker and, if it did, how such a redeeming function could be facilitated for another person.

Shame Transformed: Christina-Maria Bammel

Theologian Christina-Maria Bammel maintains that the study of shame as a theological task does not aim to develop a distinct theological theory. She holds that the task of theology is to enter into interdisciplinary dialogue and use theoretical insights from other disciplines to shed light on its own questions about God and God's relationship with humanity.[68] Part of the theological engagement with shame, according to Bammel, needs to be a debate with other disciplines about their assertions regarding Christianity's complicity in creating shame-based systems and cultures. While she finds some clues in her own study that both shame and guilt have been functionalized in Christian communities for religious purposes, she argues that sweeping claims by other disciplines about Christianity's shame-orientation need to be engaged in a differentiated manner through theological reflection. Such reflection needs to consider the emotional and psychological aspects of shame as well as the relevance of shame for an ontological understanding of the human condition.

---

68 See Christina-Maria Bammel, *Aufgetane Augen–Aufgedecktes Gesicht: Theologische Studien zur Scham im interdisziplinärem Gespräch* (Gütersloh: Gütersloher Verlagshaus, 2005), 15.

If theology claims to make true statements about the real human condition in relation to God, Bammel argues, theologians need to pay as much attention to shame as they do to guilt. Both can provide information about the existential constitution of individuals and communities, albeit in different ways. Shame, as a defining aspect of the human condition and an emotion that is closely connected to the experience of embodiment, particularly highlights those two aspects—embodiment and emotion—as theological themes and necessary subjects of theological attention and analysis.[69] Embodiment is a central aspect of the human condition. Only the embodied self can enter into community and experience the world as a person with others. At the same time, embodiment can subject human beings to exploitation and may reduce another to a mere object under the gaze of someone who refuses to see the person. Both of those possibilities as well as other experiences of one's embodied self can create suffering and become a source of shame. Under God's gracious gaze (Num 6:24–26), Bammel proposes, human beings can affirm their bodies, their physical selves, as a gift and express themselves as embodied creatures without shame and realize their purpose in life and in relationship to their environment.[70]

Bammel identifies human beings as intrinsically emotional and affective, which means that they are also fragile and vulnerable. She references, on the one hand, the Protestant-reformed tradition that insists that faith must not be mistaken for an emotion and, on the other hand, points to the fact that faith is deeply connected to a variety of emotions and that the language of faith reflects that reality. Thus, Bammel asks how faith influences and shapes human emotions, including shameful emotions, and finds that the theologies of Schleiermacher and Barth stand out as Christian theories that explore the affective structure of human existence affirmingly.[71]

Schleiermacher's exploration about the Christian faith attempts to present Christian doctrines in a comprehensive way, but he identifies faith not primarily as a belief system but as religious experience with affective power. It is a pious consciousness that seeks to relate to God and a feeling of absolute dependence. Schleiermacher never completely abandoned the

---

69 See Bammel, *Aufgetane Augen*, 188–189.
70 See Bammel, *Aufgetane Augen*, 196.
71 See Bammel, *Aufgetane Augen*, 198–199.

Moravian piety of his upbringing and held that faith is a certain emotional state that is shaped by the experience of salvation through the Jesus event.[72] For Barth, as Bammel summarizes his position, God's work of salvation in the story of the Christ demonstrates God's philanthropy and acceptance of human beings as free counterparts, who are affirmed in their full humanity, including the affective structure of their existence. Human freedom includes the freedom to feel deeply in relationship to God, fellow creatures, and the world that surrounds us and where we belong.[73] The experience of faith through which human beings can be themselves before God without pretense invites, on the one hand, the flourishing of the emotional life and, on the other hand, means that human beings are free to feel the spectrum of emotions, joy and pain, anger and fear, love and shame.

Bammel understands the meaning of reconciliation with God and the forgiveness of sin not as an eradication of shame or guilt but as a transformative event that changes the human experience of shame. When God turns toward humanity, she explains, God does not turn toward an ideal of what humanity should be. Rather, through the Jesus event, God gets involved with the reality of human existence, which is largely characterized by shame and its consequences.[74] While the God event in the Jesus story encounters human reality that is defined by shame, human beings cannot face their shame, since this would mean the exposure of their sin. Drawing upon Barth's understanding of reconciliation, Bammel argues that God's saving activity in Christ is a paradoxical event that, on the one hand, shames human beings by exposing their sin and true existence and, on the other hand, frees them to experience shame in healing ways. The worth they experience through the God event that calls upon them in the Jesus story counters alienating shame. Salvation, according to Bammel, can thus be understood as an affective experience, or more precisely, as a fundamental change in how human beings feel about themselves and their existence. Rather than being an alienating factor, in the context of salvation through the Jesus event, shame means facing oneself openly and honestly as a sinner and ultimately facilitates for

---

72 See Bammel, *Aufgetane Augen*, 201.
73 See Bammel, *Aufgetane Augen*, 203–204.
74 See Bammel, *Aufgetane Augen*, 273.

human beings the experience of grace and a transformed relationship with God and with their own shame.[75]

In Bammel's analysis, shame functions not only in the context of salvation but also in the process of sanctification. Therefore, it has theological-ethical relevance for a Christian lifestyle. She holds that the experience of shame leads to certain behaviors that express a person's relationship with God, self, and others.[76] Since shame is an essential experience and expression of concrete human existence, theological ethics needs to account for its meaning with regard to a Christian lifestyle in general. For Bammel, though, the fact that shame as such is ambivalent and can be toxic, alienating, and an expression of sin, on the one hand, and can serve protective and potentially connective functions, on the other hand, makes its use as an ethical category more difficult. However, this does not disqualify shame by default as an ethical benchmark. The fact that shame experiences are more frequent in modern Western culture than boundary violations that conjure up guilt suggests that shame indeed has ethical relevance.[77]

Bammel highlights three aspects of a theological understanding of shame that each have distinct ethical implications.[78] First, God liberates humanity from shame that is an expression of sin, which means that human beings do not need to hide anymore from God and others but can reveal themselves. Ethically, this means that human beings do not have to be self-centered and enact self-protective behavior that alienates them from community and destroys a live-giving and life-affirming ethos. Second, faith needs to be lived in a world where human beings still live as sinners and in community with sinners and will experience and encounter shame. The ethical implications are that shame can function in service of repentance and thus renew the experience of God's grace and thereby help us to see others in the same light. At the same time, shame may have a prospective and stabilizing ethical function in signaling a potential violation of values or moral boundaries. Finally, faith in a God who liberates from shame as an expression of sin affirms the totality and concreteness of human existence,

---

75 See Bammel, *Aufgetane Augen*, 274.
76 See Bammel, *Aufgetane Augen*, 282.
77 See Bammel, *Aufgetane Augen*, 283.
78 See Bammel, *Aufgetane Augen*, 284–286.

including experiences of shame, as valued, cared for, and preserved by God. Ethically, this perspective confirms the intrinsic value of human life and mandates respect for and the protection of human existence in its various expressions.

Bammel's conclusion that shame is not only a destructive and alienating force in human experience but also a constitutive aspect of human existence and Christian experience goes beyond a distinction between disgrace shame and discretion shame. It suggests implications for a praxis of spiritual care that are not specified or explored. While she does not explicitly develop a constructive theology to guide spiritual care practitioners, her work has ethical implications for exploring an understanding of the human condition and experiences that are shaped by various dimensions of shame.

An Affective Theology of Shame: Stephanie Arel

Pastoral theologian Stephanie Arel argues that understanding the role of shame in the formation of an embodied Christian self is crucial to responsibly constructing a theological anthropology.[79] While she finds that religion and theology along with cultural influences contribute to the creation of shamed bodies, the relationship between theology and shame is not one-dimensional; rather, it is complex. "The project of uncovering and highlighting where shame appears in Christian language and practice is a formidable one. Shame once recognized is often so painful it readily escapes our view. But envisioning shame as a part of the Christian self recognizes the whole self and lifts up the reality that theology both participates in and potentially disinters shame from the Christian self."[80]

While Arel points out that shame as an affect serves biological, neurological, and social purposes, she focuses on toxic, interred shame and its malignant effects. A healing response to the destructive effects of shame, according to Arel, requires a process that is diametrically opposed to what shame experiences typically trigger within the self. Rather than hiding and masking the self "to repair its toxicity, shame must be uncovered, faced, and addressed, not simply distinguished by positive affect or eradicated by

---

79 See Stephanie Arel, *Affect Theory, Shame, and Christian Formation* (London & Cham, Switzerland: Palgrave Macmillan, 2016), 2.
80 Arel, *Affect Theory, Shame, and Christian Formation*, 2.

treatment modalities. Shame displays the self at its most vulnerable—that is, socially in relationship to another person, and theologically to God."[81]

Utilizing affect theory and trauma studies to challenge the dominance of guilt in theological anthropologies, Arel proposes to formulate an affective theology of shame that considers that shame originates in the body and can become interred in the body. Arel views the human body as a source of flowing and changing energy and as the affective center of life, where shame plays a central role in shaping the embodied self.[82] Combining a biological perspective with a social perspective, affect theory takes a holistic view of human experience and postulates an innate connection between body and mind. "The immediacy of affects," explains Arel, " . . . negates differentiation between the self and the world. The events of the external environment stimulate bodily affects, usually initially without our conscious awareness, connecting us to that which lies outside of us."[83] Drawing upon psychiatrist Donald Nathanson's explanation of the affect system, Arel explains how, through conscious discernment and naming, an affect becomes a feeling, and how a feeling grows into an emotion when it aligns with a narrative that conveys meaning. Theology plays a role in this process because it explores and interprets the Christian narrative, which in turn is in Christian formation one factor that shapes personal narratives and thus contributes to defining the meaning of emotions. Arel points out that affects are crucial for the development of human attachments and in Christian formation throughout the lifespan, and that "shame, as an affect, stimulated and modulated in relationship must also be repaired in relationship."[84]

Furthermore, Arel highlights that the causative connection between trauma and shame may be missed if shame is concealed by other effects of trauma, as it often is. She explains that shame is frequently the body's physiological response to trauma in an interminable spiral where shame leads to more shame and to the denial that shame can possibly be alleviated, which may find expression in acts of violence. The task of theology is to pay attention and to envision the possibility of a healing response to shame.

---

81 Arel, *Affect Theory, Shame, and Christian Formation*, 3.
82 See Arel, *Affect Theory, Shame, and Christian Formation*, 24.
83 Arel, *Affect Theory, Shame, and Christian Formation*, 26.
84 Arel, *Affect Theory, Shame, and Christian Formation*, 31.

> *Theology as a socially relevant practice has a responsibility to those of us who experience shame. . . . Attention to innate shame's function would begin to disinter shame, fostering love, and attuned attachment rather than perpetuating cycles of toxic shame, domination, and violence. In this way, instead of the perpetuation of shame or trauma, something radically different could result. The more attention theology devotes to understanding shame's role in fostering or severing attachments to others and to God as well as comprehending its function in contributing to motivational structures of violence, the more capable tradition and practice will be at nurturing the whole self, in whom shame plays a natural part.*[85]

Arel proposes a therapeutic theology that operates both with self-awareness about the shame-inducing history and potential of Christian teachings and with awareness of shame dynamics in the formation of the Christian self.

Drawing on Augustine's theological anthropology and examining Niebuhr's treatment of sin, guilt, and shame, Arel argues for an affectively attuned theology that understands the ritualistic and therapeutic power of touch as a potentially healing response to shame. "Nurturing and nonjudgmental touch stimulates the interest that shame truncates, rendering a body both present and vulnerable or exposed. The restoration of interest or positive affect opens up the potential for the transformation of a traumatic past narrative about shame."[86] However, a healing response does not imply that shame can be eradicated from human experience. Arel treats shame as an innate affect that may be transformed or repaired in its toxic expressions but remains a necessary part of the affective life. Toxic shame sabotages secure attachments, including the Christian self's attachment to God, while innate shame points toward relationship and seeks attachment. For Augustine, as Arel points out, shame is a primary force that steers human beings toward God's grace. "Paradoxically, shame, as a corporeal affect, in its innate social function draws Christians closer to each other and God. Deeply interred shame buried by other affects and maladaptive behaviors

---

85 Arel, *Affect Theory, Shame, and Christian Formation*, 55.
86 Arel, *Affect Theory, Shame, and Christian Formation*, 138.

must be disinterred for shame to emerge and so to allow for attachment."[87] Arel discusses empathic engagement as a therapeutic practice to address and redress shame and holds that empathy incapacitates the interment of shame in the body. She sees empathy as foundational to Christian formation and locates it theologically in the mandate to love each other.[88] Through empathic engagement that values another for who they are, the self can risk being known and can thus experience a safe attachment.

Arel's pastoral theology points to the innate and essential nature of shame and its impact on embodied human existence when it becomes toxic and buried within the self, particularly when it correlates with trauma. Her understanding of the therapeutic effect of empathic engagement to repair shame underlies the principles that guide and form Christian community that can nurture the self toward wholeness. While Arel clearly locates empathy within Christian praxis, her analysis does not explore how the larger theological narrative in Christianity and the Jesus story in particular can offer perspectives that foster empathic engagement.

Sin, Shame, and Original Blessing

Referencing the yahwistic creation account as the master narrative about humanity's fall into sin, Christian theology has used the language of sin to understand the human condition in a state of alienation. The prominent understanding of sin views it as a willful act of disobedience against God's command and as a decision for human self-determination in rebellion against God. One must distinguish, however, between sin as act and sin as being, or as Tillich puts it, between behavioral sins and sin as an existential condition. Behavioral sins are acts that create or perpetuate division, fragmentation, and separation within oneself, between persons, and in relationship to the God who calls upon us. Many forms of violence, particularly if they aim to dominate or inflict abuse, can be identified as behavioral sins. Behavioral sins may be primarily identified with guilt, both in legal and psychological terms. Existential sin is a state of existence characterized by shame and the experience of alienation and fragmentation. However, shame and sin are not

---

87 Arel, *Affect Theory, Shame, and Christian Formation*, 84.
88 See Arel, *Affect Theory, Shame, and Christian Formation*, 172.

the same. Just as we need to distinguish between sin and suffering, we need to distinguish between sin and shame. Shame is the diminishing and alienating effect of existential sin and thus can be considered a form of suffering that results from sin.

Donald Capps's pastoral theological analysis of shame illustrates the distinction between sin as act and sin as being. In *The Depleted Self: Sin in a Narcissistic Age*, Capps finds that "guilt has tended to function as a convenient cover story, enabling Christian theology to ignore the experience of shame and the threat that it poses for the self and its struggle for survival."[89] Capps contends that shame rather than guilt is a primary source of the tragic estrangement from self and others, including God, and that this reality is common to both the narcissistic experience and to a Christian understanding of sin. Thus, a theology of shame alongside a theology of guilt is needed to understand the human self in its problematic state of sin. Capps sees a particular need for theology to pay attention to the problematics of the divided self, the defensive self, and the depleted self. "If theology is to be a resource of healing," Capps states, "it needs to center . . . on the problematics of the self. This, however, is only one part of its role, for theology, if it is to function as therapeutic wisdom, needs also to address the 'therapeutics of the self,' that is, the question of what it would mean for us to experience wholeness."[90]

All three of the "problematics of the self" that Capps highlights as characteristic of the state of sin are rooted in shame experiences.[91] The divided self is the self that is estranged from itself, or to use Tillich's term, the self without itself. The division within the self has been described in various ways: as the incongruency between the ideal self and the real self, as a distinction between the false self and the true self, or, in Kohut's terms, as a split between the grandiose self and the idealizing self. The defensive self focuses on strategies to avoid further shame, be it through rage, striving for power or perfection, internal withdrawal, or the transfer of blame. Finally, the depleted self is marked by the long-term effects of shame. "The words

---

89 Donald Capps, *The Depleted Self: Sin in a Narcissistic Age* (Minneapolis: Fortress Press, 1993), 85.
90 Capps, *The Depleted Self*, 100.
91 See Capps, *The Depleted Self*, 86–87.

that capture this deeper, inner experience of shame," explains Capps, "are not humiliation and embarrassment, but words like empty, exhausted, drained, demoralized, depressed, deflated, bereft, needy, starving, apathetic, passive, and weak."[92] All three problematic self-states reflect experiences of separation rather than transgression. Capps concludes that "a theology of shame centers on the sin of apathy and explores the manner in which the Christian tradition has supported but also frustrated the work of self-repair."[93] Apathy is a state of indifference and disconnection, a lack of emotions and literally an inability to engage one's experience and one's suffering as well as the suffering of others. Capps's argument contradicts a popular view that pathological narcissism is rooted in a false and exaggerated pride or hubris and suggests that, rather, a lack of empathy characterizes the narcissistic experience.

Capps's analysis further suggests that a contextual understanding of sin needs to consider cultural developments and dialogue with contemporary theories about the human condition. In the context of narcissistic culture and a prevailing theology that functionalizes shame, an understanding of sin needs to focus on threats to relationality and to wholeness within the self. Such understanding identifies sin not primarily as a condition that results from moral failure or from refusal to confess a belief in God and obey divine commands, but as a state of shame-based estrangement from one's own self, from others, and from God who calls upon us. In other words, sin is not just a theological construct but also a psychological force. A shame-focused theology of sin can support such perspectives by explaining this dynamic in the context of a theological anthropology. The early Christian teaching, for example, that described the state of sin in anatomical terms as *cor curvum in se*—the heart curved in on itself—captures the psychological experience of narcissism and the emotional pain that characterizes shame.

Foundational biblical narratives support a focus on shame because of their understanding of sin in the human experience and suggest that a contemporary, contextual theological perspective regarding shame is warranted. An awareness of shame dynamics, which shape the relationship between humans and their Creator, is clearly reflected in one of the origin narratives about the creation of humans. As philosopher of religion John Hick points

---

92 Capps, *The Depleted Self*, 99.
93 Capps, *The Depleted Self*, 99–100.

out, the mythical story about humanity's rise to self-consciousness in the Garden of Eden attempts to convey an existential truth about "the fact that ordinary human life is lived in alienation from God and hence from one's neighbors and from the natural environment."[94] The origin story explains a radical transition in human experience from being naked and not ashamed to becoming self-conscious, which means shame-conscious, needing to hide and to cover oneself. Despite its explicit reference to shame, the story became the basis for a theory of sin as a hereditary state of disobedience and guilt that became widely influential and demanded a sacrificial solution.

The notion of original sin developed early in the history of the church and influenced dogmatic theology, theological anthropology, and theories of atonement for centuries. The view that, along with individual transgressions, inherited sin affected all of humanity by being transferred from generation to generation became prominent in variations across Western theological traditions and across centuries. The classical teaching about original sin that stems from the controversy between Augustine and Pelagius has no evidential basis in the origin narrative but nevertheless has contributed to a widely accepted individualistic understanding of sin that has ignored its social dimension. If sin is individually inherited, then social systems and structures do not need to be addressed as sinful or redeemed. Rather, willful individual persons or groups of individuals become the focus of salvation from sin and the objects of conversion.

The concept of original sin attempted to explain the universality and pervasive nature of sin by explaining the transmission of sin through sexual intercourse. However, given the pervasiveness of shame in the human experience and the psychological mechanisms of its transmission through empathic failures in relationships, shame needs to be considered as the principal dimension of sin. An understanding of shame as the diminishing and alienating effect of sin supports an individual perspective of sin as a state of fragmentation and alienation and can also affirm sin as a social reality that cannot be reduced to individual choices. While sin may be a personal experience, it is also perpetuated through social structures and systems and,

---

94 John Hick, *An Interpretation of Religion: Human Responses to the Transcendent* (New Haven & London: Yale University Press, 1989), 349.

in turn, affects and shapes those systems and structures. Consequently, an understanding of salvation must include a vision for social transformation and practices that facilitate the conversion of unjust power structures.

While Capps refers to cultural forces that shape the human experience of sin, he does not address the role of power structures, nor does he explore the transformation of social inequity from a theological perspective. Rather, salvation and the therapeutic response to the human condition are focused on individuals. The biblical narratives he references about the woman who anointed Jesus (Luke 7:36–50) and had her self-trust affirmed by him as well as the crucifixion story about the new bond of love between Jesus's mother and the "beloved disciple" (John 19:26–27) both emphasize an individual perspective of restoration. Capps finds that biblical wisdom supports the notion of a therapeutic response to shame through mirroring, affirming, or confirming presence and attention to the self. Self-affirmation is essentially an individual's claim to be a self and have value, and it is confirmed and sustained by others through experiences of empathic care and compassion.

From a theological perspective, human nature is intrinsically relational. The biblical creation stories make this point not only through portraying humanity in a state of separation through the language of sin but also through the language of blessing. In contrast to the yahwistic account in Genesis 3, the priestly creation narrative does not describe in any detail the creation of human beings. It simply states that human beings were created male and female "in the image of God" and blessed by the creator, who pronounced creation and creatures as "very good" (Gen 1:27–31). However, the doctrine of original sin insisted without any scriptural basis that the image of God was corrupted through the fall of humanity into sin. In fact, the Genesis narratives nowhere suggest corruption nor that the image of God was lost. The fact that the priestly and the yahwistic creation stories stand alongside each other in the Hebrew scriptures may simply testify to the reality that both original blessing and human sin, goodness and shame with guilt coexist in the human experience.

The image of God has been interpreted in Christian theology in different ways, from explanations about physical resemblance and the capacity to reason to being given dominion over the earth and the exercise of freedom. I interpret the image of God as humanity's inherent relationality and its freedom to be in relationship. As Bonhoeffer explains in almost paradoxical terms, freedom is not a human quality or possession; rather, "it is a relation and nothing else. To be more precise, freedom is a relation between two persons. Being free means 'being-free-for-the-other,' because I am bound to the other. Only by being in relation with the other am I free."[95] Human beings are created for relationship. While sin creates a disruption within relationships with the creator and other humans, it does not erase the relational nature of human beings. Shame inhibits relational freedom, but it does not eliminate or negate it. As Bonhoeffer states, shame points to the loss of wholeness and the possibility of restored relationships.

The affirmation that human beings were created "very good" (Gen 1:31) in the image of God is humanity's original blessing. This blessing, in turn, stands alongside experiences of guilt and shame. The language of blessing speaks both about an act and a gift. As an act, blessing gives affirmation, empowers potential, and points toward possibilities. As a gift, blessing is received as an affirmation of one's intrinsic value as a person; it confirms that one is loved and belongs. The symbolism of original blessing and the image of God in human beings points to the potential to move beyond the diminishing and alienating effects of shame and to the possibility of healing and human fulfillment in relationships. To be sure, shame will always be part of the emotional human repertoire and the human condition. However, the notion of humanity's original blessing as the image of God suggests the possibility of proleptic wholeness where the effects of toxic shame are overcome. Rather than feeling alienated and diminished by self-judgment and a sense of inadequacy and worthlessness when moving toward proleptic wholeness, persons are affirmed and confirmed in their intrinsic value and dignity. They can risk intimacy in mutual relationships of care.

Conclusion

The foundational biblical narratives about the creation of humankind and the experience of alienation speak about the role of shame and the meaning of humanity's original blessing. However, neither concept has become influential in Christian teaching. Jesus emphasized the co-existence of shame and

---

95 Bonhoeffer, *Creation and Fall*, 63.

guilt within the human condition, but Christian theologies rarely hold the tension between those emotions. Instead, guilt has become the focus.

Recent theological analyses of shame engage in interdisciplinary dialogue and identify the universal nature of shame, its role in sabotaging experiences of grace and in functioning as reminder of possible wholeness, and its multi-faceted functions within human existence. While shame often functions in destructive and alienating ways, it also is a constitutive aspect of the human existence and Christian experience. A theological understanding of sin as a state that is primarily characterized by shame rather than as an act of disobedience or rebellion can account for individual as well as social dimensions of sin. Such an understanding of sin can also account for dynamics of redemption beyond classical atonement theories and rituals of forgiveness. However, theological models about the human condition and the possibility for restoration need to identify and understand more distinctively the resolution to toxic, diminishing, and alienating shame both in terms of their theological significance and in terms of a therapeutic praxis.

Part Four

EMPATHY

ASSESSMENT IS ESSENTIAL for clinical care but is not an end in itself. An assessment is ultimately worthless if it is not followed by *care-full* attention to the condition that has been identified as limiting, debilitating, or destructive. In clinical practice, a therapeutic response is typically spelled out in a plan of care that specifies outcomes and needed therapeutic interventions. In the previous section of the book, I assessed the human condition as afflicted by alienating shame. In this section, I explore empathy as an effective therapeutic response to the experience of shame.

The term *empathy* is widely used with various connotations that do not always reflect its clinical meaning and it needs to be defined clearly in reference to clinical practice. Empathy is not a general warm and fuzzy feeling toward another or an understanding of another person's situation by referencing one's own experience. Rather, it is a combination of a hospitable and accepting attitude, emotional intelligence and understanding, and therapeutic skills and techniques. All three aspects work together to understand and engage another person's experience and inner world in a way that feels intimate, communicates a sense of being known, and invites self-exploration.

Empathy is not only a psychological or therapeutic concept but can serve as a theological construct to understand the God event in the Jesus story. Christian theology is in its essence an incarnational theology, which affirms that the *logos* became flesh and entered into and shared human experience to effect salvation. Salvation, in turn, is the possibility for whole relationships with fellow creatures and creator. Salvation is based in the incarnational God event that the gospel narratives portray and that other books in the New Testament interpret.

It was not first and foremost Jesus's death that offered salvation by way of sacrifice. Rather, his life, including his death, was a saving God event that responded to the human condition in a state of alienation through shame. The Jesus event is God's empathy toward humanity and embodies God's accepting and transforming activity. The symbols of incarnation and resurrection in the Jesus story express that the God event in that story ultimately and intimately connects with human experience to create conditions for redemption, the transformation of trauma, and the flourishing of life.

7

CLINICAL THEORIES AND APPLICATIONS

EMPATHY IS BOTH a general quality of being present with others in everyday relationships and a specific and skilled therapeutic approach. Empathic attunement is a clinical skill that can inform an experience-near understanding about the human condition by attempting to know in approximation what another person might be experiencing. It is at once an introspective and an interpersonal process that is the basis for a therapeutic relationship. For that reason, empathy is, at times, misrepresented or misunderstood as a form of identification or unconscious merger between self and another. Defining empathy in clinical practice and distinguishing it from other psychological processes that combine intrapersonal and interpersonal aspects is therefore essential to understand its therapeutic use and function.

Empathy is not an unconscious or spontaneous reaction to another but a deliberate, intentional effort to know about the embodied, emotional experience of another person and about their inner world. The ancient Greek term *empátheia* literally means "in-feeling" with the possible connotation of being particularly attuned to suffering, and the German word *Einfühlung* or *Einfühlungsvermögen*, which first introduced the concept of empathy in modern psychology, reflects this meaning. The term refers to the ability to feel oneself into the experience of another person. Thus, Heinz Kohut's simplified definition of empathy seems to offer a good preliminary understanding. He identifies empathy as "the capacity to think and feel oneself into the inner life of another person ... to an attenuated degree."[1] However, additional clinical perspectives on empathy as an attitude, as knowledge, and as a skill can broaden our understanding of how empathy becomes a restorative response to the fragmented self afflicted by shame.

---

1 Heinz Kohut, *How Does Analysis Cure?*, ed. Arnold Goldberg (Chicago & London: University of Chicago Press, 1984), 82.

Clinical Theories and Practices of Empathy

Humanistic psychologist Carl Rogers and Kohut gave empathy a central place in their theories and practice of psychotherapy. Perhaps less known but nevertheless important and innovative is psychiatrist Alfred Margulies's exploration of the empathic imagination in clinical practice. More recently, clinical psychologist Arthur Clark and pastoral theologian Pamela Cooper-White have presented models of empathy for secular and spiritually integrated psychotherapy that highlight the subjective dimension of empathy. Each theory provides its own perspective on empathy as a therapeutic means to assist the self into existence or in moving toward wholeness. These models represent prominent, original, and creative approaches to an understanding and a practice of empathy.

An Empathic Way of Being: Carl Rogers

One of the empathic methods that Rogers introduced has been at times misunderstood and caricatured as using a simplistic parroting method in therapeutic conversations. His humanistic approach to psychotherapy, however, is far from simple and does not prioritize a specific method but rather focuses on the therapeutic relationship as the crucial ingredient in the growth and healing process to become "the self that one truly is."[2] For Rogers, empathy is not merely a technique to extract information from another; it is a way of being in relationships. The misunderstanding and application of Rogers's approach as a conversational method that mechanically repeats another person's words in an attempt to mirror emotions shows that the various facets of empathy need to work together. While empathy as a technique includes certain listening skills and communication methods, they need to be rooted in an empathic attitude and in emotional intelligence and knowledge. In response to distortions of his approach, Rogers recalls that he avoided for several years speaking about empathic listening and only stressed an empathic attitude without going into much detail how it is implemented. Instead, he states, "I preferred to discuss the qualities of

---

2 Carl R. Rogers, *On Becoming a Person: A Therapist's View of Psychotherapy* (1961; repr., Boston & New York: Houghton & Mifflin Company, 1995), 163.

positive regard and therapist congruence, which, together with empathy, I hypothesized as promoting the therapeutic process."[3]

Empathic understanding, however, is for Rogers at the heart of the therapeutic process that creates safety and freedom for self-exploration and personal growth. He explains that it "is only as I understand the feelings and thoughts that seem so horrible to you, or so weak, or so sentimental, or so bizarre—it is only as I see them as you see them, and accept them and you, that you feel really free to explore all the hidden nooks and frightening crannies of your inner and often buried experience."[4] *Experiencing* is an important construct in Rogers's theory. Paying close and reflective attention to another person's experience, or rather experiencing and pointing in a sensitive way to the felt meaning of that ongoing process, is the essence of an empathic relationship. The clinical examples that Rogers presents make it clear that the therapist's reflections are not statements of certainty about another's inner world but cautious, respectful, tentative explorations into the other person's experience to encourage them to engage their experience without inhibitions.

Early on, Rogers defined empathy as a state in which the therapist "is to perceive the internal frame of reference of another with accuracy and with the emotional components and meanings that pertain thereto as if one were the person, but without ever losing the 'as if' condition."[5] Over the course of his career, he changed his perspective and definition and identified empathy as a process rather than a state. In *A Way of Being*, which was written toward the end of his career, Rogers states that an

> *empathic way of being with another person has several facets. It means entering the private perceptual world of the other and becoming thoroughly at home in it. It involves being sensitive, moment by moment, to the changing felt meanings that flow in*

---

3 Carl R. Rogers, *A Way of Being* (Boston & New York: Houghton & Mifflin Company, 1980), 139.
4 Rogers, *On Becoming a Person*, 34.
5 Carl R. Rogers, "A Theory of Therapy, Personality, and Interpersonal Relationships, as Developed in the Client-Centered Framework," in *Psychology: A Study of a Science*, vol. 3, ed. Sigmund Koch (New York: McGraw-Hill, 1959), 210.

> *this other person, to the fear or rage or tenderness or confusion or whatever that he or she is experiencing. It means temporarily living in the other's life, moving about in it delicately without making judgments; it means sensing meanings of which he or she is scarcely aware, but not trying to uncover totally unconscious feelings, since this would be too threatening.*[6]

Practicing empathic understanding thus means that one becomes a trusted companion into another person's inner world and communicates what one is sensing to the other from a fresh perspective without fear. To do this effectively, Rogers highlights the need to check frequently with the other person if one's understanding is accurate. Becoming this kind of companion requires that one suspends one's own "views and values in order to enter another's world without prejudice."[7] An empathic way of being in therapeutic relationships, then, is a complex way of relating and calls for a secure self that allows one to enter the inner world of another person without fear of getting lost.

As to the effects of empathy, Rogers points to various clinical contexts that show its correlation to positive therapeutic outcomes.[8] Specifically, he identifies four change-producing effects of empathy. Empathy overcomes alienation by communicating to the other that she is valued, cared for, and accepted. Furthermore, individuals feel perceptively understood through empathic responses and, as a result, connect more closely with a wider range of their experiences. While Rogers does not address shame directly, he identifies alienation as a central human struggle that is defined by a sense of uselessness, isolation, and hopelessness.[9] Empathy, on the other hand,

---

6 Rogers, *A Way of Being*, 142.
7 Rogers, *A Way of Being*, 143.
8 See Rogers, *A Way of Being*, 150–158.
9 See Rogers, *A Way of Being*, 199. Elaborating on Rogers's biography, Brian Thorne finds reflections of shame in Rogers's own experience when, at a point in his career, he struggled to value himself and consider himself loveable. "He could imagine that people might like what *he did* but he had no concept of himself as acceptable and worthy of respect at the core of his being. In fact, he later admitted that he felt that in reality he was inferior and simply putting on a contrived front of competence and human effectiveness." As biography often inspires theory, Thorne wonders if the development of a person-centered approach to therapy was ultimately rooted in Rogers's own feelings of unworthiness and inferiority and was an attempt to find healing. Brian Thorne,

provides connection and a sense of belonging. Moreover, feeling valued and accepted in an empathic therapeutic environment invites positive self-regard and self-care. Empathic understanding can facilitate self-discovery and a deepened self-knowledge, which may result in a change of self-concept and consequently in behavioral changes.[10] Accurate empathy makes unblocked access available to one's experiencing that has previously been inhibited, and it encourages self-exploration and self-acceptance. Rogers emphasizes that empathic understanding must not be mistaken for a diagnostic effort. He insists that "true empathy is always free from any evaluative or diagnostic quality."[11] Only then does it hold the possibility of inviting and increasing self-acceptance.

Empathy as Vicarious Introspection: Heinz Kohut

Kohut emphasizes that a therapist's attunement to self-object transferences in relationship with a patient is essential to healing the fragmented self. Self-object transferences reflect latent needs that have not been sufficiently met by caregivers, so-called self-objects, during formative phases in childhood. If the formative context lacked the necessary support for the rudimentary or nascent self to gradually develop, empathy can become transformative in a therapeutic context. The theory of self psychology identifies the effect of empathic attunement to another's self-object needs and transferences as transmuting internalization, which means that, through the therapeutic process, the self internalizes functions previously assigned to outside objects.[12]

In *The Restoration of the Self*, Kohut highlights the importance of empathy for his approach to psychoanalysis. Describing the empathic stance of the analyst as essential to the practice of psychoanalysis, he states that empathy is not merely a therapeutic tool among others but is the defining element in psychoanalytic therapy. Rather than mechanisms of resistance and transference, Kohut explains, empathy "does indeed in essence define *the field* of our observations. Empathy is not just a useful way by which we have

---

Counselling and Spiritual Accompaniment: Bridging Faith and Person-Centered Therapy (Chichester, UK: John Wiley & Sons, 2012), 65.
10 See Rogers, *A Way of Being*, 155.
11 Rogers, *A Way of Being*, 154.
12 See Heinz Kohut, *The Restoration of the Self* (1977; repr., Chicago & London: University of Chicago Press, 2009), 30–32.

access to the inner life of man—the idea of an inner life of man, and thus of a psychology of complex mental states, is unthinkable without our ability to know via vicarious introspection . . . what the inner life of man is, what we ourselves and what others think and feel."[13] While everyday perception and the scientific investigation of the external world is carried out with the help of our senses, explains Kohut, the inner world of persons, that is, their psychological world of thoughts, emotions, wishes, and fantasies, has no existence in physical space and is therefore not accessible though the senses. Yet, it is as real as the external world and can be observed as existing in time.

Kohut's understanding of empathy can technically be characterized as a phenomenological method of attending to the inner world of another through a value-neutral mode of observation. When he began to formulate the theory of self psychology, Kohut defined the therapist's observation of the psychological world through empathy as vicarious introspection.[14] This definition suggests that the therapist's empathic immersion into the inner world of another happens on behalf of that person in order to understand their experience and bring it to awareness. While Kohut holds that empathy is for many human beings a natural endowment, similar to the physical senses, and that it is a primary parental function, he distinguishes the general capacity for empathy from the therapeutic skill that is honed through personal analysis, clinical supervision, and psychoanalytic study. However, both forms of empathy are most basically about "the resonance of the self in the self of others, of being understood, of somebody making an effort to understand you."[15] In clinical practice, empathy therefore requires bi-directional listening. On the one hand, it is an intentional and disciplined effort to listen to the experience of another person and how that experience reveals their inner world and reflects their self-object needs. On the other hand, it is an act of introspective listening that is attuned to the resonances of another's experience within *oneself* and uses that awareness as an interpretative, therapeutic tool.

---

13 Kohut, *Restoration of the Self*, 306.
14 See Heinz Kohut, "Introspection, Empathy, and Psychoanalysis," in *The Search for the Self: Selected Writings of Heinz Kohut 1950-1978*, vol. 1, ed. Paul H. Ornstein (New York: International Universities Press, 1978), 205–206.
15 Heinz Kohut, *Self Psychology and the Humanities: Reflections on a New Psychoanalytic Approach*, ed. Charles B. Strozier (New York: W. W. Norton & Company, 1985), 222.

As Kohut developed his therapeutic theory over time, his understanding of empathy broadened from a focus on gathering psychological data about the inner world of another person to a larger view that paid close attention to the role of empathy within the therapeutic relationship. An empathic connection, according to Kohut, is a means of instilling hope in others and "is absolutely needed for psychological survival."[16] In an interview with educational scholar David Moss about the functions and failures of an empathic environment, Kohut speaks in almost religious terms about the importance of an empathic environment for the development of the self and uses language that appropriates traditional theological concepts. He explains that a lack of empathic connection in a non-responsive environment is "the 'original sin;' it creates the feeling of deepest unworthiness without having transgressed a moral injunction. But its presence is equally undeserved within the framework of a moral outlook; it is the 'grace' of life-sustaining parental acceptance. This is the 'divine' echo, this 'peace,' this 'God' that puts the fragments together. Without it the self does not consolidate, it remains in pieces (broken)."[17] Pastoral theologian Chris Schlauch elaborates on Kohut's perspective and understands an empathic stance in pastoral psychotherapy explicitly from a theological vantage point. He argues that the capacity to relate empathically is rooted in God's creative activity and that the "empathic stance, as a style of care, is an expression of the *imago Dei*. From a Christian standpoint," he explains, "I might affirm that Jesus Christ incarnated God's empathic stance, God's *agape* for us, and in so doing modeled how we are to relate to others and to God."[18]

As a therapeutic attitude and method in self psychology, empathy is both a way of knowing and a way of relating.[19] In his last paper—"Introspection, Empathy, and the Semi-Circle of Mental Health"—which was written shortly before his death, Kohut distinguished between two levels of empathy in the therapeutic process. On the one hand, he explains, empathy can be

---

16 Kohut, *Self Psychology and the Humanities*, 222.
17 David M. Moss, "Narcissism, Empathy, and the Fragmentation of the Self: An Interview with Heinz Kohut," *Pilgrimage* 4, no. 1 (1976): 42.
18 Chris R. Schlauch, "Empathy as the Essence of Pastoral Psychotherapy," *Journal of Pastoral Care*, 44, no. 1 (March 1990), 17. See also Chris R. Schlauch, *Faithful Companioning: How Pastoral Counseling Heals* (Minneapolis: Fortress Press, 1994), 83–84.
19 See Schlauch, "Empathy as the Essence of Pastoral Psychotherapy," 6–8.

conceptualized epistemologically as a value-free mode of observation and an information-gathering activity, which collects data and is a necessary precondition for being successfully supportive and therapeutic. Within relationships, on the other hand, empathy is "a powerful bond between people" and has a beneficial and therapeutic effect in the clinical setting as well as in human life in general.[20] In other words, empathy is both an affective and a cognitive process within the therapeutic self and between persons. Both aspects cannot be separated and together they account for the centrality of the concept and the therapeutic practice in self psychology.

Empathic Imagination: Alfred Margulies
If, among those who have theorized about empathy, Rogers is considered as the warm and accepting companion on the therapeutic journey, and Kohut gathers and reveals knowledge within the context of a therapeutic relationship, then Margulies is perhaps best characterized as the contemplative poet who imagines the possibility of a self. Margulies explores the theory and practice of empathy at the intersection of phenomenology, psychoanalysis, and poetry. He identifies phenomenology and psychoanalysis as two distinct but complementary observational and creative methods of psychological investigation. While phenomenology explores and studies reports of subjective, conscious experiences, psychoanalysis attends to unconscious material in a person's experience.[21] Both approaches require the investigator to allow for surprise while entering into another person's world of experiences in order to arrive at novel perceptions. In other words, empathy is not a means to confirm what one already knows or suspects about another but is open to discovery.

Margulies's use of poetic theory underlines this viewpoint. Margulies applies the notion of negative capability, which poet John Keats identified in Shakespeare's work as the poet's dilemma, to the therapeutic process and contends that it also characterizes the therapist's dilemma. Negative capability, according to Margulies, is the ability to live with uncertainties,

---

20 See Heinz Kohut, "Introspection, Empathy, and the Semi-Circle of Mental Health," *International Journal of Psycho-Analysis*, 63, no. 4 (1982): 397.
21 See Alfred Margulies, *The Empathic Imagination* (New York & London: W. W. Norton & Company, 1989), 4.

mystery, and doubts. It is "the capacity to go against the grain of need to know."[22] Empathic attention to another's experience, thus, requires a tolerance for paradox: to attempt to know and, at the same time, not to know, to enter and experience another person's inner world in approximation while not yet knowing what the final meaning of that experience is.

Margulies finds that empathy is an inadequate translation of the German noun *Einfühlung* and that the term "has since become a highly ambiguous and technical word in psychiatry."[23] He borrows the term *inscape* from British poet and Jesuit priest Gerald Manley Hopkins, who used it to describe the poetic imagination. Making reference to Keats's sympathetic imagination, Margulies explains that inscape "captures the goal of existential psychotherapeutic work: to enter into and to share the world of the other. The existential worker, like this young poet, strives to live for a moment inside the existence of the other."[24] Elsewhere, Margulies likens the concept to an interior subjective landscape that can be entered through sensory perception.[25] Following Margulies's argument, it appears as if the word can be used both as a noun and as a verb. Inscaping, then, is the opposite of escaping. Rather than getting away from someone or from certain circumstances, one intentionally draws close and creatively imagines oneself within another's experience, fusing subjective and objective awareness. In referencing the poetic imagination and appropriating the term *inscape* to describe the therapeutic work, Margulies highlights empathy as a creative process rather than merely a receptive or resonant function of psychotherapy. As such, it is an active and searching mode of therapeutic engagement.

Margulies understands empathy as a sensory experience. It is a process of sensing the potential self or the self that is possible. Using a landscape metaphor, he portrays the clinician as a traveler who enters and takes in the inner world of another. "As I become engaged with the inner life of another," explains Margulies, "I experience a growing sense of familiarity with a built-up internal landscape. . . . I enter a private world constructed from associations and images stimulated by my patient and drawn from

---

22 Margulies, *The Empathic Imagination*, 12.
23 Margulies, *The Empathic Imagination*, 15.
24 Margulies, *The Empathic Imagination*, 15.
25 Alfred Margulies, "The Empathic Imagination: Empathy and Inscapes," *The Journal of the American Academy of Psychoanalysis* 21, no. 4 (Winter 1993): 515–517.

my own personal past experience."[26] On the one hand, empathy is work in the here-and-now by closely attending to the other and to the relationship. On the other hand, it is a creative process that imagines the possibility of the true self that may emerge. "As empathic observers," Margulies explains, "we are not only extending our experience of the inscape of the other . . . but also taking the patient into an unrealized area of her own inscape, an aspect of her world view she could not tolerate before. This new inscape, belonging to the patient, is paradoxically unfamiliar to the patient. We are into unknown areas of potential self."[27] While closely attending to another's emotional experience and psychological conflicts in the present, the therapist empathizes with the possible self and participates in its creation or consolidation.

However, Margulies's emphasis on therapeutic imagination must not be mistaken as a way of constructing from subjective observation the image of another's self and assuming it is the real thing. Like Rogers, he cautions against unchecked observations. "When all is said and done," Margulies holds, "imaginative empathy remains imaginative. Empathy must be checked and rechecked against real experience if one is not to lose one's way and make a fiction of the other."[28]

Finally, Margulies explores and clarifies the enigmatic concept of empathy with oneself. The concept is a paradoxical term that attempts to capture the fact that the self emerges in psychotherapy both through the mirror of another and through self-reflection. Therefore, empathy is simultaneously both subject and object in that process of becoming.[29] Like all of human life, the self is involved in a growth process and strives to integrate new experiences that present challenges to revise itself, gain new self-understanding, and adjust its identity and meaning-making frames accordingly. One can decide to respond to the challenges or deny them, engage the growth process or withdraw into the image of a false self. An empathic therapeutic relationship, according to Margulies, invites the other through narrative responsiveness into a self-reflective process of exploration and discovery.

---

26 Margulies, *The Empathic Imagination*, 53.
27 Margulies, *The Empathic Imagination*, 131.
28 Margulies, *The Empathic Imagination*, 18.
29 See Margulies, *The Empathic Imagination*, 108–109.

> *Empathy pushes the dialectical coil of self-reflection in motion. . . . Telling one's narrative to another helps one find and constitute oneself. The narrator lives vicariously in the world of the listener as each tries to encounter the other's perspective. The empathizer may give a more coherent viewpoint than the person empathized with may experience, ironically because the empathizer is removed from the frame and has a limited and incomplete view. . . . Empathy, in this respect, is a process which creates the self, either through the other or through empathy with oneself. That is, the self defines itself though empathy.*[30]

Empathy with oneself, then, involves an openness to know oneself at a deep level, a kind and accepting attitude toward oneself, the courage to enter yet unknown territory within one's inner landscape, and a search for meaning. It is an ability one develops in the empathic presence of another, the resonance of empathy within oneself.

Integral Empathy: Arthur Clark

Expanding Rogers's theory, counseling psychologist Arthur Clark presents a clinical fusion model that integrates multiple dimensions of empathy. *Integral empathy*, as Clark terms it, joins subjective, interpersonal, and objective empathy as ways of knowing and understanding another person's experience. "Utilizing a different conceptual framework," Clark explains, "empathy is directed toward the client from multiple vantage points in order to build a more comprehensive understanding of the individual. Diverse and potentially enlightening sources of knowledge become available when the direction of empathy extends beyond the interpersonal way of knowing."[31] The assumptions behind the model are that all three modes of knowing provide important information though empathic understanding while each mode has its limitations. Furthermore, combining different perspectives in clinical practice is inevitable and provides a more comprehensive empathic understanding. In broadening the focus of empathy, Clark attempts to gain

---

30 Margulies, *The Empathic Imagination*, 142–143.
31 Arthur J. Clark, *Empathy in Counseling and Psychotherapy: Perspectives and Practices* (2007; repr., New York & London: Routledge, 2013), 158.

a fuller and more accurate understanding of another person's experience by employing multiple perspectives of understanding.[32]

Subjective empathy is a way of knowing about another's experience by referencing one's own experience through identification, imagination, and intuition, as well as through visceral resonance or what Clark calls "felt-level experiencing."[33] While subjective knowing about another's experience is, according to Clark, an inevitable and essential part of empathic understanding, it is not sufficient by itself and needs verification. In particular, any identification needs to be transitory "because the therapist must be in a position to objectively evaluate what has been experienced in the subjective interaction when thinking about the client. . . . If a practitioner is not able to rapidly shift out of the identification phase, he or she may remain psychologically merged with the client and respond in less than therapeutic ways."[34]

Pointing to the role of imagination, Clark explains that therapeutic imagination creates images and emotional reactions and projects the self into the imagined world of the client to experience it for a moment, particularly when the client's own world and experience are significantly foreign to the therapist. However, intuitive responses are different from imaginative engagement in that they are not just about understanding or observation but also about decisions to intervene. Therapeutic intuition requires attunement to the context of another's experience and to patterns within that experience without analytic reasoning. "In this regard," Clark explains, "a counselor evokes hunches, images, and flashes of insight when intuitively interacting with a client that can provide an empathic understanding that is both enlightening and qualitatively different from intentional observation processes."[35] Subjective empathy is not just a cognitive or affective method but is a holistic, embodied practice that includes visceral resonances that a therapeutic encounter evokes. Such resonances enhance an empathic understanding of another's total experience.[36] Clark cautions that subjective empathy requires ethical controls and a high level of self-awareness due to the potential for bias and judgment error.

---

32 See Clark, *Empathy in Counseling and Psychotherapy*, 161.
33 See Clark, *Empathy in Counseling and Psychotherapy*, 171.
34 Clark, *Empathy in Counseling and Psychotherapy*, 166.
35 Clark, *Empathy in Counseling and Psychotherapy*, 169.
36 See Clark, *Empathy in Counseling and Psychotherapy*, 171.

In Clark's model, interpersonal empathy essentially represents Rogers's approach to understanding another person's experience and to communicating that understanding. The goal is to facilitate that person's self-understanding and self-discovery. While subjective empathy uses one's own internal frame of reference, interpersonal empathy is an "attempt to perceive the internal frame of reference of a client and then try to convey aspects of this understanding to the client."[37] The perception may focus on the immediate experience between oneself and another in the here-and-now, or it may attend to a person's extended, general experience of life over time. As with subjective empathy, interpersonal empathy can be liable to bias and misjudgment because one can never directly and exactly know the inner experience of another person; one seeks approximate understanding through deduction. Thus, it is imperative to state observations tentatively rather than in a diagnostic fashion and to check one's empathic understanding through therapeutic communication.

Objective empathy uses an external frame of reference to approximately understand another's experience and invite self-reflection. "Theoretical and conceptual observations of a counselor," holds Clark, "have a potential to expand a client's perceptions in a way that enables the individual to experience a deeper and more comprehensive sense of empathic understanding."[38] In other words, one's theoretical orientation provides a perceptual lens to interpret another person's experience and to make behavioral observations. As with the other facets of integral empathy, objective empathy, too, has the potential for bias and error. All theories are limited, and a therapist might be tempted to fit the other into one's theory rather than use the theory as a tool for empathic understanding. Thus, theoretical observations can inform one's approach to therapeutic conversations but, if conveyed to the other, should be tentatively expressed and checked for accuracy. An objective empathic understanding of another, even if accurate, may not always be therapeutically helpful to express. For example, while a therapist may accurately observe a client's defense mechanisms, she may decide to respect them rather than name them, assessing that client is not ready to confront his defenses and the fragile self they protect. If objective empathy

---

37 Clark, *Empathy in Counseling and Psychotherapy*, 173–174.
38 Clark, *Empathy in Counseling and Psychotherapy*, 179.

is practiced without interpersonal empathy, it can easily be mistaken and resisted as a form of labeling or as a diagnosis. "In each way of knowing," Clark summarizes his approach, "the focus of empathy is on the client and serves as a means of attuning to the experience of the individual. . . . the multiple ways of knowing provide complementary and corrective avenues for empathically understanding a client."[39]

Empathy and the Use of Self: Pamela Cooper-White

Pamela Cooper-White, a pastoral theologian and psychotherapist, explores the meaning and role of empathy in the context of countertransference from the perspective of relational psychoanalysis. Like Clark, she identifies a subjective dimension in empathic understanding or, more precisely, an *intersubjective* dimension. "Empathy," Cooper-White explains, "works primarily through the medium of countertransference, as the therapist experiences affects, resonances, fantasies, and images that are drawn from the pool of unconscious material and 'shared wisdom' in the intersubjective dynamic of the therapy."[40] While subjectivity is the perception of reality from one's own inner frame of reference, intersubjectivity includes conscious or unconscious psychological experiences and perceptions that are shared between oneself and another.

The idea of intersubjectivity is based on an understanding that human beings are in some ways unique and like no one else, in other ways like some others, and in some ways like all others. This perspective was first introduced by anthropologist Florence Kluckhohn in a 1948 collection of essays on personality, edited by psychologist Henry Murray and anthropologist Clyde Kluckhohn. Since then, it has been applied in pastoral theology and theories of pastoral counseling.[41] Empathic understanding can appreciate all

---

39 Clark, *Empathy in Counseling and Psychotherapy*, 185.
40 Pamela Cooper-White, *Many Voices: Pastoral Psychotherapy in Relational and Theological Perspective* (Minneapolis: Fortress Press, 2007), 187.
41 To my knowledge, David Augsburger was the first pastoral theologian who used the concept in exploring cross-cultural perspectives in pastoral counseling, referring explicitly to Murray and Kluckhohn. See David W. Augsburger, *Pastoral Counseling across Cultures* (Philadelphia: The Westminster Press, 1986), 49. Emmanuel Lartey, in his book on intercultural pastoral care and counseling, emphasized that all three dimensions are interrelated and interconnected in complex ways and need to be held and explored in creative and dynamic tension to each other. See Emmanuel Y. Lartey,

three aspects of human existence. Intersubjective recognition is rooted in the experience of being alike. In identifying such recognition and countertransference as a resource in the therapeutic process, Cooper-White goes beyond a classic understanding of countertransference, which viewed the therapist's subjectivity as a barrier to an effective therapeutic relationship.[42]

In the classic view, the patient or client was an object to be observed and accurately diagnosed and, thus, objectivity was valued, and subjectivity seen as a contaminant to the therapeutic relationship. In a relational paradigm, however, "subjectivity is revalued as representing the whole spectrum of ways in which both one's own and the other's realities can be understood. Subjectivity," Cooper-White explains, "does not exclude the rational sense but also incorporates affect and bodily sense as ways in which both self and other can be known."[43] Subsequently, empathic understanding in therapeutic process is at the same time a rational, an emotional, and an embodied way of knowing, integrating in a wholistic manner the "use of self" in clinical practice.

Cooper-White argues that an empathic approach that only nurtures and provides therapeutic "warmth" is ultimately not enough to effect deep change.[44] In order to heal and grow, persons need to honestly face and grieve their losses and traumatic experiences, and a clinical practitioner can facilitate that process with empathic understanding that knows about the universality of grief and does not shy away from confrontation and risking empathic failures or momentary ruptures in the therapeutic relationship. However, confrontation must not be misunderstood as an antagonistic or aggressive relational stance. Rather, it is a way of caring for another by using one's empathic understanding of their experience and of dynamics within the therapeutic relationship, bringing them to their awareness, like in a mirror, to invite a response, facilitate change, and assist healing. In other words, empathic observation is a means to an end, not an end in itself. "A psychodynamic approach," Cooper-White explains, "requires the therapist

---

In Living Color: An Intercultural Approach to Pastoral Care and Counseling, 2nd ed. (London & Philadelphia: Jessica Kingsley Publishers, 2003), 14–15.

42 See Pamela Cooper-White, *Shared Wisdom: Use of the Self in Pastoral Care and Counseling* (Minneapolis: Fortress Press, 2004), 54.
43 Cooper-White, *Shared Wisdom*, 54–55.
44 See Cooper-White, *Many Voices*, 188.

to observe the process that is occurring between therapist and patient and to act as a midwife to the patient's growing insights why his or her relationship might be unfolding as it is."[45] In this approach, support in the therapeutic birthing process must not only engage the patient's transference, as is the case in classic psychoanalysis, but also one's own countertransference.

Transference has been traditionally understood as the patient's process of "transferring" relational patterns and experiences from early childhood, particularly those based in sexual and aggressive impulses, into the therapeutic relationship and onto the therapist, manifesting themselves in distortions in the patient's perception.[46] Accordingly, countertransference has been viewed as the therapist's unconscious emotional and behavioral response to the patient that needs to be brought to awareness and kept in check, lest it interferes with therapeutic goals. Cooper-White's expansion of countertransference to regard it as a therapeutic tool, rather than an obstacle, identifies empathy as an expression and therapeutic function of countertransference, which is "the sum total of thoughts, feelings, fantasies, impulses, and bodily sensations, conscious or unconscious, that may arise in the pastoral caregiver in relation to any person who has come for help."[47] The use of self, however, needs to be coupled with an ethical commitment to disciplined self-examination on the part of the care provider, trained through clinical supervision and assisted by ongoing peer consultation as needed, to prevent abuse in the therapeutic relationship.

Empathy and Shame

Guilt and shame are related but distinct self-conscious emotions that require different therapeutic interventions. While guilt is resolved through confession and forgiveness, the effects of shame are transformed through empathic connections that help to instill a sense of being known and accepted. However, forgiveness may function in the service of self-acceptance to move beyond shame and help to mend the self without necessarily extending acceptance to another person or mending a relationship.

---

45 Cooper-White, *Many Voices*, 189.
46 See Cooper-White, *Shared Wisdom*, 11.
47 Cooper-White, *Shared Wisdom*, 5.

> Denise had joined the church after a separation from her husband. As she shared with the pastor, she blamed the separation to a large degree on her long-time depression. After several counseling sessions that focused on the effects of the depression in her life and on her losses, Denise revealed to the pastor that she was a survivor of sexual violence inflicted by her father over several years during her teenage years. Her father now lived in a different part of the country, and she had not seen nor talked to him in fifteen years. Denise explained that this was the first time she had shared with anyone about the abuse. A deep sense of shame had pervaded all her adult life as a result of the trauma she had experienced. Regular pastoral counseling continued over the next several months, and she built supportive friendships with other women in the church. One day, Denise came for counseling and let the pastor know that she felt, as a Christian, she should forgive her father. Her pastor primarily listened to Denise explain how she came to her conclusion and then she suggested that they take some time to explore her motivation and the meaning of forgiveness as it related to the abuse. After a few more counseling sessions, Denise decided to write a letter to her father, which went through several iterations, letting him know about the effects of his abuse on her life, how mental health challenges had been a dominant and oppressive force in her life for the last fifteen years, and about her newly found faith. The final version ended with the following sentences. "I forgive you, which is for me an important step towards freedom from the pain of your abuse. It means that I let go of blaming myself and hating you. I finally can accept myself but, even as I forgive you, I do not accept you as a father in my life. I do not wish to have any contact with you in the future, and I want you to know that I do not write this in anger or mean it as punishment. It is for my protection and safety alone. I truly wish for you that you will find your own healing from the past and hope that this letter can be part of it."

Through empathic connections, both in the context of formal pastoral counseling and through new friendships within the church, Denise opened up about her past and began to tell her story. The shame that was rooted in the sexual abuse she had suffered had caused her for years to withdraw from others. Now she was increasingly able to let herself be known, even with deep wounds and the pain in her life. Empathy communicated understanding and acceptance, which Denise was able to internalize over time to generate self-acceptance. For Denise, self-acceptance also meant self-protection and redefining the boundaries that were violated during her teenage years.

Arel points out that empathic relationships facilitate and support the ability of the self to engage shame intentionally and nurture a certain self-reflexivity that can be considered as both a psychological and a spiritual practice. "The ability to hold shame without interring it, without its becoming detrimental," Arel explains by referring to philosopher Edith Stein's work, "requires commitment from the self to remain both introspective and attentive to the world and the other. . . . In fact, Stein envisions empathy as interwoven into the 'psycho-physical' and spiritual becoming of the self, who is in a continual process of growth or, as Stein puts it, 'unfolding'."[48] As Denise's story shows, empathic care and engagement can instill self-worth and self-acceptance in another, which in turn can lead to a deeper understanding of oneself and to courageous actions. A self that has the potential to continually evolve can transform the debilitating effects of shame when it is supported through empathic connections. Debilitating shame can become interred and arrest self-development and growth, either for a period of time or indefinitely, if it is not assessed and therapeutically engaged. Empathic interventions, however, can disrupt the arresting effects of shame and provide the stimulus and support for self-development.

Social work professor Susan Donner emphasizes the centrality of empathy from the perspective of self psychology by pointing to its stimulating effect. "In any therapy in which relationship serves as the crucible for change, empathy is imperative, as it is the connection that sparks the relationship. Without empathy there is no meaningful relationship and no access to experiences and data by which the self becomes known. Only empathy can offer a convincingly safe invitation to a meeting attended by patient and therapist in which the subjective world of the patient creatively

---

48 See Arel, *Affect Theory, Shame, and Christian Formation*, 161.

unfolds."[49] While shame causes the self to recoil in fear of being discovered or in self-disgust, feeling not worthy of love or positive regard, empathy communicates positive regard, understanding, and acceptance. It has the capacity to draw the self out of its protective, hidden stance into a relationship of self-disclosure and self-discovery. While shame frustrates and inhibits the will to be known, empathy responds to the desire of the self to be known.

Empathic connections and understanding can lessen and even overcome the isolating and alienating effects of shame in clinical practice, but it does not eliminate shame. Like any other emotion, shame is part of the inner life and a dynamic in relationship with self and others, in both debilitating and protective ways. Healing from alienating shame does not come through elimination but through integration, which means more than accepting that shame is an inevitable reality in one's life. Integration is a psychological and spiritual process that aims to create wholeness, the integrity of the self, through recognition, engagement, and meaningful utilization of life experiences and aspects of one's inner world that one wants to deny, avoid, or hide. Empathic understanding and attunement aid and support the recognition of shame and its power and effects in one's life.

Recognition means to acknowledge the existence of one's shame, to face it, and possibly to acknowledge it to others in the context of a safe relationship. It is a first step out of hiding and away from masking the fragmented self. Engaging one's shame is a second step. It involves interaction with the emotion, allowing oneself to feel it and its impact, verbalizing it to others, exploring its origins and effects, and identifying its meaning. Discovering meaning is about understanding how shame functions in one's life, how it is significant and conveys information. Finally, being able to use shame in meaningful ways indicates that shame has lost its powerful grip on the self. Now that the self is the agent, it can attend and intentionally respond to the presence of shame and use the emotion as a resource for information about its environment and relationships rather than reacting. Meaningful utilization of shame establishes connections with others as shame experiences are integrated. Shame is a mark of our common humanity. Through

---

[49] Susan Donner, "The Treatment Process," in *Using Self Psychology in Psychotherapy*, ed. Helene Jackson (Northvale, NJ: Jason Aronson Inc., 1991), 53–54.

empathy with oneself, a spiritual care provider can model engagement with shame for another person and demonstrate solidarity with their pain of being human.

The relationship between empathy and shame is not a one-way relationship. Empathy does not only have a therapeutic effect on shame, but shame also impacts the capacity for empathy. Psychologists June Price Tangney and Ronda Dearing point to research that examines and compares dispositional empathy in guilt-prone individuals and in shame-prone individuals.[50] Shame-prone persons have less dispositional capacity for empathy than guilt-prone persons. Tangney and Dearing conclude that the capacity for empathy diminishes with shame intensity, but dispositional empathy appears to be associated with the likelihood of experiencing guilt. The results of the research studies are not surprising. Shame projects one's own self-judgment onto others but interferes with the ability to project oneself into their inner world. Indeed, individuals who are deeply wounded and alienated by shame likely do not have enough of a sense of self to let themselves resonate with another's experience. These findings have implications for clinical care providers. To be able to relate and care consistently with empathy, practitioners of spiritual care need to do the ongoing work of attending to their own shame and integrating it personally and professionally, lest it impede their ability to attend to the inner life of others.

Empathy and Vulnerability

Practicing empathy requires vulnerability and invites vulnerability in response. It invites others to make themselves known and to lower the masks of shame, risk self-exploration and self-discovery, and ultimately work toward wholeness and self-integration. But it also requires vulnerability on the part of the empathizer in various and different ways. Empathy is a journey into another person's inner world and into emotional territory that is yet unknown and may reveal a landscape shaped by trauma and the pain it inflicted. The willingness to enter such territory, not knowing what one may discover, requires a degree of emotional vulnerability. This does not

---

50 See June Price Tangney and Ronda L. Dearing, *Shame and Guilt* (New York & London: The Guilford Press, 2002), 86.

mean that through empathy one experiences the same emotions as the other person. It does not mean to feel *what* others feels but rather to know *how* they experience their situation emotionally as an embodied self, being with them emotionally and adopting their perspective, as philosopher Rowland Stout explains, and "allowing their emotional lives a place in your life."[51] Such therapeutic hospitality, according to Stout, may become threatening when one's own perspective is in conflict with the other person's perspective. It can leave the host vulnerable to her own perspective being challenged and possibly altered.

Philosopher Amy Coplan agrees with Stout that perspective-taking is a central feature of an empathic relationship. Perspective-taking, in her words, "is an imaginative process through which one constructs another person's subjective experience by simulating the experience of being in the other's situation."[52] She distinguishes between two different forms of perspective-taking that may be part of the empathic experience. Self-oriented perspective-taking means that "a person represents herself in another person's situations."[53] One imagines what it would be like for oneself to go through the other person's experience. Coplan argues that self-oriented perspective-taking is vulnerable to egocentric bias and should be excluded from a theory of empathy unless it is employed as a secondary approach alongside other-oriented perspective-taking. In other-oriented perspective-taking, the therapeutic simulation stays focused "on the other's experiences and characteristics rather than reverting to imagining based on our own experiences and characteristics."[54] Both forms of perspective-taking potentially leave the empathic practitioner vulnerable. Self-oriented perspective-taking may be vulnerable to egocentric bias and to conflating one's own perspectives with another's experience. Other-oriented perspective-taking, on the other hand, if it is not practiced with clear self-other differentiation, leaves one potentially vulnerable to a breakdown of boundaries between self and others.

---

51 Rowland Stout, "Empathy, Vulnerability and Anxiety," *International Journal of Philosophical Studies* 27, no. 2 (April 2019): 351.
52 Amy Coplan, "Understanding Empathy: Its Features and Effects," in *Empathy: Philosophical and Psychological Perspectives*, ed. Amy Coplan and Peter Goldie (Oxford & New York: Oxford University Press, 2011), 9.
53 Coplan, "Understanding Empathy," 9.
54 Coplan, "Understanding Empathy," 13.

Resonances of another self within one's own may lead to an intersubjective state of knowing that creates a vulnerability to potentially painful and distressing insights, memories, or meanings. Those may be rooted in another's perspective that becomes threatening or challenging to oneself, or they may be related to discoveries about one's own inner life. For this reason, clinical supervision that attends to dynamics of the self and its formative relationships is essential in training spiritual care providers, lest they be blindsided by emotional resonances between themselves and another in clinical encounters. After all, empathy is a therapeutic practice that ultimately seeks to effect self-discovery in another person, and, in order to do so, empathic observations and awareness need to be checked with the other regarding its accuracy. The possibility always exists that empathic understanding becomes subjectively contaminated and inaccurate, or that it does not transform self-protective resistance toward change and growth and is rejected. In other words, within a relational therapeutic paradigm, an empathic stance must accept vulnerability because it risks the possibility of empathic failure and rejection.

The most basic meaning of emotional vulnerability is being at risk of experiencing emotional pain or unwanted exposure. Vulnerability may be an involuntary and dreaded state of existence that is due to a lack of resources and defenses and feels threatening, or it may be a relational stance that is taken by choice. In case of empathic attunement, measured vulnerability is a requisite and therefore a deliberate relational stance. Measured vulnerability means that the therapeutic relationship is carefully constructed and monitored and that the risk of emotional pain and exposure on the part of the empathizer is limited by professional boundaries. Arguing that vulnerability must not be mistaken for weakness, Brené Brown identifies uncertainty, risk, and emotional exposure as defining characteristics of vulnerability.[55] All three characteristics apply to a practice of empathic attunement. Brown's argument supports the concept of measured vulnerability and makes it clear that a vulnerable stance in relationships does not mean being without boundaries. "Vulnerability without boundaries," she states, "leads to disconnection, distrust, and disengagement."[56] Since a practice of measured vulnerability

---

55 See Brené Brown, *Daring Greatly: How the Courage to Be Vulnerable Transforms the Way We Live, Love, Parent, and Lead* (New York: Gotham Books, 2012), 34.
56 Brown, *Daring Greatly*, 46.

serves ultimately a restorative purpose and invites mutuality, boundaries are essential for both partners in the therapeutic relationship to feel reasonably safe and engage the therapeutic process courageously.

The question then arises whether empathy in therapeutic relationships can become a spiritual or psychological hazard. Research on the relationship between empathy and burnout in professional care providers has raised questions about whether empathy can cause burnout, whether burnout decreases empathy, or whether empathy can protect from burnout. Evidence suggests positive answers to all three of these questions. However, the majority of those studies have focused not on psychotherapy or spiritual care but on medical settings and particularly on the correlation of both constructs in the experience of physicians and nurses.[57] Still, most studies found a negative association between empathy and burnout, meaning that as one increases the other decreases. Association or correlation, however, do not mean causality or directionality. Studies could not decisively determine whether empathy decreases burnout or whether burnout reduces empathic capacity, or if either effect could result depending on circumstances.[58] While some studies find a positive association between empathy and burnout in professional care providers, which may suggest that an empathic clinical practice can under certain circumstances increase the risk of professional burnout, the use of multiple and divergent theories of empathy have shrouded the concept and created misconceptions about the relationship between empathy and burnout.[59]

---

[57] A systematic review of ten international studies found that the research supported the suggestion that empathy and burnout were associated. In this analysis, burnout was defined as a state of emotional and possibly physical depletion that is combined with impersonal caregiving responses and a decreased sense of professional accomplishments. See Helen Wilkinson et al., "Examining the Relationship between Burnout and Empathy in Healthcare Professionals: A Systematic Review," *Burnout Research* 6, no. 6 (September 2017): 26.

[58] The question as to whether empathy can cause burnout also remains unanswered in this systematic review of research studies. While the authors define empathy based upon classic and current research as having emotional, cognitive, behavioral, and moral dimensions, the studies they analyze used various instruments to measure empathy, and it is not clear that they employ the same understanding of empathy. See Wilkinson et al., "Examining the Relationship between Burnout and Empathy in Healthcare Professionals," 19.

[59] See Marta Villacieros, Ricardo Olmos, and José Carlos Bermejo, "The Empathic Process and Misconceptions that Lead to Burnout in Healthcare Professionals," *The Spanish Journal of Psychology* 20, no. 4 (December 2017): 2.

Empathy and Compassion

Compassion is a term that is often used interchangeably with empathy in order to describe a caring practice. Both words are rooted etymologically in Greek and Latin terms *pathos* and *passion*, which have similar connotations of feeling and suffering. However, the prefix in each term is critical to understanding their meaning and their difference. The word compassion is derived from the Latin word *compati*, which means "to suffer with" another. Thus, while empathy refers to a process of entering another person's emotional and experiential frame of reference to communicate understanding and acceptance, compassion means to come alongside another in their pain and be willing to be affected by the other person's experience. In the Gospels, compassion is ascribed to Jesus when he sees individuals or groups of peoples in distress (see Matt 9:36; Mark 6:34; Luke 7:13).

The Greek verb *splanchnizomai*, which is used in several passages to describe Jesus's response, literally means "to have one's heart or inner organs turned" and viscerally describes the openness to another person's suffering and what it means to be affected by their pain. The notion of a gut-wrenching experience perhaps comes close to the meaning of *splanchnizomai*. Empathy may or may not involve resonant emotions, and if it does, they are not a main focus. Rather, the focus is on understanding the other person's emotional experience from their perspective and communicating such understanding effectively.

If empathy does not require resonant emotions, compassion does not require an understanding of the other person's inner world. It is a behavioral and emotional response to another person's experience that conveys care but does not enter therapeutically into that experience. Clinical psychologist and ethicist David Jeffrey examines empathy and compassion in the context of clinical care and medical education and argues that conceptual clarity is needed to improve clinicians' education and practice. He favors a broad concept of empathy over a vaguer understanding of compassion.[60] Compassion, as Jeffrey explains it, is generated by serious states of distress or

---

[60] See David Jeffrey, "Empathy, Sympathy, and Compassion in Healthcare: Is There a Problem? Is There a Difference? Does It Matter?" *Journal of the Royal Society of Medicine* 109, no. 12 (December 2016): 446.

suffering and implies a desire to help and relieve suffering. However, while compassion is oriented toward action and promotes relief of suffering, it may not necessarily lead to helping action.[61] Other studies have found compassion "as being broader and deeper than empathy, defining compassion in psychotherapy as connecting with the client's suffering and promoting change through action."[62] In those studies, compassion was identified with giving and having time for another, connecting and demonstrating respect with emotional resonance, and communicating with attentiveness and understanding.

Just like empathy, compassion has been understood in different ways, but the emphasis on feeling *with* another, wishing to relieve pain, and a general altruistic attitude seem to be common determinators in various definitions. Compassion is typically distinguished from sympathy, which is thought of as feeling *for* someone and as a general concern for the welfare of another in face of distress. Such concern may be expressed but does not necessarily involve an active caring response to another person's pain or suffering. While sympathy has taken on such meaning in popular understanding, the origins of the word suggest a different meaning that is closer to or even identical with compassion. While compassion is derived from the Latin, sympathy is derived from the Greek verb *sympaschō* and literally means "to suffer with" or "to suffer together." Thus, its original meaning suggests an active and more significant act of care or solidarity than what current popular understanding of the concept implies. In the letters of the Apostle Paul, for example, the verb is used to refer to discipleship in solidarity with the suffering of Christ (Rom 8:17) and to illustrate the shared suffering of believers as the "body of Christ" (1 Cor 12:26).

Empathy and compassion, while being different and distinct concepts, can complement each other in acts of care. Acknowledging the difference between empathy and compassion and their complementary potential, philosopher and ethics educator Bruce Maxwell suggests a concept and a practice of *compassionate empathy* that combines characteristics of both practices of caring. He defines compassionate empathy as "a morally enabling

---

61 See Jeffrey "Empathy, Sympathy, and Compassion in Healthcare," 448.
62 See Shane Sinclair et al., "Compassion: A Scoping Review of the Healthcare Literature," BMC Palliative Care 15, no. 6 (January 2016): 5.

affective perceptive disposition" toward others.[63] The notion of a morally enabling dynamic in relationships implies moral sensitivity and moral motivation, an awareness of a moral problem that negatively affects the well-being of another as well as an incentive to restore or increase the welfare of the other person. Furthermore, Maxwell identifies compassionate empathy as an interpersonal, emotional connection with another as well as a means of observation, perception, and knowledge.

Drawing upon philosopher Lawrence Blum's work, Maxwell identifies three key components of compassionate empathy.[64] First, it perceives in another a "compassion-grounding condition," which is a debilitating or negative condition that affects persons in the center of their being and is inconsistent with their well-being. Second, compassionate empathy is person-focused and not condition-focused. In other words, the object of compassion is a person *in* a certain condition. The third key component is a differentiating approach that appraises the various aspects of another's experience and does not necessarily view the identified negative or debilitating condition as the all-defining reality of that person's life. It is sensitive and attuned to life-limiting or life-threatening aspects of a person's experience and, at the same time, can affirm strengths, successes, and life-sustaining and life-giving dynamics in their life.

Maxwell views compassionate empathy on the one hand as a moral disposition or virtue and, on the other hand, as a skill that can be built through training and practice.[65] He emphasizes, however, that compassionate empathy is not merely an act of care or moral behavior but should be considered an "attitude of caring."[66] It entails both cognitive assessment and judgment about another's situation as well as an affective response to their experience. Four specific aspects characterize compassionate empathy as an attitude of caring: the ability to imaginatively reconstruct another's condition; concern or regard for their good; a sense of shared humanity; and the willingness and ability to sustain an affective connection with another over time. Attitudes are reflected in behavior or motivate behavior.

---

63 Bruce Maxwell, *Professional Ethics Education: Studies in Compassionate Empathy* (Berlin: Springer Science, 2008), 47.
64 See Maxwell, *Professional Ethics Education*, 47–48.
65 See Maxwell, *Professional Ethics Education*, 73–74.
66 Maxwell, *Professional Ethics Education*, 51.

Compassionate empathy as an attitude of caring, we may say, motivates acts of care that consider and appreciate others' perspectives and respond to conditions that induce emotional, spiritual, or physical pain.

Empathy in Clinical Practice

Empathy is a crucial, though not sufficient, element of a clinical practice of caregiving. A clinical practice of spiritual care involves assessing the spiritual needs and resources in the experience of individuals, groups, and communities and collaborating with those individuals, groups, or communities to implement interventions that assist effective coping, growth, transformation, and possibly healing. But what exactly does empathy look like in action? Psychologist Gerard Egan distinguishes helpfully between empathic presence and empathic responding in the clinical practice of counseling. Empathic presence is a therapeutic way of being with another person that is comforting and communicates attention and understanding.[67] Specifically, it involves dialogue, attunement to another's experience, active listening, and a way to process what one hears in order to distill meaning. Empathic responding is a communication skill that effectively shares with the other what one understands about their situation and inner world and checks for accuracy.[68] It requires perceptiveness about another's experience, knowledge about how to respond to the experience and the accompanying emotions, and assertiveness to share one's understanding of another's experience, even if that understanding presents a challenge or possibly a confrontation to the other.[69] Egan summarizes a basic formula for an empathic response as a "You feel . . . because . . ." statement.[70] In the first part of the response, one

---

67 See Gerard Egan, *The Skilled Helper: A Problem-Management and Opportunity Development Approach to Helping*, 10th ed. (Belmont, CA: Brooks/Cole, 2014), 74.
68 Egan, *The Skilled Helper*, 105.
69 Confrontation, as Ralph Underwood has shown, is not incompatible with empathy. "Respectful, considerate confrontation," holds Underwood, "goes hand in hand with empathy. This is not the kind of confrontational attitude where one says, 'It's my job to hit people between the eyes with reality, and what they do with it is their business.' Rather, respectful confrontation communicates in essence, 'Having gained some understanding of you, I now trust you to deal openly with some things you have not considered.'" Ralph Underwood, *Empathy and Confrontation in Pastoral Care* (Philadelphia: Fortress Press, 1985), 90.
70 See Egan, *The Skilled Helper*, 113.

names the emotion that is expressed by the other; in the second part of the response, one communicates an understanding of the experiences, thoughts, or behaviors that generated the emotional experience.

The following exchange exemplifies the clinical practice of empathy in a hospital setting between a chaplain and a patient diagnosed with stage four lung cancer, who was distraught after receiving the news from her medical team that "her cancer" had spread to her brain and was likely not operable. The physician had ordered a spiritual care consult due to "spiritual and emotional distress." The chaplain had first met with the patient a few days earlier, when she was admitted to the oncology unit of the hospital.

> **Chaplain:** Mary? May I come in?
>
> **Patient:** Yeah, that's fine, Chaplain. Please, come in. (She is sitting up in the bed with a sad expression.)
>
> **Chaplain:** I heard that you got some difficult news. Dr. Caldwell let me know since I am part of the team that provides care on this unit. Do you mind if I pull up a chair and sit down?
>
> **Patient:** No, not at all, please, do. You can move all the stuff that's on the chair.
>
> **Chaplain:** (Moves a chair to the bedside, sits down in an open posture, and speaks after a moment of silence.) You look sad.
>
> **Patient:** Do I? I'm not sure what I feel. I just didn't expect that news. I actually thought it was going well. The tumors shrunk, you know, and it was going well. That's what I thought.
>
> **Chaplain:** There was good progress, it seemed, and the chemo worked. You were hopeful. I can imagine that it's hard to sort out the feelings when you get thrown off course like that.
>
> **Patient:** You're damn right. (Now she sounds angry.) Pardon my language, Chaplain. I thought I was going somewhere. I thought we were on a good course and that I could beat it. And now it's like I'm lost. I don't know what's coming next. Am I dying? (She looks the chaplain directly in the eyes.)
>
> **Chaplain:** I don't know, Mary. I don't know if you are dying. What I hear is that you got some really bad news that makes you wonder

what's ahead. And you may be angry because it's not at all what you expected, and it's hard to see right now how this one will turn out. I imagine that is scary."

Patient: Yes, it is. I feel like I'm in a car that's spinning out of control and I'm about to crash in a bad way. And there is nothing I can do. It's just happening.

Chaplain: That's a terrifying image. You're afraid because it seems like you lost control and cannot maneuver anymore, much worse than when you got your initial diagnosis. You know it's dangerous.

Patient: (She looks the chaplain again straight in the eyes.) I think that's what they tried to tell me, that I will die much sooner than I had thought. (Tears well up in her eyes, and she pauses.) But there is still so much I need to do.

Chaplain: (Pause) Yes, there is still so much to do. And I feel sad when I hear your fear that you may not get to do all of it.

Mary's inner world was in turmoil. She "felt lost" and as if her life was "spinning out of control," responding with fear, anger, and sadness to the news about the spread of the cancer in her body. Through empathic listening and responding, the chaplain facilitated expression of emotions and a painful acknowledgment of the possibility that Mary's life could end sooner than expected. Mary expressed both her grief and a future-orientation that was threatened but not eliminated. Follow-up conversations assisted her to process further the meaning of her prognosis and identify goals for the time she had left to live.

Another clinical vignette illustrates the use of empathic understanding in response to a shame reaction in clinical supervision. Randy was a chaplain resident who had experienced a great degree of anxiety in clinical situations, which at times had caused him to feel utterly helpless. Nursing managers had observed this and reported it to his supervisor, wondering if he was "fit to be a chaplain." When Randy's supervisor attempted to explore the issue with Randy, Randy went into a shame spiral.

Randy: (He slumps into his chair and stares at the floor.) They hate me, don't they?! The nurse managers just hate me. I know it. I can do nothing right for them. But I'm trying. (He tears up.)

Educator: I can tell that this is difficult feedback for you to hear and it was difficult for me to share because I imagined that it would hurt you. It's upsetting to try and keep trying and not have the other person recognize and affirm your efforts.

Randy: It's so frustrating (he sounds defeated) and it keeps happening again. It's like being in that movie, "Groundhog Day." You know, the one with Bill Murray? It's like I'm doomed to mess up over and over.

Educator: I know that movie. And it sounds exhausting, being trapped in that time loop and having to repeat the same things, trying so hard and not getting affirmation. I remember how depressed Bill Murray's character was at one point in the story.

Randy: (Pause) Are you saying I'm depressed?

Educator: No, that's not what I am saying, and I didn't use the word in a clinical sense. But you sound defeated. That's how I remember that character becoming discouraged and sad.

Randy: Maybe I am discouraged. (He pauses.) Defeated? I'm not sure.

Educator: That's a helpful distinction. It sounds like you still have hope.

Randy: I think I do, but sometimes I don't know. It seems like I'm never good enough, no matter how hard I try. I finished two graduate degrees, and here I am, still craving the blessing.

Educator: Do you know *who* you want to bless you?

Randy: I'm not sure.

Educator: (Pause) Well, what if you were sure?

Randy: If I were sure? (Pause) I don't know. I guess, it would be my dad.

Educator: That sounds like a story that started way back.

Randy: Well, I remember when I gave him a drawing when I was six or so, and he looked at it and tore it up because it was not right, the way he wanted it or thought it should be. It was a picture of our house, and I didn't get it right, and I never did with him.

Educator: (Sits in silence for a moment.) That is such a sad memory, Randy. To offer that gift to someone you love and have it torn up and thrown away. For a six-year-old, it must have been like being pushed away, just when you want to give someone a big hug.

Randy: I don't know. I remember the moment, but I don't remember how I felt. It's been a long time. But telling you about it makes me sad and feel small again.

Educator: I can tell by your eyes. Maybe that's how you felt back then. (Pause) And maybe that's how you feel when the nursing managers are watching you.

Randy: What do you mean?

Educator: I wonder if you feel small and inadequate, when you work with them, and fear that they will tear up your efforts to collaborate and help. That they won't give you a chance.

The conversation surfaced a possible connection between Randy's performance and relationships with authority persons in the clinic and his personal story about rejection from an authority figure. Through empathic attention and through accurate empathic recognition, Randy discovered a painful memory and a powerful metaphor. In subsequent supervisory sessions, they provided him a way to make meaning of his experiences on the interdisciplinary team, to distinguish between past and present narratives, and to choose not to sabotage himself in his clinical work.

Conclusion

Empathy is a multifaceted and often misunderstood and conflated concept and practice. Various definitions highlight different features, from cognitive assessment and observation of another's experience to emotional resonance and availability. All theories seem to concur that empathy is an essential and crucial factor in caring relationships. It is a therapeutic skill and ability to be present with another that gathers and communicates knowledge about another's inner world and embodied, emotional experience. However, it is not only a means to understand another person's experience but also a way to convey care and a common humanity. Empathy communicates with appropriate vulnerability the willingness to know another and to respond to their will to be known. It has the potential to overcome the alienating effects of shame and to stimulate positive self-regard and self-exploration. The vulnerability involved in empathic relationships makes empathy with oneself an important aspect of professional self-care. While empathy responds to the vulnerable self, it also renders the care provider vulnerable to the experience of another. For the care provider, empathy with oneself means to be attuned to how another's story affects one's own inner world and to respond with self-care and appropriate self-other boundaries.

Empathy and compassion are related but distinct therapeutic responses. While compassion is an attitude that may lead to skillful interventions, empathy is an attitude, a therapeutic skill, and a form of knowledge about another's experience. Empathy is an advanced therapeutic skill that requires both attunement to another person's experience and the way it impacts their inner, emotional world as well as attunement to one's own inner world and how it resonates with another's experience. The notion of compassionate empathy transcends the theoretical dichotomy between both concepts and captures both the practical need for an expressively caring relationship that stays with another in their pain and the need for a skillful and disciplined way to enter and know that person's inner world.

8

A THEOLOGICAL INTERPRETATION

THE JESUS STORY, as it is narrated in in the synoptic gospels and in the Gospel of John, is the master story about salvation in the Christian tradition. While dominant interpretations of that story have focused on Jesus's death and resurrection to deliver humanity from sin and eternal judgment, the story is much larger than the passion narrative It is a story about an empathic God event that called upon those who witnessed it through Jesus's life and his public work, which provoked the authorities and eventually led to his death. However, not the cross but God's transformative empathy embodied in the life and work of Jesus is at the center of the narrative.

The Jesus Story as Theological Narrative

The gospel narratives about Jesus are neither biographies nor historical accounts. We do not have any written words by Jesus, only written words about Jesus. They are *kerygma*, theological interpretations and proclamation of a God event that occurred through Jesus, whom his early followers identified as the Christ. In other words, they are words of faith (Rom 10:8), theological narratives that use symbolic language along with prose to express the significance of the Jesus event for certain early Christian communities who did not witness the event. The fact that the Jesus story is a theological narrative in four versions, three of which are interconnected, does not negate its specific historical context. In fact, the story is inseparably linked to historical realities. Jesus was a Jewish man, who lived at a certain time in a certain place among Jewish people whose land was occupied by a military force. His death makes only sense within that context, and the theological narrative is based upon a historical narrative about a prophet and teacher from Nazareth that can be glimpsed in parts throughout the gospels. However, while the God event in the Jesus story was closely connected to a specific historical context, as a theological narrative, it points beyond that context.

Tillich among others maintains that everything that can be said about God is necessarily symbolic since "symbolic language alone is able to express the ultimate."[1] Like signs, he explains, symbols point beyond themselves to something else. Unlike signs, however, symbols participate in the reality to which they point and disclose aspects of reality that cannot be accessed in other ways. Furthermore, symbolic language is efficacious language that resonates within the self to create an awareness that would otherwise not be available. Faith in God should be considered an example of such an awareness.

Tillich seems to suggest that symbols are not human inventions but emerge somehow mysteriously from the individual or collective unconscious. However, symbols can be intentionally constructed. More importantly, such constructive process is an essential theological task in reinterpreting the Christian tradition. For example, the declaration "Christ crucified" (1 Cor 1:23) refers, on the one hand, to a historical event of the past when Jesus was executed by the Roman authorities. On the other hand, however, Christ crucified is a symbolic, theological construct that has pointed for centuries through the proclamation of the church to God's saving initiative. If symbols can be constructed, they also can be deconstructed and reconstructed, and both activities are genuinely theological tasks.

In constructing the symbol of the empathic God, I use a concept from clinical-therapeutic practice to interpret the God event in the Jesus story and to point to the means and meaning of salvation that was carried out in that event. Salvation is the name for a God event that transforms human reality to restore individuals and communities to wholeness. The symbol of an empathic God points primarily to Jesus's atoning life. It does not replace or exclude the cross. Rather, the symbol includes the cross as a sign of God's empathy and as a consequence of Jesus's passionate and compassionate public work. As is true for any human person, Jesus's death was part of his life.

A Vulnerable God

Symbols of Christ crucified and of the empathic God both point to a vulnerable God. They challenge theologies of power that assert that God is the unmoved mover, immutable and all-powerful, unaffected by human affairs

---

1 Paul Tillich, *Dynamics of Faith* (New York: Harper & Row Publishers, 1957), 41–42.

and sovereign. While the Apostle Paul contrasts the perception of foolishness in the symbol of Christ crucified with the power of God that the symbol actually portrays (1 Cor 1:18), recent interpretations of the cross have pointed to the vulnerability of God as a central aspect of the passion narratives. For example, Moltmann's relational interpretation of the cross identifies the *pathos* of God, that is, God's willingness to be affected by human affairs and suffering as a central element of the narrative about the cross of Jesus. Likewise, Frank Tupper's theology of God's providence similarly insists that Jesus's experience of Godforsakenness corresponds with God's own suffering and that God's love *for* humanity is inseparable from God's suffering *with* humanity. Vulnerability is a necessary condition for empathic encounters. Consequently, the symbol of an empathic God, like Christ crucified, implies a vulnerable God who is willing and able to be affected by human experience.

Traditional models of divine omnipotence cannot adequately convey the meaning of the God event in the Jesus story. An *all*-mighty or *all*-powerful God can ultimately not be empathic, compassionate, or loving. Love, empathy, and compassion require the willingness and ability to be vulnerable, which is not compatible with the idea of omnipotence. Outlining from prison his vision of a religionless Christianity and theology, Bonhoeffer criticizes religious models of divine power and points to the saving nature of God's vulnerability in the Jesus event.

> *God consents to be pushed out of the world and unto the cross; God is weak and powerless in the world and in precisely this way, and only so, is at our side and helps us. Matt. 8:17 makes it quite clear that Christ helps us not by virtue of his omnipotence but rather by virtue of his weakness and suffering. Human religiosity directs people in need to the power of God in the world, God as deus ex machina. The Bible directs people toward the powerlessness and the suffering of God; only the suffering God can help.*[2]

---

2 Dietrich Bonhoeffer, *Letters and Papers from Prison*, trans. Isabel Best, Lisa E. Dahill, Reinhard Krauss, and Nancy Lukens. *Dietrich Bonhoeffer Works*, vol. 8, ed. Christian Gremmels, Eberhard Bethge, and Renate Bethge, with Ilse Tödt (Minneapolis: Fortress Press, 2010), 479.

Bonhoeffer still espouses a crucicentric theology that places the cross of Christ at the center of God's saving initiative and interprets it as the primary demonstration of God's vulnerability. However, other aspects of his understanding of the Jesus event come closer to the idea of an empathic God. For example, Bonhoeffer points toward the vulnerability of God by constructing the concept of "Christ existing as community," which he formulated early in his theological work and developed throughout his writings.[3] Bonhoeffer argues that the ongoing process of reconciliation is realized within Christian community despite all its limitations. The saving God event is ultimately mediated through others in a community that reflects the compassion, inclusion, and vulnerability evident in the Jesus story. In *Life Together*, Bonhoeffer cautions against an understanding of Christian community as an exclusive, spiritual community of a higher order. "The exclusion of the weak and insignificant, the seemingly useless people, from everyday life in community," Bonhoeffer states, "may actually mean the exclusion of Christ; for in the poor sister and brother, Christ is knocking at the door."[4] The marginalized and vulnerable, those not deemed important or powerful, belong precisely because the foundation for Christian community is the belief in a vulnerable God.

While the idea of a vulnerable God stands in stark contrast to an understanding of God as all-powerful, vulnerability as such does not necessarily imply a complete lack of power. In fact, the therapeutic use of vulnerability can be powerful when used and displayed intentionally to move or motivate another person to engage in relationship at a deeper level. A vulnerable God may exercise relational power in a similar way. One of Jesus's parables shines the spotlight on the issue of power and vulnerability. Luke 18:2–5

---

[3] Bonhoeffer first introduced the idea in his doctoral dissertation in 1927. See Dietrich Bonhoeffer, *Sanctorum Communio: A Theological Study of the Sociology of the Church*, trans. Joachim Von Soosten, Reinhard Kraus, and Nancy Lukens. *Dietrich Bonhoeffer Works*, vol. 1, ed. Clifford J. Green (Minneapolis: Fortress Press, 2009). Charles March traces the theme of "Christ existing as community" throughout Bonhoeffer's writings and concludes that, for Bonhoeffer, the "experience of reconciliation is not a project of speculative reason but a life of responsibility, commitment, and risk" in community. See Charles March, *Reclaiming Dietrich Bonhoeffer: The Promise of His Theology* (New York: Oxford: Oxford University Press, 1994), 109.

[4] Dietrich Bonhoeffer, *Life Together and the Prayerbook of the Bible*, trans. Daniel W. Bloesch and James H. Butness. *Dietrich Bonhoeffer Works*, vol. 3, ed. Geffrey B. Kelly (Minneapolis: Fortress Press, 1996), 45–46.

tells the story of a widow who moves the arm of legal authority in her favor through her persistence and through the acknowledgment and display of her vulnerability. It is a curious short story because of its protagonists. The parable illustrates the contrast between the power of vulnerability and the self-serving use of power. Widows were among the most vulnerable and powerless in the society that Jesus knew and in need of protection. Judges were considered the stewards of the Torah and interpreted God's will for God's people.

This particular story challenges those traditional images and views of status, social power, and influence, so much so that biblical scholar Bernard Brandon Scott identifies it as an "anti-metaphor."[5] The widow, who was likely left vulnerable and destitute through her husband's death, apparently argued her case against an unknown opponent obstinately before the judge. She eventually succeeds and overpowers the judge with her persistence, causing him to consider the impact of her vulnerable state and a decision against her on public perception. Just as the widow does not fit the image of powerlessness, the judge in the story does not represent justice or God's will. In fact, the story states explicitly that he "neither feared God nor had respect for people" (Luke 18:2). Nevertheless, he is moved to decide in support of a vulnerable widow's case, albeit not for ethical reasons but probably out of concern for self-preservation because his public image was threatened with being tainted by the widow's persistence.

The concept of a vulnerable and empathic God is not exclusive to the Christian narrative of salvation, and it is not a new concept that supersedes theological perspectives in Hebrew scripture. Even though Jesus's public work consisted of radical teachings and a radical praxis, he was deeply rooted in the religious tradition of his people. The Torah calls attention to God's vulnerability as an aspect of the liberating God event in the Exodus. In this master story about salvation in Hebrew scripture, Yahweh is literally introduced as an event that attracts Moses's curiosity and attention (cf. Exod 3:2–4) and more specifically as an empathic God who is affected by the suffering of the Hebrew slaves in Egypt. "Then the Lord said, 'I have observed the misery of my people who are in Egypt;

---

5 See Bernard Brandon Scott, *Hear Then the Parable: A Commentary on the Parables of Jesus* (Minneapolis: Fortress Press, 1989), 175.

I have heard their cry on account of their taskmasters. Indeed, I know their sufferings . . ." (Exod 3:7).'" The Hebrew verb *yāda'* that is used here to describe God's "knowing" does not merely refer to cognitive knowledge *about* something but more importantly references deep personal knowledge and even loving awareness and attention. It can indicate intimate familiarity between persons, including sexual intimacy, which is a rather vulnerable experience.[6] The term characterizes God's knowing as an empathic understanding and a practice of relatedness rather than mere cognitive awareness that derives from observation. The God who knows the suffering of the Hebrew people is not one who observes from afar but is deeply affected and moved by the impact of their oppression and therefore initiates salvation.

Another well-known passage in the Torah points to empathy as the essence of the caring God event that enacts blessing among God's people. The priestly or Aaronic blessing in Numbers 6:22–27 evocatively communicates divine care and protection by using language and imagery that is reminiscent of an empathic relationship between a parent and an infant. The notion that God's face is lifted above God's people and shines upon them to facilitate wholeness (*shalom*) and to convey acceptance and grace suggests the image of the primal empathic gesture, a parent's face smiling with delight over the crib of an infant and making eye contact to eliminate anguish or distress, conveying a loving parental presence. The plea in cultic prayers that God may not hide God's face from worshipers (cf. Ps 102:2) in times of distress, lest they "wither away," reflects the same notion and awareness that human beings depend on God's empathic care and grace symbolized in the image of God's shining face.[7]

---

6 See G. Johannes Botterweck and J. Bergmann, "*yāda'*," in *Theological Dictionary of the Old Testament*, vol. 5, trans. David E. Green, ed. J. Johannes Botterweck and Helmer Ringgren (Grand Rapids: William B. Eerdmans Publishing Company, 1986), 464.

7 Modern psychological insight into human development during infancy and the connection between face and shame points to the importance of the empathic gaze between parent and child for self-formation and to relieve stress from shame affects. It is perhaps one of the earliest experiences of empathic receptiveness, or what Heinz Kohut calls "the resonance of the self in the self of others," and relates to the mirroring function in parental and therapeutic relationships. See Heinz Kohut, *Self Psychology and the Humanities: Reflections on a New Psychoanalytical Approach*, ed. Charles B. Strozier (New York: W. W. Norton & Company, 1985), 222.

Incarnation as At-Onement

The empathic God event in the Jesus story uses two prominent religious symbols, the incarnation and the resurrection, as bookends that frame the narrative about Jesus's atoning life. Within that narrative frame, God's empathic response unfolds through Jesus's public work of healing and inclusion, through his teaching in parables and his prophetic activity, through calling diverse people into community, and finally through his death. God's saving initiative in the Jesus event is a gracious response to the alienating effects of shame rather than a divine effort to eradicate the condemning effects of guilt through sacrifice or ransom.

The symbol of the incarnation points to a God who is at once mystery and enfleshed, a God beyond human understanding, yet whose saving activity manifests in tangible ways in human experience. Colossians 1:15–20 states that truth in quasi-paradoxical terms, identifying Jesus as the visible image of the invisible God in whom "the fullness of God" dwelled. The passage links Jesus to both God's creative activity and God's salvific initiative. The idea of incarnation is also at the center of the prologue to John's gospel. "And the Word became flesh and lived among us, and we have seen his glory, the glory as of a father's only son, full of grace and truth" (John 1:14). The poem about the divine *logos* draws from themes and from the language of the creation account in Genesis. The divine *logos* that was in the beginning and became flesh in the Jesus event is reminiscent of the creative Word that called everything into being.[8] The poem evokes the notion that God's creation was "very good" (Gen 1:31) and suggests that the Jesus event embodied the "glory" of the original blessing, the goodness of creation and humanity, and God's grace toward humanity. The enfleshed creative Word embodied divine grace, God's compassionate empathy toward humanity.

The poetic prologue to the Gospel of John explicitly highlights that Jesus was human, flesh and blood, and lived among other human beings in a certain place and time. Exploring the Son of Man traditions in Hebrew scripture and their reception in Christian theology, biblical scholar Walter Wink amplifies that very perspective. He argues that Jesus "is not the omnipotent

---

8 See Bruce J. Malina and Richard L. Rohrbaugh, *Social Science Commentary on the Gospel of John* (Minneapolis: Fortress Press, 1998), 36–39.

God in a man-suit, but someone like us, who looked for God at the center of his life and called the world to join him."[9] Jesus's connection to the God event at the center of his life, what theologian Frank Tupper calls his *Abba* relationship, was so intimate and intense that his early followers concluded that "God was in Christ" (2 Cor 5:19) and that a saving God event materialized in the Jesus story.

The relationship between an incarnate Jesus and his God was an experience of *at-onement* that was only challenged by Jesus's torture on the cross. The notion of at-onement in the Jesus event suggests connection rather than culpability, a depth of relationship rather than a bloody sacrifice, and a profound attunement to another. While the theological construct of atonement has traditionally indicated a violent act of salvation, at-onement is a relational and empathic process.

Theologian Edward Farley can help us to understand the incarnation as at-onement more clearly, even though he does not explicitly use the terminology. However, he suggests understanding Jesus's openness to his God as a particular sensibility to God's empathy and that the belief that God was in Christ points to an empathic union, in which the divine and the human come together. Farley holds that "in Jesus, relation to God and empathetic concern come to the same thing," and he concludes "that something about Jesus' relation to God orients Jesus empathically and as such to any and all he meets."[10] Jesus's faith, his Abba relationship, and his empathic concern for others unite in the way he is present to his God and to others.

Farley is suspicious of traditional interpretations of the symbol of incarnation that insist it conveys a once-for-all meaning and ignore or deny its historical context. Furthermore, he rejects interpretations of the incarnation as a means of revelation or as a means of identifying Jesus as the perfect example of divine-human relation. Instead, he highlights two principles to interpret the symbol of the incarnation. First, any interpretation of the statement that God was in Christ needs to affirm the full humanity of Jesus without implying that any aspect of Jesus's humanity was superseded

---

9 Walter Wink, *The Human Being: Jesus and the Enigma of the Son of Man* (Minneapolis: Fortress Press, 2002), 11.
10 Edward Farley, *Divine Empathy: A Theology of God* (Minneapolis: Fortress Press, 1996), 281.

through divine presence. Second, any interpretation of the incarnation needs to affirm both the uniqueness of Jesus as "the through-which" of the redeeming God event that created a new community and that "Jesus is not an exception to the way God can be 'in' or present to other human beings."[11] The Jesus event exemplifies God's activity in the world. The symbol of the incarnation, while pointing to a unique event that unfolded in the Jesus story at a certain time and place in history, does not signify an exceptional event that excludes the possibility of a God event manifesting God's saving activity through other events, persons, or relationships.

Farley further argues that, in affirming Jesus's full humanity, we need to acknowledge that "Jesus embodies the general agential structures of human existence. This means that he too is constituted by bodily passions, experiences the tragic ambiguities of existence, and participates in the deep social structures of a specific culture already infected by corporate evil."[12] It is precisely Jesus's humanity that establishes his profound God connection because a central aspect of his humanity is his sensibility and specifically his sensibility to God's empathic suffering. Farley's interpretation means that the symbol of the incarnation does not point to a God who miraculously transfers into human existence while also somehow retaining the divine nature. Rather, it signifies an attunement to the mystery of a God event that called upon Jesus and that inspires empathy toward others. The movement that the symbol points to is not from the divine realm into the human realm but it is a movement that unites the human with the divine. While the empathic union that Farley describes may be reminiscent of mystic experiences, it transcends the meaning of those experiences. Mystic experiences typically lift the human spirit into the realm of the divine (cf. 2 Cor 12:2–4). The empathic union that Farley identifies, however, directs Jesus's public work toward the realm of human suffering.

In constructing his theology of God, Farley uses the concept of empathy differently than this clinical theology. Farley focuses on the empathic quality of Jesus's Abba relationship and consequently on how God appears in the Jesus event. His understanding of empathy draws from philosophical perspectives rather than from a clinical, experience-near perspective, and he specifically

---

11 Farley, *Divine Empathy*, 280.
12 Farley, *Divine Empathy*, 281.

references Edith Stein's work. Combining the concepts of empathy, sympathy, and compassion that Stein distinguishes, Farley creates a broadly defined and inclusive understanding of empathy that integrates "participative suffering, self-impartation, perception of our experiencing, and compassion."[13] Divine empathy, for Farley, merges this collection of metaphors into an inclusive interpretation of the notion that God was in Christ. While a clinical theological approach affirms that the Jesus event embodies and conveys God's empathy toward humanity, it does so primarily by focusing on the human condition rather than the empathic union between Jesus and his God. From a clinical-theological perspective, God's empathy in the Jesus event is God's saving, restorative intervention in response to human suffering and to the shame that characterizes the human condition. The incarnation is therefore at once a symbol of God's solidarity with humanity and a symbol of God's initiative toward salvation.

Jesus's Public Work of Healing

Jesus's mission announcement in Luke 4:18–19 is remarkable for what it says and for what it does not say. Jesus announces that a God event called upon him to "bring a good report" to the poor, to proclaim healing to the sick and freedom to the oppressed, and that this is symbolic of the Jubilee year, which was a period of liberation and restoration ordered in the Torah (cf. Lev 25:8–10a). Jesus announces salvation in a broad manner primarily as a response to suffering at the margins of society. He does not forecast his death as part of his mission, nor does he promise eternal life to those who accept his death as a sacrifice. Rather, he focuses on conditions that diminish or can destroy life and have the potential to induce or increase, pointing to the possibility of flourishing life.

Jesus does not suggest a spiritualized understanding of salvation as the means to enter the next life but rather seems to suggest that salvation is about the work of liberation and restoration in this life. According to Luke 4, the trajectory of Jesus's mission is not toward the cross but toward the suffering of those around him to provide restorative interventions. Immediately after

---

13 Farley, *Divine Empathy*, 296.

Jesus's mission statement and his subsequent rejection by some, Luke makes it clear in his account of the Jesus story that the announcement was not an eschatological vision but an agenda for salvation in the here-and-now. Four healing narratives follow Jesus's mission statement, along with accounts of calling disciples as participants in the work of salvation, as if to illustrate how the mission translates into concrete healing events and how salvation takes place though a community of those called upon to care.

Jesus was famous as a teacher and as a healer (cf. Matt 4:24), and he was infamous for keeping company with "sinners" (cf. Matt 9:10–11), those who were marginalized by religious authorities and regulations. Both aspects of his reputation reflect the same truth, namely that Jesus embodied and enacted God's compassionate empathy to overcome marginalizing, alienating, and life-limiting conditions. Traditionally, the healing narratives in the gospels have not been interpreted in their own right but as signs of the coming reign of God. In other words, interpreters understood that they pointed to a larger, more abstract, and future-oriented reality than the concrete experiences of suffering that Jesus encountered and engaged.

However, all four gospels seem to agree that Jesus's healing ministry was essential to his mission, not just as a collection of acts that point to the fullness of possibilities for liberation and restoration in the future but as therapeutic responses to the suffering of real persons that he encountered in real time. Not only did Jesus practice a healing ministry, but he also asked his disciples to follow his lead, "proclaim the good news," and engage in a ministry of healing and restoration (Matt 10:8). If Jesus's healing encounters were merely meant to legitimize him as the Son of God who was ushering in the reign of God with supernatural powers, why would Jesus instruct his followers to heal, even though they did not have those powers available to them? It appears then that just as a healing and restorative practice in response to human suffering was an essential aspect of Jesus's mission and public work, it is also essential to following in the way of Jesus. An incarnational interpretation that affirms Jesus's full humanity combined with the fact that Jesus instructed his disciples to imitate or participate in the practice of healing suggests that Jesus' healing ministry was not a series of miraculous, supernatural events. Rather, Jesus's own practice and his charge to his followers was in the realm of human abilities and skills.

The gospels do not introduce the healing narratives as miracles but literally as "deeds of power" (cf. Matt 11:20–23) or as "signs" (cf. John 2:23), which seems to shift the meaning of the events away from a supernatural interpretation. Gerhard Lohfink reminds us that the distinction between natural and supernatural is a modern way of looking at the world. In the so-called miracle stories in Hebrew and Christian scripture, he explains, it "was not about 'natural laws' in the modern sense and most certainly not about breaking them. For the Bible a miracle is something unusual, inexplicable, incomprehensible, disturbing, unexpected, shocking, something that amazes and explodes the ordinary, something by which God plucks people out of their indifference and causes them to look at him."[14] We may think of miracles as God events that call upon those present and involved in astonishing and, perhaps, even alarming ways. Lohfink further argues that, to understand the so-called miracle stories in the gospels, we must consistently apply a theology of grace, which means, on the one hand, that those events are expressions of God's grace and, on the other hand, that God does not impose salvation but calls people to participate in salvation.[15] God's freedom to intervene in the world and to engage in saving activity does not take away human freedom or replace human action. Rather, God's grace empowers human freedom and action. In the narratives about Jesus's healing work, the collaborative nature of a healing event is regularly indicated by an inquiry about what the person in need of healing wants or by referencing their faith.

The narrative about the healing of the woman with a hemorrhage in Mark 5:25–34 shows, perhaps more than any other healing story, how physical illness and shame can be closely linked and how a compassionate and empathic response needs to attend to both. It is an example how Jesus's ability to heal interacts with the woman's initiative and faith. Similar to present times, illnesses could carry a stigma in the ancient near Eastern context. Serious life-limiting physical illness prevented persons from maintaining an honorable position in society, forced them often to the margins of society, and forced them to become dependent as beggars.[16] Illness could exclude

---

14 Gerhard Lohfink, *Jesus of Nazareth: What He Wanted, Who He Was*, trans. Linda M. Maloney (Collegeville: The Liturgical Press, 2012), 140.
15 See Lohfink, *Jesus of Nazareth*, 140–141.
16 See Malina and Rohrbaugh, *Social Science Commentary on the Gospel of John*, 111.

them as unclean from their ritual and religious communities, confronting them regularly with the disgust of others. This exclusion would have been almost certainly true for this woman, who was restricted from being in physical contact with others by purity laws (cf. Lev 15:19–30) because of chronic vaginal bleeding. She was not just suffering physically and economically but had also been cut off from affective human relationships for years. Her desperation is evident in the fact that she was breaking the law and risking repercussions by getting close to Jesus and touching his garment with the hope to be healed. Her shame and her fear are evident in the fact that, after she realized that she was cured, she attempted to go back into hiding and become invisible.

The gospels describe Jesus as exhibiting a special sensibility to others. The writer of the Gospel of Mark emphasizes that Jesus knew that a powerful connection had occurred when the woman, who was considered unclean, touched his clothes. One has to wonder why Jesus would cause this woman to come forward, make herself publicly known, and possibly risk repercussions due to her violation of ritual law. Why not just let her go, particularly since Jesus was on another mission to attend to the critically ill daughter of one of the leaders of the synagogue and since time seemed to be of the essence? It can be argued that the reason Jesus called upon this woman was to respond and attend to her shame that rendered her healing incomplete. According to the narrative, she apparently had been cured physically, but the effects of her illness on her psyche and her spirit were still forcefully at work by compelling her to become invisible again. Emerging from hiding among the crowd and making herself known to Jesus with "fear and trembling" (Mark 5:33), the woman acted against her shame when Jesus paid attention to meet her with compassionate empathy and affirm her dignity and her faith.

In his classic introduction to narrative medicine, physician Howard Brody, a veteran researcher of the placebo response, explores the relationship between medicine, storytelling, and sickness. His discussion possibly can help us to understand the underlying dynamics at work in the healing encounter described in Mark 5 and in other gospel narratives where Jesus's empathy and ability to heal resonated with the other person's faith. Brody argues that meaning has an important role in the healing experience and likens it to the placebo response when actual physical changes occur because of the symbolic or emotional impact of a healing encounter. He explains that "a positive placebo response seems most likely to occur when the meaning of the illness experience is altered in a positive direction."[17] According to Brody, such a change in meaning-perspective may occur by gaining a sense of agency and control or trusting the power of others to effect positive change; by being able to rely on trustworthy care by others, which is conveyed through empathic understanding; or by finding an acceptable explanation for the illness experience within the framework of one's belief system or worldview.

At least two of the conditions that Brody describes are present in the narrative in Mark 5. The woman recognizes and seizes a hopeful opportunity. She claims her own agency and power, even though it means acting in violation of the law, and at the same time, she trusts the power that her faith invests in the healer who is passing by. When Jesus responds to the woman, he seems to affirm precisely what modern placebo research suggests, namely that a patient's hope and trust in a healer and the meaning attached to the treatment that is being offered can bring about positive, physiological changes. Jesus's subsequent response not only affirms the power of her faith but also counteracts her shame by addressing her publicly as a beloved daughter, someone who belongs, is cherished, and is valued.

Parables as Empathic Imagination

Along with his healing work, the gospel narratives, particularly the synoptic gospels, portray Jesus as a teacher. More specifically, they introduce him as an activist teacher who disrupted not only the status quo but also the theological and ideological worlds of his listeners. A primary tool for his activism were the stories he told and for which he was apparently famous. Jesus's parables are imaginative and provocative stories that are not without humor, drawing inspiration from the agrarian society he knew, from family life, and from social relationships. They invite listeners to engage the story in order to discover something about themselves and the God event that is calling upon them even through the story. There are good reasons to believe that

---

17 Howard Brody, *Stories of Sickness*, 2nd ed. (Oxford & New York: Oxford University Press, 2003), 13.

the parables originated with the public teachings of the historical Jesus, even if we cannot reconstruct the factual narrative about Jesus's life.[18] They are woven into the fabric of the synoptic tradition about the Jesus event.

Like Jesus's healing work, interpreters have related the parables to the coming reign of God. Many of Jesus's parables indeed identify the reign of God or the kingdom of heaven explicitly as a point of reference. One should not assume, however, that the formular about the reign of God necessarily points to an event or process in the future or that the parables contain the theological teaching points related to an eschatological event. The parables speak, in their own right, truth about how God events call upon persons and communities in surprising and sometimes disturbing ways. Biblical scholar William Herzog suggests that the parables need to be interpreted in the larger context of Jesus's public work. How one understands the meaning of Jesus's work ultimately determines how one understands his parables.[19] Interpreting Jesus's work as prophetic activity of liberation and as activism that sought to establish just relationships, Herzog draws on Paulo Freire's educational philosophy to explore many parables as subversive stories about economic and political realities that imaginatively exposed oppression and exploitation and invited practices of protest and liberation. The stories Jesus told were not just clever sermon illustrations but were means of salvation, sacraments for change and liberation.

Interpreters of the gospels have described Jesus's parables in various ways, depending on their hermeneutical perspectives, as riddles to be deciphered, metaphors to be translated, allegories or short symbolic fiction, to name just a few interpretative categories. Herzog correctly suggests understanding them not merely as illustrations or theological teaching points but in salvific terms and, more specifically, as therapeutic communication through empathic imagination. If we understand Jesus's public work to

---

18 See Amy-Jill Levine, *Short Stories by Jesus: The Enigmatic Parables of a Controversial Rabbi* (New York: HarperCollins Publishers, 2014), 10–11. Levine argues that the parables reflect concerns that are found elsewhere in the synoptic gospels, such as economics, relationships, and prioritizing; that they are consistent with his representation in the gospel narratives; and that they frequently reflect the theme of celebration, which seems to have prominently shaped Jesus's reputation, particularly as it concerns his companionship around the table with a wide variety of persons.

19 See William R. Herzog, *The Parables as Subversive Speech: Jesus as a Pedagogue of the Oppressed* (Louisville: Westminster John Knox Press, 1994), 14.

embody God's empathy toward humanity, the parables can be considered imaginative, empathic interventions. Recall that the empathic imagination is closely related to the poetic imagination in that it enters the world of others to envision possibilities of becoming and to engage those possibilities. Empathic imagination is as much a creative process as it is a therapeutic process. Biblical scholars Kenneth Bailey and John Dominic Crossan have discussed the parables as creations of Jesus's poetic imagination and more specifically as poetic metaphors and parabolic ballads.[20] As such, the parables function to convey a deep knowledge about the human experience in its various dimensions and how God events call upon persons to realize possibilities that can transform their experience.

Following Herzog's argument that Jesus was a pedagogue of the oppressed and that many of his parables functioned as subversive speech, we can also see how the parables are empathic interventions in response to shame. Oppression and abusive or exploitative violence are likely to inflict shame on individuals and communities, as Toni Morrison's novel illustrates. Structural shame is an integral part of systems of oppression, disempowering those who are being used and abused and keeping them in line. The so-called parable of the talents in Matt 25:14–30 (cf. Luke 19:11–27) may make more sense if it is read with such understanding. Two of the enslaved persons[21] in the story who are charged to create revenue for their master perform under the power of shame to prove their worth and avoid humiliation and punishment by their master, who is portrayed as abusive and brutal. They stay within the rules and expectations that a system of oppression and exploitation has established. A third enslaved person, who is traditionally seen as playing it safe by burying the money given to him to make a profit for his master, is the one who is speaking up subversively to expose the slave

---

20 See Kenneth E. Bailey, *Poet and Peasant* (1976; repr., William B. Eerdmans Publishing Company, 1990), 72–74.
21 Biblical scholar Mitzi Smith argues that the word "servant" (*doulos*) in the Gospel of Luke refers to enslaved people, including Luke's Jesus, who was born to a *doulē* and, according to Smith, lived the life of an enslaved person from birth to death. See Mitzi J. Smith, "Abolitionist Messiah: A Man Named Jesus Born of a *Doulē*," in *Bitter the Chastening Rod: Africana Biblical Interpretation after Stony the Road We Trod in the Age of BLM, Say Her Name, and MeToo*, ed. Mitzi J. Smith, Angela N. Parker, and Ericka S. Dunbar Hill (Lanham, MD & London: Lexington Books/Fortress Academic, 2022), 53–70.

master's unjust practices, even at the risk of making himself vulnerable to mistreatment.[22]

Jesus's parables do not only usher an invitation to restore wholeness in relationship with God, others, and oneself, they also envision what wholesome relationships look like and what undermines them. Wholesome relationships are just relationships that confront and work to transform oppression and injustice rather than use violent and oppressive power to pursue change (Mark 12:1–12; Matt 18:24–35). They are relationships shaped by grace, the unconditional affirmation and acceptance of self and others as valued and valuable instead of measuring the worth of individuals by their performance and rewarding productivity (Matt 20:1–15). Wholeness means acting truthfully and with integrity rather than meeting expectations and proving one's worth, even if one risks vulnerability by speaking truth to brutal power (Luke 19:11–27). It means belonging with others in community and depending on their care, rather than being separated and abandoned (Luke 15:4–6). Flourishing life is a pursuit and a process, not a static condition. It is a search for that which is worth great investment and sacrifice (Matt 13:45–46). Becoming whole is ultimately the result of *metanoia*, a restorative change of mind, heart, and behavior. Jesus's parables invite metanoia through imaginative and empathic narratives with transformative calls upon listeners to live inside the visions that the narratives reveal and to realize them.

The New Community

The Jesus event created a new community. From the beginning of his public work, Jesus enacted God's empathy with a group of disciples whom he recruited and invited to join his mission as close collaborators.[23] The group of

---

22 See Herzog, *The Parables as Subversive Speech*, 162–166.
23 While the group of disciples was likely selected from a larger community of followers of Jesus, the gospel narratives specify a certain number of disciples, which may have represented the restored tribes of Israel. Even though the social system of the twelve tribes of Israel did not exist anymore in Jesus's time, and only the tribes of Benjamin, Judah and half of Levi had survived, the traditional religious hope expected that God would restore the twelve tribes in God's time. See Gerhard Lohfink, *Jesus and Community*, trans. John P. Galvin (Philadelphia: Fortress Press, 1984), 10.

disciples reflected the social, geographical, and seemingly political diversity of society. We do not know the occupation and background of all the disciples, but we know about fishermen from northern Galilee, a tax collector from the Decapolis area on the opposite side of the Sea of Galilee, a Zealot identified as "the Cananaean" (Matt 10:4), and one named Judas Iscariot, who may have come from the town of Kerioth in the south of Judea. Lohfink points out that this group of disciples included extreme opposites.[24] While tax collectors collaborated with the occupying Roman authorities, members of the Zealot movement were nationalists and freedom fighters who fiercely opposed Roman rule and threatened those who cooperated with the oppressors. Thus, it appears that the gospel narratives paint the group of disciples around Jesus unequivocally as one that included individuals from diverse backgrounds and even political enemies to unite them in a common cause. Apparently, it was a community that was challenged to create a space where each member was accepted and valued.

Farley identifies the new community connected to the Jesus event as the ecclesial Christian community that began to form in response to the narrative about Jesus's death and resurrection. "The new community that arose as a resolution of the event of Jesus as Christ," he argues, "is a universalized form of the faith of Israel. That is to say, it is a social form of Israelite faith that can exist in connection with any of the ways human beings organize themselves in societies, cultures, or ancestral groups."[25] As a universalized form of Israelite faith, Farley explains, the *ecclesia* is a non-ethnic expression of Israel's faith, presenting a legitimate form of that ancient faith alongside Judaism and not in opposition. However, if all theology is ultimately contextual, and if faith is in essence the personal practice of theology, one may raise the question if there truly can be a universalized faith in the way that Farley identifies it. Additionally, even though Farley argues against a displacement theology in the long tradition of Christian anti-Semitism, his overall case nevertheless seems to imply that the new community based in the Christ event is less limited and more evolved than Jewish forms of Israel's faith. I contend that the new community that the Jesus event brought forth preceded the community that formed into the Christian *ecclesia* around the

---

24 See Lohfink, *Jesus and Community*, 11.
25 Farley, *Divine Empathy*, 257.

story of the Christ. The gospel accounts point to themes of a new community in Jesus's public work and not just when referring to the group of disciples, envisioning a larger community that is structured to reflect God's intention for change, restoration, and wholeness.

If one follows the gospel narratives closely, it almost seems paradoxical that Jesus called his closest disciples, those who accompanied him on his journey, to leave their families (Mark 1:20) to find a new family (Mark 10:29–30). Why replace one community with another? Lohfink suggests that the theme of the new family points to the reality of a new community. It symbolizes the changes the Jesus event initiates by calling upon individuals and communities in radical ways, including changes in social structures.[26] Mark 3:20f; 31–35 spells out the reality of that new community, which was likely not restricted to the close circle of disciples. The narrative specifically points out that a "crowd was sitting around" Jesus (v. 32) when he named them as his family of choice. More importantly, it was not a community established by family ties and commitments, but "whoever does the will of God" makes up this new community (v. 33). Was Jesus talking about those who followed the Torah? That explanation seems unlikely since it can be assumed that Jesus's family, who was the object of the exchange in Mark 3, was obeying Jewish law. Rather, it appears that Jesus envisioned a new community that was not structured according to hierarchical principles of middle eastern patriarchy but that responded to the God event calling upon them through Jesus's life and public work and that was willing to participate in God's saving activity. From what we know about Jesus's healing ministry and the way that he interpreted the law, we may conclude that the will of God is "to do good" and "save life" (Mark 3:4), to restore persons and communities to wholeness.

One of the best-known gospel narratives highlights the connection between community and salvation. Luke 19:1–10 tells the story about Zacchaeus, apparently a man of diminutive stature, who held a lease from the Roman authorities to collect taxes for them from Jewish citizens in Jericho as the chief revenue officer. The fact that he had become wealthy suggests that he had been in the business for a long time. Because tax collectors enriched

---

26 See Lohfink, *Jesus and Community*, 39–42.

themselves at the expense of fellow Jews and collaborated with the occupying forces, he and those who worked in similar positions elsewhere or worked for him were despised and shunned, particularly by the Pharisee guilds.[27] The narrative explains that Zacchaeus was curious about Jesus, wanting to see him on his way through Jericho, but his view was blocked by a crowd of spectators. So he climbed a tree to get a better view. While the story does not explicitly name the experience of shame, one can imagine that climbing a tree in this situation would have been a humiliating effort by someone in Zacchaeus's position and that his short statue had perhaps even created body-shame throughout his life. Being shunned and despised for his profession by fellow Jewish citizens also certainly could have been a source of shame for Zacchaeus. Disgust, after all, is a powerfully shaming force.

Reading the narrative from the perspective of an empathic clinical-therapeutic practice, the turn the story takes when Jesus interrupts his journey to pay close attention to Zacchaeus demonstrates his empathic attunement. Jesus intervenes by offering community to one who was despised, announcing almost demonstratively that he wanted to be a guest in Zacchaeus's house. As the story goes, Zacchaeus welcomes Jesus with joy, while those who witnessed it had misgivings about Jesus inviting himself into the house of someone labeled as a sinner. Not only does Zacchaeus welcome Jesus, but he also commits to making amends to those he defrauded and to practice *tzedakah*, as the Torah demands, giving part of his wealth to charity.

However, there is an enigmatic conclusion to the narrative when Jesus announces that "salvation has come to this house" (v. 9). While the announcement directly follows the mention of Zacchaeus's resolution to make amends and give to the poor, Jesus could not have possibly referred to this act of repentance, lest salvation was an act of human volition. If we understand the encounter between Jesus and Zacchaeus as an act of empathic care, salvation means in this instance deliverance from the alienating effects of toxic shame by offering communion, sharing a meal in an act of acceptance, and affirming that Zacchaeus fully belonged among God's people, that he "too was a son of Abraham" (v. 9). The affirmation here functions similarly to

---

27 See Helmut Merkel, "telōnēs," in *Exegetical Dictionary of the New Testament*, vol. 3, trans. John W. Medendorp and Douglas W. Stott, ed. Horst Balz and Gerhard Schneider (Grand Rapids: William B. Eerdmans Publishing Company, 1993), 349.

the one Jesus ushered to the woman who was healed from hemorrhaging, bestowing a sense of dignity and belonging. Zacchaeus's response testifies to the effectiveness and transforming power of the intervention. He takes responsibility and becomes responsive to others with an intention to care.

A therapeutic process to facilitate such development and transformation could, of course, not possibly be accomplished in a dinner meeting or even a lengthy home visit. The gospel narratives are, after all, not historic reports but imaginative, symbolic stories that condense theological truth into metaphors, narrative plots, and images to express in pointed ways theological and arguably therapeutic meanings. They interpret and reflect on the God event in the Jesus story, rather than documenting historical events in a chronological order. The therapeutic dimension in the gospels has to do with matters of salvation, healing, restoration, and wholeness. The literary case studies of Sethe and Buechner both resonate with the story of Zacchaeus and its therapeutic dimension. The theme of re-membering is particularly present in Sethe's story when she becomes reconnected with her past through the disturbing presence of Beloved and when she reconnects at the end of the novel with a community of women who had previously shunned her but then remember her, know her suffering, and invite her into healing community. Likewise, healing from emotional trauma and deeply rooted shame came though community for Buechner. The Jesus event powerfully affirms the potentially therapeutic and transformative power of community and, more specifically, calls upon those who become involved with the event to become a community, where life can flourish within transformed social relationships.

Prophetic Empathy

The vision of flourishing life within transformed social structures is supported by Jesus's prophetic activism. Jesus announced his calling in the tradition of the prophets along with his healing work in his mission statement in Luke 4. The Gospel of John identifies Jesus's mission similarly as enabling "life in its fullest" (John 10:10). Jesus's work was about making possible the flourishing of life, which deeply resonates with the prophetic tradition. As biblical scholar Walter Brueggemann explains, the work of the prophets was the formation of a new, alternative community with an alternative consciousness that could criticize and dismantle the dominant community and thus create conditions for flourishing life. He identifies Jesus of Nazareth as "the fulfillment and quintessence of the prophetic tradition."[28] Brueggemann contends that Jesus's prophetic authority was intrinsically connected to his inner life and his self-empathy. "The authority of Jesus, his power to transform strangely, was found precisely in his own poverty, hunger, and grieving over the death of his people. In his poverty he had the power to make many rich (2 Cor 8:9). In his hunger he had the capacity to fill others. In his capacity to grieve he had the power to bring joy and wholeness to others."[29] Along with his empathic sensitivity to God, it was Jesus's self-empathy that energized his prophetic activism and solidarity with those marginalized and oppressed by the dominant culture and also his compassion for those who held privilege in the dominant culture.

Prophetic empathy is a deep understanding of human experiences of injustice followed by a response that seeks transformation through confrontation. Jesus confronted religious and political authorities with prophetic empathy through his healings (cf. Mark 3:4), through his parables (cf. Luke 18:1–8), and through direct action and challenge (cf. Mark 11:15–19). He identified himself as a prophet when he was rejected in his hometown (Mark 6:4 par), and the crowd that welcomed him at his entrance into Jerusalem apparently recognized him as popular prophet (Matt 21:11). Through his empathic public work, which consisted primarily of healing work and teaching, Jesus had gained a reputation as a prophet. Herzog echoes Brueggemann's assessment, pointing out that Jesus's actions and teaching clearly reflected his prophetic identity and the prophetic tradition, in particular the tradition of Israel's oracle prophets. He explains that "Jesus was a peasant prophet who interpreted the Torah not as representative of the great tradition emanating from Jerusalem but as one who embodied the little tradition found in the villages and countryside of Galilee. . . . he attracted crowds because he embodied the yearnings of the villagers of Galilee, who were increasingly separated from their land and traditions by an alien network of

---

28 Walter Brueggemann, *The Prophetic Imagination*, 2nd ed. (Minneapolis: Fortress Press, 2001), 102.
29 Brueggemann, *The Prophetic Imagination*, 112.

Roman domination, Herodian exploitation, and temple control."[30] Jesus's empathy for those who lived on the margins and the periphery of society, where the "little tradition" was rooted, and his understanding of their world, both external and internal, is reflected in many of his parables. It is at the heart of his prophetic activism.

Herzog argues that the Pharisees used shaming as a strategy to exercise control and to discredit Jesus.[31] Just as they attempted to shame Jesus by labeling him and calling him names, their imposition of purity laws and rituals of the temple cult on everyday life, using those laws to identify some as clean and others as unclean, functioned similarly to induce social shame. Jesus's prophetic empathy aimed at liberation from shame and challenged the use of religious means as a form of social shaming and control (Matt 15:1–9). He explicitly valued and paid tribute to the experience and the world of peasants and to village life by making them models for the reign of God in many of his parables. However, as Herzog points out, Jesus's public work went beyond that of the prophets, in that he became a "broker of Yahweh's justice" and "claimed that he was the mediator of God's healing and saving power, evidenced by his own healing and exorcisms."[32] Thus, Jesus's work for liberation from shame, his healing work, and his activism to establish just relationships must be considered central aspects of his atoning life.

The Rule of God

Some would argue that the rule of God is at the center of the Jesus story, that his whole existence was about God's rule, and that his work was one of proclaiming and explaining the rule or the reign of God and pointing to

---

30 William R. Herzog, *Jesus, Justice, and the Reign of God: A Ministry of Liberation* (Louisville: Westminster John Knox Press, 2000), 70. The "great tradition," according to Herzog, is how the dominant culture describes the world and exercises social control, using religion to define reality and to identify it with the current social, political, and economic order. The "little tradition," on the other hand, is the perspective on the world, God, and reality from the margins and the periphery of society that supports resistance to domination.
31 Herzog, *Jesus, Justice, and the Reign of God*, 154.
32 Herzog, *Jesus, Justice, and the Reign of God*, 208.

its salvific purpose through healings and exorcisms.[33] Literally, the gospels use kingdom, or *basileia,* terminology to speak about the rule of God. In the history of the church, the notion of God's kingdom took on a literal meaning at various times and led to conquests and colonialization in the name of the Christian faith. The kingdom metaphor could easily imply a God event with imperial dimensions and overwhelming power.

Given that Jesus proclaimed and explained the rule of God in his parables as a dynamic and subversive event, the notion of kingdom as a theocratic institution does not seem to capture the meaning of the event adequately. Jesus proclaimed the rule of God as an event that was happening and in motion. It was to "come" (Matt 6:10) and "among" (Luke 17:21) people, hidden like a treasure to be discovered (Matt 13:44) and creating surprises (Mark 4:26–29). The gospel narratives speak about the *basileia* as an event that is in process or proceeding. Thus, translating it as the rule or the reign of God, we capture perhaps better the dynamic and subversive nature of the event.

While the notion of God's reign is a prominent theme in the gospel narratives, it did not originate with Jesus's public work. It is deeply rooted in Israel's history, going back to the foundational narrative about salvation, the story of the Exodus (cf. Exod 19:6), contrasting Yahweh's reign with pharaoh's reign. However, the way Jesus interpreted and taught about the rule of God was unique. Most significantly, Jesus announced the rule of God not as a political or eschatological spectacle sometime in the future but as a present and emerging reality (Luke 17:20–21). God's rule is the empathic and salvific God event that overcomes alienation now and calls upon individuals and communities to create just relations.

Given Jesus's announcement about the rule of God in Luke 17, we may ask *how* God's rule emerged as a present reality. The Greek phrase *entos hymōs,* which is typically translated to indicate that the reign of God is "among you," can also mean "between you."[34] If we consider this possible translation, God's rule would appear to be a relational God event that seeks to establish connection and community rather than a theocratic institution or an eschatological victory. Furthermore, the dynamic nature of the event

---

33 See, for example, Lohfink, *Jesus of Nazareth,* 24.
34 See Lohfink, *Jesus of Nazareth,* 51.

reflected in Jesus's teaching and the fact that he explains the rule of God in terms of communal life would support such understanding. However, Jesus did not only proclaim and explain the rule of God, but he also identified it with his mission. The Jesus story is one about God's rule embodied in the life and public work of a prophet and a healer from Nazareth. In other words, the rule of God is the empathic God event in the Jesus story that established a new community with a new mindset as an alternative to the dominant community and the dominant mindset. It called upon this new community to participate in the movement of salvation. Just as the liberating God event in the Exodus narrative aimed to establish a covenant community, so did the rule of God that Jesus proclaimed and enacted through his work create a new community, called upon to share in his mission to heal and to liberate.

The Shame of the Cross

Traditional atonement models view Jesus's death as the center of God's saving initiative toward humanity and hold that the trajectory of his ministry pointed from the beginning toward Golgotha. New Testament scholar Scot McKnight examines the passion predictions in the gospels and finds that "death for Jesus is not a tragedy but the *telos* of his mission."[35] At the same time, McKnight argues that, even though Jesus likely thought he might die prematurely and sought to connect the script of his life with the teachings of his faith to understand his death in accordance with God's plan, it is not at all clear that Jesus viewed his death as atoning. The belief that Jesus's death was an act of substitutionary atonement is spelled out clearly for the first time by the Apostle Paul (cf. Rom 5:6–17), who understood Jesus's death and resurrection as complementary events that accomplished God's plan for salvation. Paul offered a theological interpretation of two select aspects of the Jesus event, which he regarded as central and which have prominently shaped Christological models throughout the history of theology. He applied a particular eschatological perspective, which intentionally did not consider other aspects of the event, including his prophetic activity, healing work, and teachings.

---

35 Scot McKnight, *Jesus and His Death: Historiography, the Historical Jesus, and Atonement Theory* (Waco: Baylor University Press, 2005), 225.

However, to understand the meaning of Jesus's death, we need to understand it as part of his life. The cross is not the apex of Jesus's mission but a consequence of his prophetic work and his empathic imagination. Through his storytelling, Jesus suggested possibilities of living in whole and just relationships with God and others. However, his prophetic and poetic vision and activity were considered subversive to the political and religious systems of his time. Examining Jesus's parables as stories that exposed systems of oppression, Herzog argues that Jesus's teachings threatened the powers that ruled the political and the religious domains.[36] Jesus's arrest, trial, and execution were direct results of his teaching and his public activity. His proclamation of God's rule as an empathic God event that established a new community and envisioned just relations, combined with the fact that he taught "with authority" (cf. Mark 1:22), disturbed the religious leaders and eventually the political rulers enough to take action against him. Jesus died as a prophet who set himself against political and religious interest groups that could not tolerate his challenge and his vision.[37] His body was traumatized, and he was degraded and humiliated by the authorities to discredit his message.

Jesus's death was not a sacrifice demanded for the forgiveness of human transgression against God's will. Rather, it was a political sacrifice (cf. John 11:50; 18:14) and a brutal act of deterrence on part of the occupying Roman forces. However, even if we assert that Jesus's death was not central but consequential to his public work, we must acknowledge that the notion that "Christ died for us" (Rom 5:8) is a fundamental conviction of Christian faith, and we need to understand this theological claim in the context of the empathic God event in the Jesus story. A liberationist perspective can help us not only understand that Jesus's death was a historical consequence of his life but also to comprehend the theological claim that his death was "for us" (Rom 5:8).

Essential to liberationist hermeneutics and praxis is the notion of solidarity. From a liberationist perspective, Christian praxis is based on Jesus's praxis of solidarity.[38] Jesus's solidarity with humanity is expressed both in the

---

36 Herzog, *The Parables as Subversive Speech*, 27.
37 See Herzog, *Jesus, Justice, and the Reign of God*, 241.
38 See Leonard Boff, *Passion of Christ, Passion of the World: The Facts, Their Interpretation, and Their Meaning Yesterday and Today*, trans. Robert R. Barr (Maryknoll, NY: Orbis Books, 1987), 99–101.

symbol of the incarnation and in the symbol of the cross. By interpreting Jesus's death as an ultimate expression of solidarity, we can understand it as an empathic experience within the God event that made a claim on Jesus's life. Jesus's death on the cross was not only a consequence and expression of his solidarity with those who sought liberation from forces of oppression but also an ultimate display of solidarity with humanity bound by shame. Crucifixion was not simply a mode of execution among others in the Roman world but was a torturous and even sadistic act of humiliation and deterrence.[39] Jesus's traumatized body was exposed and displayed publicly to a staring crowd in a cruel act of violence as an ultimate symbol of shame.

The view that the physical trauma that Jesus had suffered was somehow salvific shaped interpretations of his death from early on in Christian writings. The author of the first letter attributed to the Apostle Peter proclaims that "by his wounds you have been healed" (1 Pet 2:24; cf. Isa 53:5–6). The verb *iaomai*, which is used in this passage, points to the stories about Jesus's healing work in the Gospels and to God's salvific and liberating work in the history of the Hebrew people. *Iaomai* can refer to ordinary and extraordinary healing events.[40] The context of the statement presents Jesus's suffering "for you" (1 Pet 2:21) as a model for believers to follow. For that reason, the passage has been interpreted as an example of martyr theology.

However, there is no direct reference to martyrdom. Rather, the passage speaks of the abuse and the suffering that enslaved individuals endured. It instructs enslaved believers to accept their situation and not to rebel against their owners. Rather, they should understand their unjust suffering as an imitation of Jesus's passion. From a liberationist perspective, the argument is problematic. It demonstrates how a cruciform view of Jesus's work can shape a Christian praxis that colludes with violent behavior and unjust structures in society. However, the close connection that is made in this passage between the suffering of enslaved persons and Jesus's passion is intriguing because shame has a role in both experiences of suffering. From a clinical perspective, Jesus's physical and emotional wounds have therapeutic impact in light of

---

39 See Herzog, *Prophet and Teacher*, 228.
40 See Ragnar Leivestad, "iaomai," in *Exegetical Dictionary of the New Testament*, vol. 2, trans. James W. Thompson and John W. Medendorp, ed. Horst Balz and Gerhard Schneider (Grand Rapids: William B. Eerdmans Publishing Company, 1991), 170.

his solidarity with all of humanity in the experience of shame. Shame loses its alienating power when it is openly disclosed. The cross as a humiliating display of trauma is at the same time a symbol of shame and forsakenness as well as a symbol of God's empathy with humanity. The shame of the cross that instilled in Jesus a sense of forsakenness (cf. Mark 15:34) also points to the possibility of restoration and transformation toward wholeness.

Resurrection and the Transformation from Trauma and Shame

If the cross is paradoxically a symbol of shame and separation as well as a sign of God's empathy, the resurrection is at once a symbol of continuity and of transformation that becomes possible as a result of Jesus's life, public work, and his death. The transformation out of trauma into life again is, as pastoral theologian Shelly Rambo points out, a complex process that does not happen quickly. The resurrection stories in the Gospels use various narrative tools to describe fear, disorientation, and isolation among the disciples. The stories also describe Jesus's emergence from a dark tomb and his gradual reconnection with community and recognition among his followers. The gospel narratives portray the resurrection not primarily as a divine act that defies the laws of nature but rather as an event that unfolds over time between individuals as a creative and constructive process that recreates community.

In *Resurrection and Discipleship*, theologian Thorwald Lorenzen identifies Jesus's resurrection, on the one hand, as a God event that has a *novum* character, breaking all categories and expectations, and, on the other hand, as an event that needs to be understood in theological continuity with Jesus's life.[41] Following Lorenzen, the question about the content of Jesus's life and its continuity with the narrative of the resurrection is crucial to a Christian praxis. What can be discerned about Jesus's life and his life's intention that led to his death defines a resurrection faith and a post-resurrection praxis of those who follow in the way of Jesus. I have argued that Jesus's life and public work was characterized by empathic attunement to his *Abba* relationship and to human suffering. He proclaimed God's liberating rule to

---

41 See Thorwald Lorenzen, *Resurrection and Discipleship: Interpretative Models, Biblical Reflections, Theological Consequences* (Maryknoll, NY: Orbis Books, 1995), 242.

establish just relations, exposing and confronting authorities who excluded those deemed "unclean" to the margins. Jesus's resurrection from trauma and shame stands as a symbol of continuity, a confirmation that his life intent continues, regardless of theological arguments about whether or not his traumatized body was supernaturally reanimated. The issue of theological continuity between Jesus's life, death, and resurrection is not about the historicity of an event that seemingly defies the laws of nature; it is about the question of whether the God event in the resurrection is consistent with the God event that made a claim upon Jesus's life.

The Jesus event created a new community, healed those who were marginalized by their illness, reconnected them with their ritual group, and called upon others to live in just relations. Lorenzen holds that the God event in the resurrection is a relational reality that is in continuity with Jesus's life and public work, overcoming fear and alienation. "By raising the crucified Christ from the dead, God has revealed that humanity is not strange to his being, and more so, he has opened his very being to the estranging power of sin. Thereby God, in his very being, has bridged the gulf between God and humanity, between heaven and earth, between transcendence and immanence. He is not far but near; and this nearness is not qualified by morality and fear but by unconditional love and grace."[42] The resurrection narratives are a confirming declaration of God's availability and grace. Incarnation and resurrection are interlocking book ends to the Jesus story. Both themes within the story express symbolically God's availability and nearness, God's at-onement with the prophet from Nazareth, who lived God's empathy and shared the shame of humanity in ultimate solidarity at the cross.

Jesus's resurrection, however, is not only a symbol of continuity but also a symbol of transformation. It is a *novum* that points to the possibility that shame does not have to define a life. Rather, shame can be transformed toward wholeness. The resurrection narratives declare that Jesus was raised from the trauma and shame of the cross into a new and transformed existence.

The theme of Jesus's transformation appears in two curious Gospel stories about disciples who initially did not recognize the resurrected Jesus (cf. Luke 24:13–32; John 20:14; 21:4). The narratives suggest that Jesus's

---

42 Lorenzen, *Resurrection and Discipleship*, 256.

physical appearance after the resurrection was somehow transformed. Jesus did not look familiar and appeared unrecognizable as a stranger. However, transformation and continuity intersect when two people within the larger circle of disciples recognize Jesus's presence during a shared meal and, in retrospect, through his teaching style (Luke 24:31–32). The resurrection narratives symbolically talk about how community that seemed lost was recreated in a surprising and disturbing God event, how separation was overcome, and how those who were hiding and utterly disoriented found hope and courage. These narratives deeply resonate with Sethe's and Buechner's stories in that the promise of salvation and restoration toward wholeness is intrinsically linked to the re-creation of a community where one can be known, accepted, and transformed into a new existence. In that sense, Buechner's and Sethe's stories are resurrection narratives in their own respects.

Conclusion

The Jesus story is about one whose life was claimed to embody God's empathy. It is at once a narrative about the empathic union between a prophet from Nazareth and his Abba God as well as a narrative about God's empathy toward the world embodied in the Jesus event. The early Christian proclamation that God was in Christ reconciling the inhabited world to Godself (2 Cor 5:19) points toward both aspects of the narrative. It speaks about the empathic God event in the Jesus story as a salvific union to overcome fragmentation and separation and to restore the wholeness and goodness of creation. While the union between the prophet from Nazareth and his God was a historical event in the past that shaped a theological narrative, the salvation toward wholeness, which it initiated, was proleptic and is ongoing, as the passage in 2 Corinthians indicates. As Paul concluded, the message and ongoing work of reconciliation has been entrusted to those who follow in the way of Jesus. From a clinical perspective, salvation from shameful self-fragmentation and its alienating effects toward wholeness is indeed an ongoing process of healing and not something that is accomplished once for all. It is a process toward wholeness rather than a one-time restorative event.

Part Five

PRACTICING AT-ONEMENT

A CLINICAL INTERPRETATION of the empathic God event in the Jesus story ushers a call to participate in the ongoing process of salvation toward wholeness in individuals and in communities. Spiritual care practitioners, who may work in various clinical environments that include congregational settings, regularly encounter opportunities to support persons in their journey toward wholeness and restoration by engaging shame in therapeutic ways. A purposeful, clinical theology not only explores the meaning of a God event from a clinical perspective and experience but also suggests a praxis of spiritual care that is rooted in such clinical-theological reflection. More specifically, a clinical theology of an empathic God points to an empathic praxis of spiritual care that can assess and attend in caring and healing ways to shame and its alienating effects. While shame creates division and fragmentation, an empathic practice of spiritual care attempts to restore connection within the self, in relationships with God and others, and within and between communities.

Exploring crucial aspects of an empathic praxis of spiritual care establishes the "so-what" of clinical-theological reflection. Such an exploration also establishes the meaning of a clinical Christian praxis of salvation as it tends to individuals and communities to facilitate wholeness. Such wholeness, in turn, is not a state of existence devoid of pain or limitations. Rather, it is a growth process that includes knowledge and acceptance of one's full humanity and vulnerability in connection to the source of all being, to others, and to oneself. Wholeness is a relational reality, an ongoing process of restoration within a matrix of relationships. A praxis of spiritual care that facilitates and supports this process of restoration participates in the relational nature of the God event that works for salvation. It is a praxis of at-onement that joins and accompanies others in their struggles and suffering to help sustain them and possibly to effect transformation.

9

TOWARD AN EMPATHIC PRAXIS OF SPIRITUAL CARE

THE GOSPEL NARRATIVES not only proclaim Jesus's work of salvation but explicitly point out that Jesus empowered his disciples to participate in his healing work of salvation (cf. Matt 10:1; Luke 9:1–2). The Christian narrative affirms that God's saving initiative in the Jesus event did not end on the cross or on Easter morning but continues through the work of those who follow in the way of Jesus and work to restore wholeness in persons and communities. An empathic Christian practice of spiritual care, using interdisciplinary knowledge and therapeutic skills along with the wisdom and practices of its religious tradition, responds to the call that the empathic God event in the Jesus story ushers.

Defining Spiritual Care

The use of certain terminology has important implications for exploring aspects of spiritual care as a participatory praxis of salvation. Over the years, I have changed terminology from pastoral care to spiritual care for two reasons. First, strictly applied, the qualifier *pastoral* references exclusively the Christian tradition of *poimenics*. When constructing a clinical theology using the Christian salvation narrative, one could argue that the notion of pastoral care is appropriate. However, while my argument primarily addresses caregivers in the Christian tradition, we need to consider that a clinical theology applies not just in Christian contexts for caregiving but also in clinical contexts that are more diverse where Christian care providers attend to those of all faiths and of no faith. Furthermore, the gospel narratives about the Jesus event highlight the inclusive nature of God's salvation. Therefore, restrictive and potentially exclusive language is not useful in describing a praxis of participatory salvation that is based on narratives about inclusion. Second, the term *pastoral* care is often understood as referring to the person providing the care. That is, it is care given by a person in a pastoral role or position. The term *spiritual care*, on the other hand, focuses not on the person providing the care but identifies the nature and focus of care.

A focus on the spiritual dimension of experience, however, should not imply that spiritual care pays attention only to one particular aspect in the life of individuals and communities. Rather, the notion of spiritual care is akin to an understanding of *Seelsorge*, the care of souls, as German theologian Eduard Thurneysen formulated it in the late 1920s. Thurneysen explained that *Seelsorge* was not care for a person's soul but rather care for the person as soul.[1] While his definition should not be mistaken for a radical, holistic approach to the praxis of spiritual care, it reflects a central aspect of biblical anthropology. The Hebrew concept of *soul* does not refer to an immaterial and unique entity separate from the body. Rather, *nephesh*, which is typically translated as "soul" literally means "throat" and refers *pars pro toto* to the living, breathing human being who does not have a soul but *is* a soul.[2] As such, a person is dependent on God's sustaining care. Thurneysen suggested that when spiritual care practitioners attend to persons as a soul, they can assume a perspective of faith that views others as connected to

---

1 See Eduard Thurneysen, "Rechtfertigung und Seelsorge," in *Seelsorge: Texte zum gewandelten Verständnis und zur Praxis der Seelsorge in der Neuzeit*, ed. Friedrich Wintzer (Munich: Christian Kaiser Verlag, 1988), 85. Thurneysen's 1928 essay defined pastoral care in light of the Lutheran doctrine of justification by grace alone and argued that the notion of "soul" defined persons as those who are called upon by God through Christ, and that the primary act of pastoral care is to see another as one whom God has claimed in Christ. In his later book about a theology of pastoral care, Thurneysen seemed to revise his earlier definition, declaring that pastoral care "means and is care for the soul of man" and argued that body and soul are distinct entities. However, Thurneysen explained that both define a person's humanity and "are to be conceived as a unity, which makes up the totality of his life as well as each individual act." Eduard Thurneysen, *A Theology of Pastoral Care*, trans. Jack A. Worthington and Thomas Wieser (Richmond, VA: John Knox Press, 1962), 54–55.
2 See Hans Walter Wolff, *Anthropology of the Old Testament*, trans. Margaret Kohl (London: SCM Press, 1974), 10. The notion of soul in Hebrew scripture is not necessarily how Jewish theology has constructed or interpreted models of the soul in an ongoing dialogue with the tradition. Depending on scholarly perspectives, interpretations vary widely, ranging from mystical and kabbalistic perspectives, which postulate that that soul has different components and exists on various planes, to rationalistic models that view the soul as controlling the body and cognitive functions. See Andrew Newberg and David Halpern, *The Rabbi's Brain: Mystics, Moderns and the Science of Jewish Thinking* (Nashville: Turner Publishing Company, 2018), 22–26.

the sacred in specific ways and on their own terms, or they can suspend a religious perspective and meet others in solidarity as fellow human beings with common needs. Following Thurneysen's early definition of soul care, a preliminary understanding of spiritual care may postulate that it is the care of persons as embodied spiritual beings who evolve within a relational matrix, dependent on care by others and by God.

The meaning of spirituality and our understanding of the human spirit also helps clarify our understanding of spiritual care. The notion of spirituality has been used in a variety of ways, ranging from references to traditional religious beliefs and practices to vague ideas about human nature and its connection to the universe. For the purpose of clinical care, a definition of spirituality that was developed by a workgroup of interdisciplinary educators and clinicians in the field of palliative care is particularly useful. The group identified spirituality as "the aspect of humanity that refers to the way individuals seek and express meaning and purpose and the way they experience their connectedness to the moment, to self, to others, to nature, and to the significant or sacred."[3] This definition is useful both clinically and theoretically for two reasons. On the one hand, it clearly specifies the parameters of the spiritual life through references to meaning making and connectedness. On the other hand, it is inclusive and applies to a wide variety of religious and spiritual orientations and practices. Individuals may construct meaning in life and experience their connectedness through traditional religious faith perspectives and practices or in non-religious ways.

Alienating shame distorts meaning-perspectives and prevents authentic connection with self and others. It has the potential to severely impair spiritual life and needs to be considered a primary threat to spiritual development and spiritual growth. In supporting meaning making and assisting individuals and communities to nurture or restore connections, spiritual care offers a therapeutic response to potential or actual impairment. The spiritual life, or spirituality, is how the human spirit finds connective expression. Christian scripture views the human spirit as a life force within persons (cf. Matt 27:50; John 19:30; Rev 11:11). In some places, the concepts of *spirit* and

---

[3] Christina M. Puchalski, Robert Vitillo, Sharon K. Hull, and Nancy Reller, "Improving the Spiritual Dimension of Whole Person Care: Reaching National and International Consensus," *Journal of Palliative Medicine* 17, no, 6 (June 2014): 643.

soul are used alongside each other or interchangeably to describe human beings in their wholeness and totality (cf. 2 Cor 7:1; 1 Thess 5:23). We may think of the human spirit as the essential aliveness of persons that transcends mere physical animation and strives toward wholeness and fulfillment.

Spiritual care is the empathic praxis of at-onement toward persons as embodied, spirited beings and seeks to facilitate proleptic wholeness for individuals and communities. It does so by supporting meaning-perspectives or assisting to revise those perspectives and by offering others a compassionate and empathic relationship that aids them to strengthen their connections in the world, including their connection to God, the Sacred, or the Significant. At-onement defines the therapeutic process of spiritual care as a skillful empathic effort to establish a relationship of trust and safety in which another can experience caring solidarity, an understanding and accepting presence, and a shared humanity that create a space to be known. As a praxis of at-onement, spiritual care is a process of joining and knowing others and their experience in a caring and therapeutic way. Aiming to facilitate a therapeutic process toward proleptic wholeness, spiritual care does not ignore or deny limitations and adversity. In fact, the recognition and acceptance of life-limiting or adverse conditions that cannot be remedied may be a characteristic of proleptic wholeness in persons that is never completely achieved but is always in process as something to anticipate.[4] Wholeness is not a state of being but a process that integrates various aspects of one's life experience through a unifying meaning-perspective to facilitate or support a hopeful response to life as it is.

Salvation and Wholeness

The relationship between salvation and health has theological significance for health care ministries, including chaplaincy, pastoral counseling, and spiritually integrated therapy. Pastoral theologian Edward Thornton states

---

4 Miroslav Volf and Matthew Croasmun have applied the concept of prolepsis to theological articulation and the process of sanctification in Christian life. Citing Paul's reference to "having the treasure in jars of clay" (2 Cor 4:7), they conclude that imperfection and the awareness that one is imperfect are essential to Christian formation and the development of a spiritual identity. See Miroslav Volf and Matthew Croasmun, *For the Life of the World: Theology That Makes a Difference* (Grand Rapids: Brazos Press, 2019), 130.

that "God intends to meet us with salvation in every experience of life."[5] He argues that the Jesus story revealed a God event that intends to meet us in the midst of physical and mental illness to effect healing as a penultimate manifestation of salvation and that pastoral counseling as a form of spiritual care participates in the salvific process by facilitating experiences of God's grace. I would add to Thornton's argument that healing may not necessarily mean a cure. Given an understanding of wholeness as a process toward integration and a hopeful response to life, healing may occur even if a cure is not possible.

In *Salvation and Health*, pastoral theologian James Lapsley proposes a dynamic process model for relating salvation and health that describes various levels of participation in the process of salvation. Lapsley explores salvation and health as "interlocking processes" that can be analyzed and understood separately but that "are inseparable in actual occurrence, and mutually dependent in some respects."[6] He concludes that healing in the lives of individuals is never fully complete but must be ongoing, similar to an understanding in Christian theology that persons are continually in need of grace. Lapsley refers to the traditional concept of sanctification, interpreting it not as a form of religious purification but "in terms of fulfillment of potential for participation in the salvatory process."[7] His interpretation comes close to identifying health and healing in the context of salvation as a process of proleptic wholeness, which means that God's work of salvation does not accomplish personal and relational wholeness but rather sets a process in motion that aims at fulfillment.

Ethicist Stanley Hauerwas foreshadows more recent considerations about social determinants of health and emphasizes the importance of community for sustaining care for those who are sick and health for those who recover. Arguing that pain and illness can alienate individuals from themselves and from others, he advocates for health care providers and spiritual care practitioners to be instrumental in overcoming such alienation by being present to those who suffer with pain and illness. Furthermore, he

---

5 Edward E. Thornton, *Theology and Pastoral Counseling* (1964; repr., Philadelphia: Fortress Press, 1967), 27.
6 James N. Lapsley, *Salvation and Health: The Interlocking Processes of Life* (Philadelphia: The Westminster Press, 1972), 86.
7 Lapsley, *Salvation and Health*, 129.

sees the church as a community that can exemplify and sustain a habit of presence to those in need of care and healing.[8] The need for restorative and redemptive relationships is increased by the fact that the alienating factor in illness and pain can induce shame. "To be in pain means we need help, that we are vulnerable to the interests of others, that we are not in control of our destiny. Thus, we seek to deny our pain. . . . But the attempt to deal with our pain by ourselves or to deny its existence has the odd effect of only increasing our loneliness. For exactly to the extent I am successful, I create a story about myself that I cannot easily share."[9] While Hauerwas does not explicitly use the concept of relational wholeness, he argues that care and healing must not be limited to the mechanics of the human body; care and healing need to use relationships and a community that is called upon by a God who is always present to us in our failures and successes.

The salvific God event in the Jesus story was not a sacrificial act of atonement but was an empathic life of at-onement that was closely attuned in an exemplary fashion to the Abba whom Jesus knew and to his fellow human beings, particularly to those who suffered from illness, exclusion, and oppression. At-onement describes the empathic union with the God event that called upon Jesus (cf. John 10:30) and his public work to establish a new community and to facilitate wholeness in individuals. In Matthew's version of the sermon on the mount, Jesus calls those who listen to his teachings toward wholeness (Matt 5:48). Jesus's call is often translated to "be *perfect* as your heavenly Father is perfect" due to the Greek word *teleios* that is used in this passage. However, this translation can be misleading, as it may suggests moral or spiritual perfection. Perfectionism is by no means a spiritual virtue but is rather a psychological and behavioral defense against shame and sabotages wholeness. If the Jesus event exemplifies God's empathic initiative to overcome the alienating effects of shame, it seems unlikely that Jesus would have ushered a call to perfection.

While *teleios* may be translated as "perfect," it does not mean to be without fault or blemish but rather points to a state of wholeness or completeness. The context of Jesus's call in Matthew 5:43–48 makes it clear

---

8 See Stanley Hauerwas, "Salvation and Health," in *The Hauerwas Reader*, ed. John Bergman and Michael Cartwright (Durham & London: Duke University Press, 2001), 553.
9 Hauerwas, "Salvation and Health," 550.

that he did not challenge his listeners to engage in a process of constant self-improvement but rather to love wholeheartedly beyond one's tribe and overcome the fragmentation of enmity. His charge to his followers to be "whole, therefore, as your heavenly Father is whole" points them toward relational wholeness that involves even those who are against them by means of transformative initiatives.[10] The parallel passage in the Gospel of Luke supports an interpretation that focuses on relational wholeness and invites participation in the work of salvation. According to Luke, Jesus called upon those who listened to become "compassionate as your Father is compassionate" (Luke 6:36).[11] God's compassionate empathy, as it was embodied in the Jesus event, thus became the model for early Christian communities of how to live and relate in a world of enmity.

Relational wholeness and personal wholeness are closely related. Relational wholeness is the result of healing that occurs in fragmented relationships and communities through caring interventions that overcome alienation. Personal wholeness is the result of caring interventions that facilitate or support the healing of fragmentation within the self. It is the restoration of a wholesome relationship with oneself that acknowledges and integrates the various aspects of one's existence. Neither form of wholeness implies the absence of conflict. However, in the process of proleptic wholeness, conflict is engaged as an opportunity for growth, learning, and transformation rather than as a dividing strategy.

Developing a Clinical Hermeneutic of Curiosity

Spiritual care as a praxis of empathic at-onement needs to be rooted in a method that invites and interprets the stories of others with openness and curiosity. Therapeutic curiosity does not pry into the private lives of others but pays respectful attention to their stories and allows them to

---

10 See, for example, Matt 5:21–43. The concept of *transformative initiatives* has been introduced by Glen Stassen in his theological ethics for peacemaking. Stassen found evidence for a Christian praxis of peacemaking though transformative initiatives both in the Jesus story as Matthew and Luke relate it and in the Pauline letters. See Glen H. Stassen, *Just Peacemaking: Transforming Initiatives for Justice and Peace* (Louisville: Westminster John Knox Press, 1992), 53–88.

11 Author's translation.

emerge on their own terms through empathic connection. It is a therapeutic attitude that listens for meaning, which may lie below the surface of personal narratives and may reveal surprising discoveries. I suggest that spiritual care clinicians who practice at-onement need to develop a *clinical hermeneutic of curiosity* to gain interpersonal knowledge and to interpret the stories they learn. A hermeneutic of curiosity integrates theoretical perspectives relevant to the praxis of spiritual care and to therapeutic interpretation with empathic attunement to the experience and inner world of others. Spiritual care practitioners who use a hermeneutic of curiosity do not approach others with certitude based on assumptions or theoretical categories but use theory cautiously to explore the meaning of the stories that emerge between them and another. They do not listen to confirm their theory or assessment but to understand at a deep level. In other words, a hermeneutic of curiosity is a necessary element of therapeutic interpretation that guides spiritual care practitioners to approach another's struggle, distress, or pain not as a diagnosis to be made but as a story to be told and to be explored.

Pastoral care pioneer Anton Boisen, one of the founders of the CPE movement, famously referred to the patients he worked with as living human documents. We do not know exactly when he first used this terminology, but in his 1936 book about *The Exploration of the Inner World*, he points out that the basis of spiritual healing is not to be found in textbooks or in certain therapeutic techniques but "in the living human documents in all their complexity and in all their elusiveness and in the tested insights of the wise and noble of the past as well as of the present. To the ability to read these human documents in the light of the best human understanding there is no royal road. It calls for that which is beyond anything that books or lectures or schools can impart and to which only a few can attain."[12] Boisen's proposition that therapeutic knowledge about the human condition can be gathered from clinical encounters with persons in crisis informs an understanding of a hermeneutic of curiosity. If human persons can indeed be read as living human documents, similar to written sources from which knowledge can be

---

12 Anton T. Boisen, *The Exploration of the Inner World: A Study of Mental Disorder and Religious Experience* (Chicago: Willet and Clark, 1936), 248–249.

gleaned, such reading and subsequent interpretations need to be guided by an understanding about the hermeneutical process.[13]

However, the study of living human documents is less arcane than Boisen seems to suggest and can be learned and practiced by spiritual care clinicians. Furthermore, while empathy may not be the royal road that Boisen speaks about, it is a principal therapeutic approach to understanding living human documents. In the context of empathic at-onement, a hermeneutic of curiosity is dialogical and does not impose an expert interpretation on human experience. Rather, it uses empathic listening and understanding in dialogue with the other to determine accuracy, establish connection, and explore meaning.

A hermeneutic of curiosity is process-oriented rather than defined by certain theoretical perspectives. While it uses theory to interpret narratives of the self, it does not construct its own theoretical perspective, nor does it prescribe the use of a certain theory. Rather, by engaging in a process of open and appreciative inquiry and empathic attunement that allows for another's story to emerge and possibly to surprise, spiritual care practitioners can choose theoretical perspectives depending on context, their theological or philosophical orientation, methodological considerations, or their assessment of spiritual needs and resources. Such therapeutic-hermeneutical process is not unidirectional but bidirectional. It requires that spiritual care practitioners not only attend to the inner world of others but also to their own inner world and know how to interpret their responses to the stories they invite. The praxis of empathic at-onement allows for the resonance of the self through an intersubjective process. Utilizing a hermeneutic of curiosity, spiritual care practitioners thus need to be attuned and curious about such resonance within themselves and interpret it in relationship to the stories they invite and learn. In the context of spiritual care relationships, any form of countertransference should be engaged reflectively as a source

---

[13] Charles Gerkin revisited Anton Boisen's metaphor to suggest a hermeneutic of the self that connects the documents of the Christian faith with the living human document and integrates concepts and language from the biblical-theological tradition with the interpretative process in pastoral counseling. See Charles V. Gerkin, *The Living Human Document: Re-Visioning Pastoral Counseling in a Hermeneutic Mode* (Nashville: Abingdon Press, 1984), 55–75.

of information about the therapeutic relationship and about another's life narrative, and it needs to be explored with openness and curiosity.

Facets in Spiritual Care

A praxis of spiritual care that is anchored in the theory and practice of empathic at-onement and guided by a hermeneutic of curiosity has various facets. My use of the term *facet* is a deliberate reference to the appearance of a cut gem that reflects light in various ways. While compassionate empathy is at the heart of spiritual care and defines its essence, a praxis of at-onement finds expression through various modalities of care. The choice of modality may depend on the circumstances of the clinical situation, the assessment of spiritual needs, and interventions called for as a result, each facet uniquely reflecting the empathic God event in the Jesus story.

Spiritual Care as Witnessing

Spiritual care through empathic at-onement is an act of witnessing. The act of bearing witness through spiritual care is not the kind of witnessing that curious bystanders tend to exhibit. Neither does it mean to profess one's religious faith in the context of caregiving. Rather, witnessing as an aspect of spiritual care is a focused involvement in the lives of others that communicates interest, attentiveness, and recognition. Interest in another's life and experience is an attitude of caring concern that genuinely desires to be involved with the experience of others, learn about it, and seek to understand it. Attentiveness is a function of interest. It is a mindful and observant approach to situations and lives of others, a way to be present with others and to collect the details and dynamics of their experience in order to assess their needs and resources. Finally, recognition views others in their shared humanity, acknowledging and affirming the validity of their experience and of related emotions.

The act of witnessing in spiritual care is a hopeful activity that can claim its theological roots in the liberating God event of the Exodus, which began with an act of witnessing the suffering of the Hebrew people. At the same time, spiritual care as witnessing is a therapeutic activity that corroborates subjective experience and pain and acknowledges its reality, impact, and importance in the life of another. It is the gift of caring presence and attention to others who may want to hide behind one of the masks of shame. Clinical psychologist Louis Cozolino explains the impact of therapeutic witnessing.

> The witness to horror can never be overestimated. Someone who is willing to go with us to the ground zero of our pain helps us to be able to sit with it ourselves. Having to communicate our story to another encourages us to articulate an experience that may only be a series of images, bodily sensations, and emotions. Having to make our experiences comprehensible to another person allows us to grasp them in a clearer and more empowering way. Telling the story also provides us with the opportunity to see the reaction of the other, which helps us to grasp the emotional meaning of our experiences. In addition, telling the story to others provides us with a new memory of the story that now includes a witness, making it a public experience.[14]

According to Cozolino, a therapeutic practice of witnessing facilitates meaning making and makes public what is hidden or private. It can be argued that it also accomplishes its goal by creating a safe and accepting space to look at oneself and to show oneself to another.

Witnessing gives significance to that which is being witnessed and to those who are involved and affected. The witness becomes one who confirms the truth of their experience even when that truth is still emerging. Identifying experience and acknowledging it as significant is the first step toward meaning making. Clinical psychologist Kenneth Pargament argues that both the exercise of religion and a person's coping with distress are similar processes in that they represent a search for significance. Both are dynamic processes that unfold over time. While the exercise of religion necessarily involves experiences of the sacred, coping may or may not include a connection to the sacred.[15] While the praxis of spiritual care in the Christian tradition

---

14 Louis Cozolino, *Why Therapy Works: Using Our Minds to Change Our Brains* (New York & London: W. W. Norton & Company, 2016), 57.

15 See Kenneth I. Pargament, *The Psychology of Religion and Coping: Theory, Research, Practice* (New York: The Guilford Press, 1997), 90.

is theologically rooted in the Jesus story and attempts to support coping through that perspective, spiritual care providers must not impose religious beliefs or interpretations on others in an attempt to assist meaning making.

Pargament explains that significance is "a phenomenological construct involving feelings and beliefs associated with worth, importance, and value. It embodies the experience of caring, attraction, or attachment."[16] He further elaborates that the search for significance not only involves emotional awareness but is also object oriented, and that such orientation may be material, physical, psychological, or spiritual in nature. The objects of significance that people attach to when receiving empathic spiritual care are primarily psychological and spiritual in nature and thus are intangible but nevertheless real. They may include a sense of feeling seen, being known and accepted, discovering meaning, having a sense of purpose, or feeling close to God or to a caring individual.

Shame, however, seeks to evade witness. It is the emotion that makes persons want to hide and remain undetected.

> *Martin was in his mid-seventies when he was diagnosed with advanced cancer after he was brought to the Emergency Department following a fall. Imaging revealed a tumor in his brain. Over the next few days, he tried to adjust to the reality of his diagnosis and built a relationship with the chaplain, who visited him daily. He used his sarcastic humor both to connect and to mask his emotions. When the chaplain visited with him on the morning before the first exploratory procedure and asked if prayer might be supportive, Martin said: "Honestly, chaplain, I would not know how to show up for prayer and what to pray for. I have done many things in my life that I am ashamed of and, believe me, I have done it all. But I want you to pray with my family once I am in the operating room. They will need you." The chaplain affirmed her support for his family, and then said: "Martin, I want you to know that I care for you as much as I care for your family. I wonder, if you did know how to show up, what you might want to pray for."*

---

16 Pargament, *The Psychology of Religion and Coping*, 92.

> *Martin became silent, broke eye-contact for a moment, and then re-connected, saying "I want the good that I did to matter more than the bad." The chaplain listened and then replied: "I pray for that, Martin, and really would like to hear about the good that you did once you are done with this procedure and have recovered."*

Martin's shame tried to hide in the undergrowth of thorny sarcasm that attempted to keep others at bay just enough not to detect his desire to be known. The chaplain's expressed curiosity, attentiveness, and interest in the context of a caring relationship invited for a brief moment self-disclosure. He wanted his life—the "good" in it—to matter, to have significance, and the chaplain offered to be a witness to "the good" in Martin's life.

Shame is self-sabotaging in the literal sense of the word in that it denies the self the experience of positive significance. It diminishes the self through self-judgment and a sense of inadequacy and unworthiness. Compassionate empathy counteracts the self-sabotaging function of shame by communicating acceptance when witnessing another's inner experience with understanding. At-onement, the caring praxis of paying close attention and connecting with another through empathy at a significant level, affirming her humanity and value, is a potentially transformative intervention in response to self-sabotaging shame. When being seen and having one's experience witnessed is perceived as an act of care rather than an act of exposure, it poses a positive, disorienting dilemma that requires a new meaning-perspective. A praxis of at-onement aims to transform self-defeating meaning-perspectives into self-accepting perspectives by affirming significance in the lives of others and assisting them to transform the alienating effects of shame.

Spiritual Care as Parabolic Engagement

Spiritual care that is informed by God's empathic initiative in the Jesus event is a practical theological response to the lives of individuals and communities, particularly those impacted by spiritual distress, pain, and suffering. It is outcome-oriented as it participates in God's ongoing work of salvation and seeks to assist change, growth, and possibly healing. On the one hand, spiritual care is a praxis that is deeply rooted in the Jesus story of God's compassionate salvation, and, on the other hand, it is a therapeutic process that has been informed by various theories of empathic care. Empathic at-onement points beyond clinical-therapeutic intervention to God's salvific initiative without explicitly identifying a theological perspective. Therefore, we can understand it as parabolic engagement with others.

The gospel narratives convey Jesus's teachings primarily through parabolic stories. They communicate truth about the ways the liberating God event calls upon people by using narrative symbols, and they serve subversive purposes to confront and transform oppressive structures. Spiritual care as a parabolic process integrates both aspects of Jesus's public work. It points through a praxis of empathic at-onement to the compassionate God event in the Jesus story, and it is subversive by therapeutically confronting internal and external forces that sabotage wholeness.

Empathy and confrontation are distinct therapeutic concepts and interventions. However, as pastoral theologian Ralph Underwood points out, they are not mutually exclusive. Underwood explains that empathy "educes clarity if not wisdom from the person being helped, whereas confrontation demands that one recognize what one has been denying. Empathy is based on the possibility of harmony if not unity between two persons; confrontation aims to make use of tension between persons for creative challenge."[17] Underwood suggests that empathy and confrontation share a partially overlapping cluster of therapeutic skills. Confrontation that is ultimately grounded in empathy can cause others to encounter themselves and their situation with a different perspective that encourages change.[18] Like empathy, confrontation seeks to facilitate in others a therapeutic encounter with themselves through an encounter with another. Metaphorically speaking, therapeutic confrontation is an act of holding up a mirror to another person at a certain angle so that he may see and understand himself more fully and consider engaging change or growth opportunities. While empathy accomplishes the therapeutic task primarily through listening and responding skills and through an authentic and accepting relationship, confrontation uses direct feedback and self-disclosure to challenge others, ideally at their strength and by engaging their potential.

---

17 Ralph Underwood, *Empathy and Confrontation in Pastoral Care* (Philadelphia: Fortress Press, 1985), 15.
18 See Underwood, *Empathy and Confrontation in Pastoral Care*, 90–91.

Spiritual care has long recognized the importance of stories in the lives of individuals and in communities. The skill to invite another's story and identify its themes and plot is central to the practice of spiritual care. Persons are storied beings. Practical theologians Herbert Anderson and Edward Foley highlight the significance of a storied existence in the context of spiritual care. "Stories are privileged and imaginative acts of self-interpretation. We tell stories of a life in order to establish meaning and to integrate our remembered past with what we perceive to be happening in the present and what we anticipate for the future. We weave many stories together into a life narrative that conveys what we believe to be essential truths about ourselves and the world."[19] Our stories are essential in constructing our personal world and how we communicate the truth we believe about that world to others. Depending on the themes and the storyline, they may contribute to the flourishing of life, or they may limit life.

Anderson and Foley point out that our stories may be revealing in hopeful ways or they may conceal the shame of our life in self-deceptive ways.[20] Spiritual care practitioners can support hopeful stories and facilitate a deeper understanding and utilization of those stories. Practitioners also need to be prepared to empathically confront self-sabotaging or self-defeating stories and assist others in transforming their narratives about the self. Spiritual care as parabolic engagement takes a narrative approach that reflects the Jesus story of God's empathy while carefully attending to the stories of others. Narrative spiritual care, as pastoral theologian Karen Scheib points out, "invites us to become story companions to one another, listening in the midst of suffering, listening as life unfolds, listening for the presence of God. Story companions give attentive reverence to the other and the other's story, and such companions open themselves to learn from the other."[21]

Anderson and Foley offer a perspective similar to Scheib's approach, identifying the integration between divine and human narratives as a central aspect of spiritual care. Pointing to the parabolic nature of such integration process, they argue that it "is necessary so that we will have a language to

---

19 Herbert Anderson and Edward Foley, *Mighty Stories, Dangerous Rituals: Weaving Together the Human and the Divine* (1998, repr., Minneapolis: Fortress Press, 2019), 5.
20 Anderson and Foley, See *Mighty Stories, Dangerous Rituals*, 9–12.
21 Karen D. Scheib, *Pastoral Care: Telling the Stories of Our Life* (Nashville: Abingdon Press, 2016), 61.

speak about our human struggles that will, at the same time, open us to possibilities beyond the present struggle.... Weaving together human and divine narratives has, as its ultimate goal, the transformation of individual and communal life."[22] The integration between human and divine narratives in spiritual care may happen explicitly, using sacred narratives as a resource for meaning making and transformation when caring for persons who value those narratives. It also can function implicitly by using sacred stories as hermeneutic tools to understand the stories of persons, who may not choose to relate to sacred narratives in meaningful ways. Integrating sacred and human narratives is not a matter of naming the meaning of another's story from a religious perspective. Rather, it is about a process of discovering metaphors, symbols, and meaning-perspectives that may have the potential to transform the experience and relationships of individuals and communities.

> *Mary had come to the trauma room of the Emergency Department while suffering a heart attack. Ever since, she had experienced abdominal pain, which became so debilitating that she was brought back to the hospital where initial tests revealed that she was bleeding internally. When the chaplain saw her lying disheveled and obviously in pain on a stretcher in one of the emergency room bays, he stopped at her side to see if he could provide support. After telling the story about her recent illness and sharing with the chaplain that her faith was "the only thing that brings strength and comfort" to her, the chaplain asked Mary how her faith was supporting her right now. She said, "You know, when the pain is the worst, I imagine Jesus with the crown of thorns before he was crucified. His pain must have been so much worse. And that helps me to deal with my pain when it's really bad." "That image of Jesus with the crown of thorns connects your pain to his," the chaplain responded. "Yes," said Mary, "I know it's not the same, but it means that he knows what it's like and that he knows worse."*

---

22 Anderson and Foley, *Mighty Stories, Dangerous Rituals*, 41.

For Mary, the passion narrative about Jesus's suffering connected in a meaningful way with her own suffering with pain and made her feel known in the experience of her illness. Her own experience was implicated in the story of Jesus's suffering, and her story of illness and pain resonated with the sacred story, providing her with a means of coping through her faith.

Spiritual Care as Re-Membering
Pastoral theologian John Patton explores spiritual care as a practice of re-membering, drawing both from biblical theological themes and from the theory of feminist family therapist Deborah Luepnitz. Patton's theological premise is that "God created human beings for relationship with God and with one another. God continues in relationship with creation by hearing us, remembering us, and bringing us into relationship with one another."[23] He further argues that spiritual care, as a function of caring religious communities, practices hearing and remembering in analogy to God's care for humanity. In clinical-therapeutic praxis, Patton explains, the notion of re-membering captures both the reflective process as well as the restructuring of relationships that spiritual care can facilitate within others to bring about change and growth.[24]

It also can be argued that God's ongoing work of salvation does not only aim to transform alienation between persons but also aims to bring persons into an accepting relationship with themselves. This argument resonates with Patton's contextual approach to spiritual care. However, the process of re-membering therapeutically is not primarily one that happens within or through the recipient of care but as a process that evolves between those who care and those who open themselves to care. Re-membering as a facet in spiritual care is both an expression of care as well as an outcome of care. As an expression of care, re-membering participates in the ongoing event of salvation and reflects God's empathy in the Jesus story. As an outcome of care, it is about the restorations of relationships, including the relationship with oneself, and the connection to communities, small or large, that nurture healing and the flourishing of life. Re-membering can be a function

---

23 John Patton, *Pastoral Care in Context: An Introduction to Pastoral Care* (Louisville: Westminster John Knox Press, 1993), 6.
24 See Patton, *Pastoral Care in Context*, 50–52.

of an individual relationship of care or the act of a caring community, such as the community of women that Toni Morrison describes at the end of *Beloved* who gathered in a circle of solidarity to chant and to re-member Sethe by calling upon her to rejoin their community.

Re-membering as an act of care counteracts the alienating and isolating effects of shame. Shame hides and attempts to be amnesic, using various psychological defenses toward those ends. Spiritual care as a practice of re-membering invites others into community and invites their attention to the past without judgment. It reflects the story about the God event that met Zacchaeus on the road, remembered that he, too, was "a son of Abraham" (Luke 19:9), and re-membered him into community. Re-membering includes intentional therapeutic efforts to recollect another—to understand and hold together the various aspects and experiences of another life as much as possible—and to share one's understanding in a non-judgmental way with unconditional acceptance. As Patton points out, drawing upon sociologist Clifford Geertz's method of social ethnography, one who provides spiritual care in the mode of re-membering must be "a keen observer who becomes able to tell a story of the persons cared for that includes their myths, rituals, daily activities, and problems. The pastoral carer 'believes in the primacy of experience' and, 'like the poet and the painter,' is strongly drawn to the details of a person's life, perhaps respecting and seeing in them far more than the person herself sees and values."[25] A practice of re-membering entails faithful and sustained attention to another and another's story, along with an invitation to enter into a relationship that is both therapeutic and parabolic in nature, pointing toward the God who re-members us and calls us into relationships.

Spiritual care providers who re-member another do so to assist them therapeutically to re-member themselves. A practice of re-membering creates space for the other to face themselves and explore meaning in their story and their relationships. Based on a dream he once had, Buechner describes the space where re-membering can happen as a room one can choose to enter. Buechner's metaphor can be expanded to say that empathic spiritual care is a way of furnishing the room, providing what is needed, and

---

25 Patton, *Pastoral Care in Context*, 45.

making it inviting and safe enough for another to enter. Personal therapy and Buechner's involvement in the recovery community assisted Buechner to enter the room and re-member pieces of his story that had remained unspoken and unattended for a long time. In his essay about *A Room Called Remember*, Buechner argues that re-membering needs to be an intentional and purposeful process.

> *So much has happened to us all over the years. So much has happened within us and through us. We are to take time to remember what we can about it and what we dare. That's what entering the room means, I think. It means taking time to remember on purpose. It means not picking up a book for once or turning on the radio, but letting the mind journey gravely, deliberately, back through the years that have gone by but are not gone. It means a deeper, slower kind of remembering; it means remembering as a searching and finding.*[26]

Spiritual care practitioners are companion-guides on this journey and in the searching process. They not only prepare the room, they also share the room with the other for a while. While assisting others to re-member their life, the pieces of it that they have owned and disowned, they attend to their discoveries with empathic understanding to offer a confirming presence and facilitate self-reflection and self-understanding.

The process of re-membering through spiritual care is not unlike the process that Rambo identifies as redemption from the middle when one must live with the impact of trauma. Both processes have in common the recollection of experiences that may linger and may not quickly or easily integrate with one's life narrative, where pain remains and needs to be acknowledged and attended. They also share a movement toward re-connection in community. In Rambo's theology of trauma, the middle is the space where remnants of death remain and the movement of life in the aftermath of trauma is a promise that can barely be discerned. Like Buechner, Rambo

---

26 Frederick Buechner, *A Room Called Remember: Uncollected Pieces* (New York: Harper-Collins Publishers, 1984), 6.

uses figurative language to identify a place of survival where recovery is not a linear process but where "death and life are inextricably bound."[27] It is a place where the witness to suffering is redemptive and supports the promise of life in the aftermath.

Rambo suggests that the redemptive process from the middle involves two related movements. Both movements should be considered aspects of re-membering. The first movement is about tracking how the remnants of trauma rise to the surface of life and consciousness and how they recede. Part of this movement is tracking and marking the presence of the sacred in the experience of trauma and in its aftermath.[28] Spiritual care practitioners can facilitate and support this movement as witnesses to another's narrative and memory of suffering. Through empathic understanding, they can provide a therapeutic response to shame that may result from trauma and thus can facilitate attention to loss and grief. The second movement is toward sensing life again. It is a hopeful process and engages the imagination to re-member the possibility of life. "For trauma healing to happen," explains Rambo, "the capacity to imagine one's life beyond a radical ending, to imagine life anew, must be restored."[29] Just as spiritual care practitioners are witnesses to the remnants of death and loss, they also witness the possibility of coming to life again. In other words, spiritual care as re-membering is a hopeful practice that engages another's imagination to envision a future where life can be restored, assisting them in identifying possibilities to realize the vision and move toward the future. Re-membering as redemption from the middle, which, in turn, is a practice toward at-onement, brings together past, present, and future narratives. More importantly, it brings together persons in relationships that support, sustain, and restore life.

Spiritual Care as Solidarity

Both the Hebrew scriptures and the Jesus story speak of the God event that initiates salvation as one that also effects liberation. While salvation and liberation are not the same, they cannot be separated. The traditional Christian

---

27 Shelly Rambo, *Spirit and Trauma: A Theology of Remaining* (Louisville: Westminster John Knox Press, 2010), 156.
28 See Rambo, *Spirit and Trauma*, 160–61.
29 Rambo, *Spirit and Trauma*, 162.

interpretation holds that the saving God event liberates individuals and communities from the condemning power and eternal consequences of sin, where sin is understood as disobedience against God through transgression of God's commands. An incarnational theology, however, affirms that salvation and its effects are not otherworldly events but parts of a process that unfolds in the world we inhabit and shape, and that sin is an alienating force in history that has personal, social, and political dimensions. Salvation as a process that restores wholeness and overcomes alienation addresses persons not just as individuals but as human beings who need connection and community to survive and to thrive. Salvation must include the restoration of wholeness in communities and of wholesome connections and therefore liberation from oppressive social, political, and psychological forces. Consequently, a praxis of spiritual care that participates in the ongoing event of salvation needs to be a liberating praxis.

Developing an intercultural theory of spiritual care, pastoral theologian Emanuel Lartey suggests that such care needs to be liberative and empower people in situations of oppression. "The power to define one's own experience on one's own terms," Lartey holds, "is a vital part of liberation."[30] He sees spiritual care practitioners as uniquely equipped to engage in a liberative praxis because of their listening skills. A liberative praxis begins with listening to the concrete, lived experience of people. Through what Lartey calls "interpathic listening," practitioners of spiritual care can "enter into the real-life, human experience of people who struggle to recover their humanity in situations of oppression in all communities in the world."[31]

From a liberationist perspective, spiritual care as empathic at-onement is a practice of solidarity. At the most basic level, caregiving as an act of solidarity means joining another or a community with a deep awareness of a shared humanity. That awareness includes both an appreciation for the potential for growth that we share as human beings as well as knowledge about the potential for being deeply wounded and in pain. Joining another

---

30 Emmanuel Y. Lartey, *In Living Color: An Intercultural Approach to Pastoral Care and Counseling*, 2nd ed. (London & Philadelphia: Jessica Kingsley Publishers, 2003), 126.
31 Lartey, *In Living Color*, 125. Lartey uses the term "interpathy," which originated with David Augsburger's early work about cross-cultural pastoral care, to define an empathic response to the experience of others that crosses cultural boundaries. See David W. Augsburger, *Pastoral Care Across Cultures* (Philadelphia: The Westminster Press, 1986), 29.

or a community in their attempt to change, grow, or heal is an empathic act of entering their physical and emotional world in order to support liberation.

While liberation and healing may be linked, they are not the same. Liberation from the power of oppressive forces such as shame or racially motivated exclusion may be a prerequisite for healing to occur. When spiritual care practitioners join others in solidarity, they come alongside, affirming their humanity in attempts to empower and support change. The praxis of joining another in solidarity to offer care and support in her suffering or in her struggle to be free from oppression is the gift of presence that conveys therapeutic attentiveness, mutuality in the context of a professional relationship, and interdependence.

Therapeutic attentiveness is both an attitude and a skill. As an attitude, it is an openness to others who need care and healing, while recognizing and acknowledging realistically oppressive forces that work against their well-being and wholeness. As a skill, therapeutic attentiveness pays close attention to the lives of others and listens empathically to their stories to understand the dynamics of oppression that prevent them from moving toward proleptic wholeness. Mutuality in therapeutic relationships prevents therapeutic attentiveness from creating disempowering spiritual care interventions. It affirms the dignity of others by engaging them as partners in the care process who have unique resources to contribute to a mutual effort to overcome oppressive forces within the self and within communities and move toward wholeness. This means that, even though spiritual care practitioners have special expertise, they are not *the* experts who are called in to prescribe a course of healing for the lives of others. Rather, they are skilled companions on a journey who know about the vulnerabilities inherent in our common humanity. A spiritual assessment of needs should not imply that the person who is being assessed becomes an object of care, and it should include an assessment of another's spiritual assets or resources along with their needs. The notion of interdependence in caring relationships of solidarity is closely related to an understanding of mutuality. Therapeutic interdependence does not negate professional boundaries in spiritual care, nor does it suggest that spiritual care practitioners engage in the process of caring to meet their own emotional needs. However, it means that spiritual care practitioners and those who enter into a care partnership with them are affected by each other in the process of care and depend on each other for growth. While recipients of care depend on the expertise of spiritual care practitioners and on the reliable and caring relationships they offer, spiritual care practitioners depend on clinical experience in therapeutic partnerships to help them to grow and develop as professionals.

A liberationist perspective requires caring attention in solidarity with individuals, yet it points beyond individual distress to address oppression, trauma, and suffering at communal and systemic levels. With few exceptions, the modern practice of spiritual care in Western Europe and North America has traditionally focused on therapeutic relationships with individuals and small groups and has been widely influenced by therapeutic models from individual psychotherapy and group therapy. Spiritual care as an empathic practice of solidarity needs to pay attention to the larger context of human suffering and to communities affected by trauma and oppression. Discussing the nature and role of spiritual care for oppressed populations, pastoral theologian Karen Montagno points out that it "requires taking the impact of oppression seriously. It is a call to solidarity and the work of justice. Context and community are interrelated and inform the perspectives of both caregiver and receiver. Serious consideration of these reveals challenges as well as wisdom and insight. Further, the interrelated nature of context and community suggests that pastoral care is a holistic practice that attends to whole persons—mind, spirit, and body—in community."[32]

One of the challenges when engaging in community-focused spiritual care is that it may require spiritual care practitioners to cross contexts and join communities that are not their own as an aspect of an empathic practice of at-onement.

In response to the police shooting of Breonna Taylor, a group of #BlackLivesMatter protesters had held regular vigils every Saturday in downtown Louisville, demanding justice and police reform. One Saturday, a local network of clergy informed its members

---

32 Karen B. Montagno, "Midwifes and Holy Subversives: Resisting Oppression in Attending the Birth of Wholeness," in *Injustice and the Care of Souls: Taking Oppression Seriously in Pastoral Care*, ed. Sheryl A. Kujawa-Holbrook and Karen B. Montagno (Minneapolis: Augsburg Fortress Press, 2009), 12.

that right-wing militia groups had announced an armed march upon the downtown area to confront the protesters. Members of the clergy from various denominations were asked to come to the area where the vigil was held in their robes and with stoles as signs of their vocation to form a peaceful barrier between the protesters and the militia groups. Several healthcare chaplains received the notice and decided to join the intervention. Almost every day, they cared for victims of violence and for their families. On this day, they decided to join an initiative to prevent violence and to stand in solidarity with people that demanded justice. They gathered at a downtown church with other clergy and marched together to the square where the vigil was being held. They were welcomed by the community that protested, and for several hours they stood between those who protested on one side of the street, a wall of police officers in the middle of the street, and sympathizers of white-nationalist organizations on the other side of the street. Mostly white bodies in clergy robes standing in the buffer zone between mostly black bodies and uniformed bodies. Armed militia members fortunately did not turn out in great numbers, and no violence erupted during the day. The chaplains along with other clergy members stood in solidarity, trying to engage protesters, bystanders, and police in conversation to make connections across dividing lines.

Practices of practical solidarity such as this clergy intervention in response to a threat in their community may need to cross cultural and class boundaries to join with oppressed groups of people, bridge divisions, and contribute to justice work. Spiritual care as a practice of solidarity attends to those who have been wounded and limited by systems of oppression. Such practice finds guidance in the Jesus story to cross contexts and be subversive by supporting efforts to confront systems of oppression and exclusion.

Pastoral theologian Brita Gill-Austern explains that practices of practical solidarity respect diversity while recognizing the sustaining power of interdependence. Such practices therefore "require developing a capacity to recognize our common humanity and our common need of one another for individual wholeness and for the healing of our world."[33] Claiming the biblical principle of mercy as a precondition for justice and foundational for practices of solidarity, Gill-Austern proposes three movements and three associated practices of solidarity. It can be argued that those practices of solidarity can inform an empathic praxis of spiritual care as justice work to counteract what Gill-Austern identifies as practices of exclusion and abandonment. Exclusion may happen through direct expulsion from community, by eliminating the unique identity of others through assimilation, by subjugating others and designating them as inferior, or by abandoning them through indifference.[34]

The first movement that Gill-Austern identifies is toward self-awareness about one's biases and assumptions about others and about one's privilege. A disciplined self-awareness is an indispensable prerequisite for spiritual care practitioners and has been a primary focus in CPE. The corresponding practice of practical solidarity includes self-examination, confession, and repentance with regard to one's own participation in practices of exclusion and to one's privilege and sense of entitlement in a world of division and marginalization.[35] The second movement is to leave what is familiar and comfortable and to practice constructive engagement with otherness. "To have a constructive engagement with otherness," holds Gill-Austern, "requires that we step out of the familiar into the unknown place where we have to struggle alongside others and learn to see the world from their perspective, and in so doing simultaneously find ourselves developing empathic identification."[36] The final movement is about returning home, transformed by new allegiances and able to confront one's complicity in oppression. Gill-Austern identifies as a corresponding practice of solidarity partnering with others in building "communities that embody lives of mercy and justice" and that are empowered through partnerships.[37]

---

33 Brita L. Gill-Austern, "Engaging Diversity and Difference: From Practices of Exclusion to Practices of Practical Solidarity," in *Injustice and the Care of Souls: Taking Oppression Seriously in Pastoral Care*, ed. Sheryl A. Kujawa-Holbrook and Karen B. Montagno (Minneapolis: Augsburg Fortress Press, 2009), 35.
34 See Gill-Austern, "Engaging Diversity and Difference," 31–32.
35 See Gill-Austern, "Engaging Diversity and Difference," 38–39.
36 Gill-Austern, "Engaging Diversity and Difference," 42.
37 Gill-Austern, "Engaging Diversity and Difference," 44.

She reminds practitioners of spiritual care that such partnerships require humility, both by recognizing that we need the other and by acknowledging that we do not know what best benefits others. Partnership in solidarity with others, therefore, is an inclusive practice and promotes equal participation.

Spiritual Care as Hospitality

Closely related to a practice of solidarity is hospitality. Hospitality means offering space for others to heal and to become known in a caring relationship with another and in relationship with themselves. The practice of hospitality is a biblical theme and a tradition that characterizes God's people. Welcoming the stranger is a core principle in Judaism and is explicitly commanded in the Torah (cf. Lev 19:33–34). Among early Christian literature, Luke's writings in particular highlight in several places that Jesus's followers and likely Jesus himself depended on the hospitality of others to do their public work (Luke 10:1–8; 24:28–30; Acts 9:43–10:48).[38] At the same time, the gospel narratives portray Jesus as one who offered hospitality to those on the margins of society. He became infamous for welcoming "sinners" to share meals with him (cf. Mark 2:13–16). Jesus's hospitality embodied God's welcome to all and particularly to those who were considered "the other" and who were largely excluded from communal life and common religious practices.

Feminist theologian Letty Russell suggests that to understand the depth of the biblical concept of hospitality and its relevance for a contemporary praxis of care, we need to reframe our common idea of hospitality as a nice evening around the table with friends to be able to see it as a radical practice of unity without uniformity that provides space for "the other" who is not like me. Quoting a Jewish participant at a conference for Muslim-Christian relationships, Russell describes hospitality as an empathic practice where one does not see others through one's own eyes the way one wants to see

---

38 In a sociological reading and analysis of the synoptic Gospels and parts of Josephus's writings, Gerhard Theissen has shown that hospitality was essential to the development of the early Jesus movement, since the inner circle of Jesus's followers, who were essentially charismatic vagabonds, depended on local congregations of sympathizers who supported them and offered them shelter. See Gerd Theissen, *Sociology of Early Palestinian Christianity*, trans. John Bowden (Philadelphia: Fortress Press, 1978), 17–23.

them but attempts to see them as they see themselves.[39] Hospitality is not a one-sided invitation or an act of charity; rather, it is an empathic partnership with others that involves a deep respect and appreciation for them and for what they have to offer. At the same time, as Russell points out, the biblical-theological concept of hospitality means creating safe space for the other and with the other. The notion of safe space is rooted in the Hebrew and Christian traditions of sanctuary, which are holy or sanctified spaces of protection. Russell explains that the "right of protection for all persons is derived from God's holiness and provides the basic theological understanding of hospitality in both Hebrew and Christian scriptures: Human beings are created by God and are to be holy, and are to be treated as holy or sacred: 'You shall be holy, for I the LORD your God am holy,' says Leviticus 19:2."[40]

Public health expert and social justice activist Sandra Bloom contends that sanctuary space needs not only to provide a physically safe space but also psychological safety and social safety. Psychological safety, she explains, "refers to the ability to be safe with oneself, to rely on one's own ability to self-protect against any destructive impulses coming from within oneself or deriving from other people, and to keep oneself out of harm's way."[41] Social safety involves creating a therapeutic environment where corrective experiences that support recovery can occur. For Bloom, such a space is characterized by shared fundamental assumptions, goals, and practices that allow persons "to maximize their emotional and intellectual functioning in an integrated way."[42] It could be argued that sanctuary also involves the need for spiritual safety. A spiritually safe space is characterized by non-judgmental attention that allows for a variety of meaning-perspectives to emerge and be explored, and for diverse connections that sustain the self. Spiritual safety requires the deconstruction of traumatic or traumatizing religious symbols and the construction of symbols that aid the flourishing of life.

---

39 See Letty M. Russell, *Just Hospitality: God's Welcome in a World of Difference*, ed. J. Shannon Clarkson and Kate M. Ott (Louisville: Westminster John Knox Press, 2009), 80–81.
40 Russell, *Just Hospitality*, 87.
41 Sandra L. Bloom, *Creating Sanctuary: Toward the Evolution of Sane Societies*, rev. ed. (New York & London: Routledge, 2013), 132.
42 Bloom, *Creating Sanctuary*, 134.

In the practice of spiritual care, hospitality that provides safe space for another is particularly relevant to the care of persons who have suffered trauma. Trauma happens in unsafe spaces, and the experience of trauma creates unsafe space. A sense of vulnerability and threat in an unsafe world lingers with those who have suffered trauma, as the many symptoms of post-traumatic stress disorder demonstrate. The wounds of trauma may be physical, emotional, or spiritual, or they may radiate with a combination of various remnants of pain. They may stem from individual injury or abuse, or they may reflect the sustained pain of oppressed communities through historical and intergenerational trauma. Spiritual care as an act of hospitality for those who live with the remnants of trauma provides safe space to attend to the wounds inflicted by trauma. Hospitable space, in turn, allows others to name what happened to their body, psyche, and spirit, and to connect safely with their story in the presence of someone who joins them in caring solidarity. Spiritual care practitioners, then, may assist others to discern meaning in examining the past, understanding their present condition, and envisioning a future where healing is a possibility.

In the clinical vignette about Denise, who had suffered childhood trauma through sexual abuse, she had felt lost after her marriage had ended and sought support in a local congregation. The pastor was literally hospitable when Denise walked unannounced into his office. He invited the stranger in and offered her a space to voice her despair. However, he did not only open his office to Denise but was hospitable to her story and her pain. The church office and, more importantly, the pastoral relationship that began there became a safe space for a woman who had been deeply wounded by trauma. By listening with empathy and meeting Denise with acceptance, the pastor helped her to move slowly against her shame, make herself known, and expose a deep wound that had not ceased radiating with pain since her childhood days. When Denise felt that her newfound faith required her to forgive her father, who perpetrated the abuse, a hospitable pastoral relationship helped her to take time to examine that proposition and discern its meaning. In a safe space, she was able to decide what forgiveness would look like for her and to courageously address the perpetrator, claiming her power to define the relationship with him on her terms.

Rogers's understanding of empathy along with his concept of unconditional positive regard describe well what hospitality looks like from a clinical, therapeutic perspective. Paradoxically, empathy and unconditional positive regard shape the therapeutic process that is hospitable to another's experience by entering their inner world and grasping on a deep level with respect and without judgment the experience as the other person sees and feels it. In Rogers's terms, a safe and hospitable therapeutic space where one experiences empathic care and unconditional regard creates change by modeling acceptance and understanding. It nurtures self-acceptance and self-understanding in another and assists them to move forward in becoming the self they truly are.[43] What appears like a paradox essentially reflects the empathic God event in the Jesus story where a prophet from Nazareth entered the lives and the homes of others, extending acceptance, doing the work of healing, and proclaiming liberation. A praxis of spiritual care that participates in the process of God's ongoing work of healing and salvation not only models therapeutic understanding and acceptance but also reflects God's hospitality in the Jesus story.

Conclusion

A Christian praxis of spiritual care is rooted in the religious traditions of Christianity and specifically in the narrative about the Jesus event that revealed God's saving initiative. It participates in God's ongoing work of salvation. Depending on the context or therapeutic situation, Christian spiritual care practitioners may or may not choose to assume explicitly a faith perspective. However, a Christian praxis of spiritual care nevertheless reflects the saving intent expressed in the foundational theological narrative that is embedded within the Christian tradition, albeit without any attempts to impose religious beliefs or practices on others. The Jesus event calls upon spiritual care practitioners to develop a reflective practice of care that participates in the ongoing work of God's salvation, which is a liberating, therapeutic endeavor to restore wholeness in individuals and communities.

---

43 See Carl R. Rogers, *On Becoming a Person: A Therapist's View of Psychotherapy* (1961; repr., Boston & New York: Houghton Mifflin Company, 1995), 63.

Such wholeness is always in process and anticipatory, working against internal and external forces that oppress and inhibit or deny the flourishing of life. Among those forces, shame is a primary threat to the spiritual life as it imposes self-defeating meaning-perspectives, denies significance, and makes connections unsafe. A caring praxis of at-onement that is grounded in the empathic God event in the Jesus story and joins others to know them and their experience in therapeutic ways has the potential to transform the oppressive, alienating, and threatening effects of shame. While spiritual care has various facets, all of them reflect the empathic nature of the God event in the Jesus story. Witnessing, parabolic engagement with others, re-membering, acts of practical solidarity, and the practice of hospitality are empathic practices that join persons together to effect change, growth, and healing. However, their effectiveness does not primarily rely on the mastery of certain skills but rather on the ability to establish genuine relationships of trust and safety.

BIBLIOGRAPHY

Abelard, Peter. *Commentary on the Epistle to the Romans.* Translated by Steven R. Cartwright. The Fathers of the Church Mediaeval Continuation, vol. 12. Washington, DC: The Catholic University of America Press, 2011.

American Psychiatric Association. *Diagnostic and Statistical Manual of Mental Disorders.* Fifth edition. Washington, DC: American Psychiatric Publishing, 2015.

Anderson, Herbert, and Edward Foley. *Mighty Stories, Dangerous Rituals: Weaving Together the Human and the Divine.* Minneapolis: Fortress Press, 2019. First published in 1998 by John Wiley & Sons, Inc. (New York).

Anselm of Canterbury. *The Major Works.* Edited by Brian Davies and G. R. Evans. Oxford World's Classics. Oxford & New York: Oxford University Press, 1998.

Arel, Stephanie N. *Affect Theory, Shame, and Christian Formation.* London & Cham, Switzerland: Palgrave Macmillan, 2016.

Augsburger, David W. *Pastoral Counseling across Cultures.* Philadelphia: The Westminster Press, 1986.

Aulén, Gustaf. *Christus Victor: An Historical Study of the Three Main Types of the Idea of Atonement.* Translated by A. G. Herbert. 1931. Reprint, Eugene, OR: Wipf & Stock, 2003.

Bailey, Kenneth E. *Poet and Peasant.* Grand Rapids: William B. Eerdmans Publishing Company, 1990. First published in 1976 by William B. Eerdmans (Grand Rapids).

Bammel, Christina-Maria. *Aufgetane Augen—Aufgedecktes Gesicht: Theologische Studien zur Scham im interdisziplinärem Gespräch.* Gütersloh: Gütersloher Verlagshaus, 2005.

Bannister, Jenny A., Colvonen, Peter J., Angkaw, Abigail C., and Sonya B. Norman. "Differential Relationships of Guilt and Shame on Posttraumatic Stress Disorder Among Veterans," *Psychological Trauma: Theory,*

Research, Practice, and Policy 11, no. 1 (January 2019): 35–2. https://doi.org/10.1037/tra000392.

Barth, Karl. *Church Dogmatics*, vol. IV.2. Translated by G.W. Bromiley. Edited by G.W. Bromiley and T. F. Torrance. London & New York: T. & T. Clark, 1958.

Bettenson, Henry, ed. *Documents of the Christian Church*. Second edition. London, Oxford & New York: Oxford University Press, 1963.

Bevans, Stephen B. *Models of Contextual Theology*. Revised edition. Maryknoll: Orbis Books, 2002.

Binau, Brad A. "When Shame Is the Question, How Does the Atonement Answer?" *Journal of Pastoral Theology* 12, no. 1 (January 2002): 89–113. https://doi.org/10.1179/jpt.2002.12.1.008.

Bloom, Sandra L. *Creating Sanctuary: Toward the Evolution of Sane Societies*. Revised edition. New York & London: Routledge, 2013.

Blumenthal, David R. *Facing the Abusing God: A Theology of Protest*. Louisville: Westminster John Knox Press, 1993.

Blythin, Suzanne P. M., Nicholson, Hannah L., Mcintyre, Vanessa G., Dickson, Joanne M., Fox, John R. E., and Peter J. Taylor. "Experiences of Shame and Guilt in Anorexia and Bulimia Nervosa: A Systematic Review." *Psychology and Psychotherapy: Theory, Research and Practice* 93, no. 1 (March 2020): 134–159. https://doi.org/10.1111/papt.12198.

Boff, Leonardo. *Jesus Christ Liberator: A Critical Christology for Our Time*. Translated by Patrick Hughes. Maryknoll, NY: Orbis Books, 1978.

Boff, Leonardo. *Passion of Christ, Passion of the World: The Facts, Their Interpretation, and Their Meaning Yesterday and Today*. Translated by Robert R. Barr. Maryknoll, NY: Orbis Books, 1987.

Boisen, Anton T. *The Exploration of the Inner World: A Study of Mental Disorder and Religious Experience*. Chicago: Willet and Clark, 1936.

Bonhoeffer, Dietrich. *Creation and Fall: A Theological Exposition of Genesis 1–3*. Translated by Douglas Stephen Ba., *Dietrich Bonhoeffer Works*, vol. 3. Edited by John W. DeGruchy. Minneapolis: Fortress Press, 1997.

———. *Ethics*. Translated by Reinhard Krauss, Charles C. West, and Douglas W. Scott. *Dietrich Bonhoeffer Works*, vol. 6. Edited by Clifford J. Green. Minneapolis: Fortress Press, 2005.

———. *Letters and Papers from Prison*. Translated by Isabel Best, Lisa E. Dahill, Reinhard Krauss, and Nancy Lukens. *Dietrich Bonhoeffer Works*, vol. 8. Edited by Christian Gremmels, Eberhard Bethge, and Renate Bethge, with Ilse Tödt. Minneapolis: Fortress Press, 2010.

———. *Life Together and Prayerbook of the Bible*. Translated by Daniel W. Bloesch and James H. Burtness. Dietrich Bonhoeffer Works, vol. 5. Edited by Geffrey B. Kelly. Minneapolis: Fortress Press, 1996.

———. *Sanctorum Communio: A Theological Study of the Sociology of the Church*. Translated by Joachim Von Soosten, Reinhard Kraus, and Nancy Lukens. Dietrich Bonhoeffer Works, vol. 1. Edited by Clifford J. Green. Minneapolis: Fortress Press, 2009.

Botterweck, G. Johannes, and J. Bergmann. "*yāda'*." In *Theological Dictionary of the Old Testament*, vol. 5, translated by David E. Green, edited by J. Johannes Botterweck and Helmer Ringgren, 456–464. Grand Rapids: William B. Eerdmans Publishing Company, 1986.

Bouson, J. Brooks. *Quiet as It's Kept: Shame, Trauma, and Race in the Novels of Toni Morrison*. Albany: State University of New York Press, 2000.

Brock, Rita Nakashima. *Journeys by Heart: A Christology of Erotic Power*. New York: Crossroad Publishing Company, 1988.

———, and Rebecca A. Parker. *Proverbs and Ashes: Violence, Redemptive Suffering, and the Search for What Saves Us*. Boston: Beacon Press, 2001.

———, and Rebecca A. Parker. *Saving Paradise: How Christianity Traded Love of This World for Crucifixion and Empire*. Boston: Beacon Press, 2008.

Brody, Howard. *Stories of Sickness*. Second edition. Oxford & New York: Oxford University Press, 2003.

Brown, Brené. *Daring Greatly: How the Courage to Be Vulnerable Transforms the Way We Live, Love, Parent, and Lead*. New York: Gotham Books, 2012.

———. *I Thought It Was Just Me (But It Isn't): Making the Journey from "What People Think" to "I Am Enough."* New York: Avery, 2008. First published in 2007 by Gotham Books (West Hollywood).

Brueggemann, Walter. *The Prophetic Imagination*. Second edition. Minneapolis: Fortress Press, 2001.

Buechner, Frederick. *The Clown in the Belfry: Writings on Faith and Fiction*. New York: HarperCollins Publishers, 1992.

———. *A Crazy Holy Grace: The Healing Power of Pain and Memory.* Grand Rapids: Zondervan, 2017.

———. *A Room Called Remember: Uncollected Pieces.* San Francisco: HarperCollins Publishers, 1984.

———. *The Sacred Journey.* San Francisco: HarperCollins Publishers, 1982.

———. *Secrets in the Dark: A Life in Sermons.* New York: HarperCollins Publishers, 2006.

———. *The Son of Laughter.* San Francisco: HarperCollins Publishers, 1993.

———. *Telling Secrets.* San Francisco: HarperCollins Publishers, 1991.

Capps, Donald. *The Depleted Self: Sin in a Narcissistic Age.* Minneapolis: Fortress Press, 1993.

Caputo, John D. *Cross and Cosmos: A Theology of Difficult Glory.* Bloomington: Indiana University Press, 2019.

———. *In Search of Radical Theology: Expositions, Explorations, Exhortations.* New York: Fordham University Press, 2020.

———. *The Insistence of God: A Theology of Perhaps.* Bloomington & Indianapolis: Indiana University Press, 2013.

———. *The Weakness of God: A Theology of the Event.* Bloomington: Indiana University Press, 2006.

Carson, Timothy L. *Liminal Reality and Transformational Power.* Lanham, MD: University Press of America, 1997.

Clark, Arthur J. *Empathy in Counseling and Psychotherapy: Perspectives and Practices.* New York & London: Routledge, 2013. First published in 2007 by Lawrence Erlbaum Associates (Mahwah, NJ).

Clark, Carrie, Classen, Catherine C., Fourt, Anne, and Maithili Shetty. *Treating the Trauma Survivor: An Essential Guide to Trauma-Informed Care.* London & New York: Routledge, 2015.

Clark, Theodore R. *Saved by His Life: A Study of the New Testament Doctrine of Reconciliation and Salvation.* New York: The Macmillan Company, 1959.

Cone, James H. *A Black Theology of Liberation.* Maryknoll, NY: Orbis Books, 1986. First published in 1970 by J. B. Lippincott Company (Philadelphia).

———. *The Cross and the Lynching Tree*. Maryknoll, NY: Orbis Books, 2011.

Cooper, Rhonda S. "The Palliative Care Chaplain as Story Catcher." *Journal of Pain and Symptom Management* 55, no.1 (January 2018):155–158.

Cooper-White, Pamela. *Many Voices: Pastoral Psychotherapy in Relational and Theological Perspective*. Minneapolis: Fortress Press, 2007.

———. *Shared Wisdom: Use of the Self in Pastoral Care and Counseling*. Minneapolis: Fortress Press, 2004.

Coplan, Amy. "Understanding Empathy: Its Features and Effects." In *Empathy: Philosophical and Psychological Perspectives*, edited by Amy Coplan and Peter Goldie, 3–8. Oxford & New York: Oxford University Press, 2011.

Cozolino, Louis. *Why Therapy Works: Using Our Mind to Change Our Brains*. New York & London: W. W. Norton & Company, 2016.

Crites, Stephen. "The Narrative Quality of Experience." In *Why Narrative? Readings in Narrative Theology*, edited by Stanley Hauerwas and L. Gregory Jones, 65–88. Grand Rapids: William B. Eerdmans Publishing Company, 1989. First published 1971 in *The Journal of the American Academy of Religion*, XXXIX: 291–311.

Crumpler, Michael J. "Give Us What Magic Johnson Got! Spiritual Care for Black Lives, Living with HIV and Aids in the Era of #Black Lives Matter." In *Spiritual Care in an Age of #Black Lives Matter*, edited by Danielle J. Buhuro, 102–113. Eugene, OR: Cascade Books, 2019.

DeYoung, Patricia A. *Understanding and Treating Chronic Shame: A Relational/Neurobiological Approach*. New York & London: Routledge, 2015.

Donner, Susan. "The Treatment Process." In *Using Self Psychology in Psychotherapy*, edited by Helene Jackson, 51–70. Northvale, NJ: Jason Aronson Inc., 1991.

Egan, Gerard. *The Skilled Helper: A Problem-Management and Opportunity Development Approach to Helping*. Tenth edition. Belmont, CA: Brooks/Cole, 2014.

Eller, Jack David. *Cruel Creeds, Virtuous Violence: Religious Violence across Culture and History*. Amherst, NY: Prometheus Books, 2010.

Evans, Amanda, and Patricia Coccoma. *Trauma-Informed Care: How Neuroscience Influences Practice*. London & New York: Routledge, 2014.

Fairbairn, Donald, and Ryan M. Reeves. *The Story of Creeds and Confessions: Tracing the Development of the Christian Faith.* Grand Rapids: Baker Academic, 2019.

Farley, Edward. *Divine Empathy: A Theology of God.* Minneapolis: Fortress Press, 1996.

Flores, Philip J. *Addiction as an Attachment Disorder.* Lanham & Oxford: Jason Aronson Inc., 2004.

Freire, Paulo. *Pedagogy of the Oppressed.* Translated by Myra Bergman Ramos. New York & London: Continuum, 2000. First published 1970 by Penguin Random House (London & New York).

Ganz, Zev. "God as Selfobject and the Therapeutic Potential of Divine Failure." *Clinical Social Work Journal* 45, no. 4 (December 2017): 332–343. https://doi.org/10.1007/s10615-016-0608-z.

Gerkin, Charles V. *The Living Human Document: Re-Visioning Pastoral Counseling in a Hermeneutic Mode.* Nashville: Abingdon Press, 1984.

Gill-Austern, Brita L. "Engaging Diversity and Difference: From Practices of Exclusion to Practices of Practical Solidarity." In *Injustice and the Care of Souls: Taking Oppression Seriously in Pastoral Care*, edited by Sheryl A. Kujawa-Holbrook and Karen B. Montagno, 29–44. Minneapolis: Augsburg Fortress Press, 2009.

Gilligan, James. "Shame, Guilt, and Violence." *Social Research* 70, no. 4 (Winter 2003): 1149–1180. https://doi.org/10.1353/sor.2003.0053.

———. *Violence: Reflections on a National Epidemic.* New York: G. P. Putnam's Sons, 1996.

Girard, René. *I See Satan Fall Like Lightning.* Translated by James G. Williams. Maryknoll: Orbis Books, 2001.

———. *The Scapegoat.* Translated by Yvonne Freccero. Baltimore: Johns Hopkins University Press, 1986.

Gottschall, Jonathan. *The Storytelling Animal: How Stories Make Us Human.* Boston & New York: Houghton Mifflin Harcourt Publishing Company, 2012.

Gutiérrez, Gustavo. *A Theology of Liberation: History, Politics, and Salvation.* Revised edition. Translated and edited by Sister Caridad Inda and John Eagleson. Maryknoll, NY: Orbis Books, 1988.

Hauerwas, Stanley. "Salvation and Health." In *The Hauerwas Reader*, edited by John Bergman and Michael Cartwright, 539–555. Durham & London: Duke University Press, 2001.

Heim, Mark S. *Saved from Sacrifice: A Theology of the Cross*. Grand Rapids & Cambridge, UK: William B. Eerdmans Publishing Company, 2006.

Herman, Judith L. *Trauma and Recovery: The Aftermath of Violence—From Domestic Abuse to Political Terror*. New York: Basic Books, 1992.

Herzog, William R., II, *Jesus, Justice, and the Reign of God: A Ministry of Liberation*. Louisville: Westminster John Knox Press, 2000.

———. *Parables as Subversive Speech: Jesus as Pedagogue of the Oppressed*. Louisville: Westminster John Knox Press, 1994.

———. *Prophet and Teacher: An Introduction to the Historical Jesus*. Westminster John Knox Press, 2005.

Hick, John. *An Interpretation of Religion: Human Responses to the Transcendent*. New Haven & London: Yale University Press, 1989.

Irenaeus, Saint. *Five Books against Heresies: The Standard Greek and Latin Text for Over a Century with Detailed English Commentary*. Vol. 2. Edited by W. Wigan Harvey. Rochester, NY: St. Irenaeus Press, 2013. First published 1857 by Typis Academicis (Cambridge).

Jeffrey, David. "Empathy, Sympathy, and Compassion in Healthcare: Is There a Problem? Is There a Difference? Does It Matter?" *Journal of the Royal Society of Medicine* 109, no. 12 (December 2016): 446–452. https://doi.org/10.1177/0141076816680120.

Kähler, Martin. *The So-Called Historical Jesus and the Historic Biblical Christ*. Translated by Carl E. Braaten. Philadelphia: Fortress Press, 1964. Originally published as *Der sogenannte historische Jesus und der geschichtliche, biblische Christus*. Zweite erneuerte Auflage. Leipzig: A. Deichert,1896.

Kaufman, Gershen. *The Psychology of Shame: Theory and Treatment of Shame-Based Syndromes*. Second edition. New York: Springer Publishing Company, 1996.

———. *Shame: The Power of Caring*. Third revised edition. Cambridge, MA: Schenkman Books, 1992.

Kertelge, Karl. "diakaiosynē." In *Exegetical Dictionary of the New Testament*, vol. 1, edited by Horst Balz and Gerhard Schneider, 325–330. Grand Rapids: William B. Eerdmans Publishing Company, 1990.

Kilborne, Benjamin. "Oedipus and the Oedipal: Shame and Shame Dynamics." *The American Journal of Psychoanalysis* 64, no. 4 (Fall 2004): 289–297.

Kohut, Heinz. *The Analysis of the Self: A Systematic Approach to the Psychoanalytic Treatment of Narcissistic Personality Disorders*. Chicago: University of Chicago Press, 2009. First published 1971 by International Universities Press (New York).

———. *How Does Analysis Cure?* Edited by Arnold Goldberg. Chicago & London: University of Chicago Press, 1984.

———. "Introspection, Empathy, and Psychoanalysis." In *The Search for the Self: Selected Writings of Heinz Kohut 1950–1978*, vol. 1, edited by Paul H. Ornstein, 205–232. New York: International Universities Press, 1978.

———. "Introspection, Empathy, and the Semi-Circle of Mental Health." *International Journal of Psycho-Analysis*, 63, no. 4 (1982): 395–407.

———. *The Kohut Seminars on Self Psychology and Psychotherapy with Adolescents and Young Adults*. Edited by Miriam Elson. New York: W. W. Norton and Co., 1987.

———. *The Restoration of the Self*. Chicago & London: University of Chicago Press, 2009. First published 1977 by International Universities Press (New York).

———. *Self Psychology and the Humanities: Reflections on a New Psychoanalytic Approach*. Edited by Charles B. Strozier. New York: W. W. Norton & Company, 1985.

———. "Thoughts on Narcissism and Narcissistic Rage." In *The Search for the Self: Selected Writings of Heinz Kohut 1950–1978*, vol. 2, edited by Paul H. Ornstein, 615–658. New York: International Universities Press, 1978.

Koolish, Lynda. "'To Be Loved Is to Cry Shame': A Psychological Reading of Toni Morrison's *Beloved*." *MELUS* 26, no. 4 (Winter 2001): 169–195. https://doi.org/10.2307/3185546.

Krumholz, Linda. "The Ghosts of Slavery: Historical Recovery in Toni Morrison's *Beloved*." In *Toni Morrison's Beloved: A Casebook*, edited by William L. Andrews and Nellie Y. McKay, 107–125. New York & Oxford: Oxford University Press, 1999.

Lapsley, James N. *Salvation and Health: The Interlocking Processes of Life.* Philadelphia: The Westminster Press, 1972.

Lartey, Emmanuel Y. *In Living Color: An Intercultural Approach to Pastoral Care and Counseling.* Second edition. London & Philadelphia: Jessica Kingsley Publishers, 2003.

Lasch, Christopher. *The Culture of Narcissism: American Life in an Age of Diminishing Expectations.* New York & London: W. W. Norton & Co., 1979.

———. "For Shame: Why Americans Should Be Weary of Self-Esteem." *The New Republic* (August 10, 1992): 29–34.

Lebron, Christopher J. *The Color of Our Shame: Race and Justice in Our Time.* Oxford & New York: Oxford University Press, 2013.

Leith, John H., ed. *Creeds of the Churches: A Reader in Christian Doctrine, from The Bible to the Present.* Third edition. Atlanta: Westminster John Knox, 1982.

Leivestad, Ragnar. "iaomai." In *Exegetical Dictionary of the New Testament,* vol. 2, translated by James W. Thompson and John W. Medendorp, edited by Horst Balz and Gerhard Schneider, 169–170. Grand Rapids: William B. Eerdmans Publishing Company, 1991.

Lester, Andrew D. *The Angry Christian: A Theology of Care and Counseling.* Louisville: Westminster John Knox Press, 2003.

———. *Hope in Pastoral Care and Counseling.* Louisville: Westminster John Knox Press, 1995.

Levine, Amy-Jill. *Short Stories by Jesus: The Enigmatic Parables of a Controversial Rabbi.* New York: HarperCollins Publishers, 2014.

Lewis, C. S. *The Lion, the Witch, and the Wardrobe.* London: Fontana Lions/William Collins Sons & Company, 1980. First published 1950 by Geoffrey Bless (London).

Lewis, Helen Block. *Shame and Guilt in Neurosis.* New York: International Universities Press, 1971.

Lewis, Michael. *Shame: The Exposed Self.* New York: The Free Press, 1992.

Litz, Brett T., Stein, Nathan, Delaney, Eileen, Lebowitz, Leslie, Nash, William P., Silva, Caroline, and Shira Maguen. "Moral Injury and Moral Repair in War Veterans: A Preliminary Model and Intervention Strategy." *Clinical Psychology Review* 29, no. 8 (December 2009): 695–706. https://doi.org/10.1016/j.cpr.2009.07.003.

Lohfink, Gerhard. *Jesus and Community*. Translated by John P. Galvin. Philadelphia: Fortress Press, 1984.

———. *Jesus of Nazareth: What He Wanted, Who He Was*. Translated by Linda M. Maloney. Collegeville: The Liturgical Press, 2012.

Lorenzen, Thorwald. *Resurrection and Discipleship: Interpretative Models, Biblical Reflections, Theological Consequences*. Maryknoll, NY: Orbis Books, 1995.

Luther, Martin. *Die Reformatorischen Grundschriften*, vol.1. Edited by Horst Beintker. Munich: Deutscher Taschenbuch Verlag, 1983.

Malina, Bruce J., and Richard L. Rohrbaugh. *Social-Science Commentary on the Gospel of John*. Minneapolis: Fortress Press, 1998.

March, Charles. *Reclaiming Dietrich Bonhoeffer: The Promise of His Theology*. New York: Oxford: Oxford University Press, 1994.

Margulies, Alfred. *The Empathic Imagination*. New York & London: W. W. Norton & Company, 1989.

———. "The Empathic Imagination: Empathy and Inscapes." *The Journal of the American Academy of Psychoanalysis* 21, no. 4 (Winter 1993): 513–524. https://doi.org/10.1521/jaap.1.1993.21.4.513.

Maxwell, Bruce. *Professional Ethics Education: Studies in Compassionate Empathy*. Berlin: Springer Science, 2008.

May, Samuel J. "Margaret Garner and Seven Others." In *Toni Morrison's Beloved: A Casebook*, edited by William L. Andrews and Nellie Y. McKay, 25–36. New York & Oxford: Oxford University Press, 1999.

McClendon, James A., Jr. *Systematic Theology*. Vol. 2, *Doctrine*. Nashville: Abingdon Press, 1994.

McConnell, T. Mark. "From 'I Have Done Wrong' to 'I Am Wrong'." In *Locating Atonement: Explorations in Constructive Dogmatics*, edited by Oliver D. Crisp and Fred Sanders, 168–188. Grand Rapids: Zondervan, 2015.

McKnight, Scot. *Jesus and His Death: Historiography, the Historical Jesus, and Atonement Theory*. Waco: Baylor University Press, 2005.

Merkel, Helmut. "telōnēs." In *Exegetical Dictionary of the New Testament*, vol. 3, translated by John W. Medendorp and Douglas W. Stott, edited by Horst Balz and Gerhard Schneider, 348–350. Grand Rapids: William B. Eerdmans Publishing Company, 1993.

Mezirow, Jack. *Transformative Dimensions of Adult Learning.* San Francisco: Jossey-Bass, 1991.

Miceli, Maria and Cristiano Castelfranchi. "Reconsidering the Differences between Shame and Guilt." *Europe's Journal of Psychology* 13, no. 3 (2018): 710–733. https://doi.org./10.5964/ejop.v14i3.1564.

Miller-McLemore, Bonnie J. "Feminist Theory in Pastoral Theology." In *Feminist and Womanist Pastoral Theology,* edited by Bonnie J. Miller-McLemore and Brita L Gill-Austern, 77–94. Nashville: Abingdon Press, 1999.

———. "The Living Human Web: A Twenty-Five Year Retrospective." *Pastoral Psychology* 67, no. 3 (June 2018): 305–321. https://doi.org/10.1007/s11089-018-0811-7.

Moltmann, Jürgen. *The Crucified God: The Cross of Christ as the Foundation and Criticism of Christian Theology.* Translated by R. A. Wilson and John Bowden. New York: Harper & Row, 1974.

———. "The Crucified God—Yesterday and Today: 1972–2002." Translated by Margaret Kohl. In *Cross Examinations: Readings on the Meaning of the Cross,* edited by Marit Trelstad, 127–138. Minneapolis: Augsburg Fortress Press, 2006.

Montagno, Karen B. "Midwifes and Holy Subversives: Resisting Oppression in Attending the Birth of Wholeness." In *Injustice and the Care of Souls: Taking Oppression Seriously in Pastoral Care,* edited by Sheryl A. Kujawa-Holbrook and Karen B. Montagno, 3–12. Minneapolis: Augsburg Fortress Press, 2009.

Morrison, Andrew P. *The Culture of Shame.* Northvale, NJ & London: Jason Aronson Inc., 1998. First published in 1996 by The Ballantine Publishing Group (New York).

———. "Shame, Ideal Self, and Narcissism." In *Essential Papers on Narcissism,* edited by Andrew P. Morrison, 348–372. New York: New York University Press, 1986.

Morrison, Toni. *Beloved.* New York: Vintage Books, 2004. First published 1987 by Alfred A. Knopf (New York).

———. *The Source of Self-Regard: Selected Essays, Speeches, and Meditations.* New York: Vintage Books, 2020. First published 2019 by Alfred A. Knopf (New York).

Moss, David M. "Narcissism, Empathy, and the Fragmentation of the Self: An Interview with Heinz Kohut." *Pilgrimage* 4, no. 1 (1976): 26–43.

Myers, Chad. *Binding the Strong Man: A Political Reading of Mark's Story of Jesus*. Maryknoll, NY: Orbis Books, 1988.

Nathanson, Donald L. *Shame and Pride: Affect, Sex, and the Birth of the Self.* New York & London: W. W. Norton & Company, 1992.

New Oxford American Dictionary, Third edition. Oxford & New York: Oxford University Press, 2010.

Newberg, Andrew B. *Principles of Neurotheology*. London & New York: Routledge, 2016.

———, and David Halpern. *The Rabbi's Brain: Mystics, Moderns and the Science of Jewish Thinking*. Nashville: Turner Publishing Company, 2018.

Oates, Wayne E. *Christ and Selfhood*. New York: Association Press, 1961.

Otto, Rudolf. *The Idea of the Holy: An Inquiry into the Non-Rational Factor in the Idea of the Divine and Its Relation to the Rational*. Translated by John W. Harvey. Second edition. Oxford and New York: Oxford University Press, 1950.

Pargament, Kenneth I. *The Psychology of Religion and Coping: Theory, Research, Practice*. New York: The Guilford Press, 1997.

Pattison, Stephen. *Saving Face: Enfacement, Shame, Theology*. Farnham & Burlington: Ashgate Publishing, 2013.

———. *Shame: Theory, Therapy, Theology*. Cambridge, UK & New York: Cambridge University Press, 2000.

Patton, John. *Is Human Forgiveness Possible? A Pastoral Care Perspective*. Nashville: Abingdon Press, 1985.

———. *Pastoral Care in Context: An Introduction to Pastoral Care*. Louisville: Westminster John Knox Press, 1993.

Pears, Angie. *Doing Contextual Theology*. New York: Routledge, 2010.

Pembroke, Neil. *The Art of Listening: Dialogue, Shame, and Pastoral Care*. Edinburgh & New York: T. T. Clark/Handsel Press; Grand Rapids: William B. Eerdmans Publishing Company, 2002.

Petry, Ray C., ed. *A History of Christianity: Readings in the History of the Church*, vol. 1. Grand Rapids: Baker Book House, 1981. First published 1962 by Prentice-Hall International (London).